A PURPOSE RIDDEN

RYAN CORREY

A

PURPOSE

RIDDEN

RMB

Rocky Mountain Books
www.rmbooks.com

Library and Archives Canada Cataloguing in Publication

Correy, Ryan, author
        A purpose ridden / Ryan Correy.

Issued in print and electronic formats.
ISBN 978-1-77160-064-4 (pbk.).—ISBN 978-1-77160-065-1 (epub).—
ISBN 978-1-77160-066-8 (pdf)

        1. Correy, Ryan. 2. Cyclists—Canada—Biography. 3. Cycling.
4. Extreme sports. I. Title.

GV1051.C69A3 2015   796.6092   C2015-900985-5
                                                     C2015-900986-3

Front cover photo: Long ride © Fertnig

Printed in Canada

Rocky Mountain Books acknowledges the financial support for its publishing program from the Government of Canada through the Canada Book Fund (CBF) and the Canada Council for the Arts, and from the province of British Columbia through the British Columbia Arts Council and the Book Publishing Tax Credit.

  Canadian   Patrimoine   Canada Council   Conseil des Arts
                      Heritage   canadien   for the Arts   du Canada

  BRITISH COLUMBIA
                      ARTS COUNCIL
                      Supported by the Province of British Columbia

This book was produced using FSC®-certified, acid-free paper, processed chlorine free and printed with vegetable-based inks.

"All men dream: but not equally. Those who dream by night in the dusty recesses of their minds wake in the day to find that it was vanity: but the dreamers of the day are dangerous men, for they may act their dream with open eyes, to make it possible."

—T.E. Lawrence

"His father watched him across the gulf of years and pathos which always must divide a father from his son."

—John Phillips Marquand

CONTENTS

FOREWORD

Nine years ago, shortly after returning from a journey along Borneo's north coast, I was asked to make a presentation at Calgary's Mount Royal College as part of their Distinguished Speaker Series. After the keynote, several dignitaries joined me on stage for a discussion on the subjects of risk and adventure. The student representative on the panel was Ryan Correy, the author of this book.

At the time, he had just returned from a record setting bicycle ride on the Pan-American Highway, travelling the 25,000 kilometres – from Prudhoe Bay, Alaska, to Ushuaia, Argentina – in 131 days, nine days ahead of the previous record. There was something contagious about Ryan's energy. He was dreaming big dreams. Modern life, with all its hectic obligations and responsibilities, had dulled none of his youthful aspiration.

After a cocktail reception, Ryan and I strolled together to our cars, and on the way, he mentioned a documentary film he had shot and produced, called *Longest Road*. It would be premiering at a local cinema the coming weekend. Despite the substantial physical and logistical challenges of his bike journey, Ryan had still managed to record enough video footage to create an hour-long movie. I was impressed, for it would have been far easier to drop the project when the going got tough – as it surely did. My wife and I made a point of attending.

From those two events – the panel discussion and the film – I developed a good sense for the young, ambitious man who has now written this book. What impressed me most, beyond the obvious physical achievements, were his stark honesty (emotions and tumultuous relationships are often glossed over in adventure tales) and his commitment to helping others less fortunate than himself (his Pan-American ride became a successful fundraiser for the Make-A-Wish Foundation.)

Over the years ahead we stayed in touch. At one point I acted as a mentor for a third-year business course. Ryan was eager to glean all the advice and wisdom he could from me, for twenty years earlier I'd left my own nascent engineering career to pursue dreams of adventure, photography and writing. While I gladly shared experiences and lessons learned, my fundamental message was this: it is not easy to live a life less ordinary, something beyond the invisible scaffolding erected by society, beyond the 9-to-5, with its pensions and cubicles, and vacations crammed into two short weeks. Frankly, it's darn tough. For a relentless pressure alternatively pushes and coaxes one back toward familiarity, toward the known, toward a career and a home and a job you can explain with a single word. Such forces are strongest at times of uncertainty, when the future looks bleak. To persevere, one must choose Robert Frost's proverbial "road less traveled" – again and again and again.

But if such a path is in your heart – as it clearly was in Ryan's – then there is no choice but to follow it; blindly, and with faith. For despite all its challenges, such a life is deeply rewarding. So I encouraged Ryan to press on.

Today, Ryan has travelled far down that uncharted trail. And this book – *A Purpose Ridden* – is an account of his journey, both inner and outer.

Once again, the physical accomplishments are simply staggering. From the Pan-American Highway to RAAM

(Race Across America) to Olympic training to the Tour Divide, Ryan has biked more than 100,000 kilometres since we first met, over one quarter of the distance to the moon!

Along the way, his honesty remains unflinching – painfully unflinching at times – in both his assessment of himself and of others. This story will, I suspect, make a reader want to turn their eye from the page at times, and take a deep breath before reading on as they surely will be drawn to do. There is value and vitality in this, for without it, we would never know the true toll of such accomplishments. And there is humanity in it, too, for amid Ryan's tumult we recognize our own.

In his introduction, Ryan declares that "publishing a book is tough." Indeed it is; far tougher than most imagine. But following dreams, challenging the status quo and living the life of one's choice is tougher still. This book tells the story of one young man's journey – his struggles and joys, frustrations and successes – as he seeks to find his own way in the world. Ryan's determination and efforts show again and again that when nothing is certain, anything is possible. His story is a reminder of the possibilities that lie within us all.

Bruce Kirkby

AUTHOR'S INTRODUCTION

Publishing a book is tough, I don't care what anyone says.

I first began writing this story after cycling the length of the Pan-American Highway (25,000 kilometres from Alaska to Argentina) in 2005. That first draft involved locking myself away at my parents' cottage in British Columbia, thinking I would bang off a compelling manuscript in a week. But no.

I realized I had accumulated an engaging series of anecdotes about flawed aspiration and cycling great distances, but not an enthralling story arc.

My second attempt was after the Race Across America ("The Toughest Sporting Event in the World," once touted *Outside Magazine*) in 2008. Having my father involved as crew chief really brought out a meaningful element, first introduced in Part I, "Manhood Training" (when he and I cycled across Canada when I was 13).

But I stopped writing a few months after that, realizing I only had two acts of a three-part story.

Delete.

It was not until the 2012 Tour Divide (the self-proclaimed 'Longest Mountain Bike Race in the World') that the pendulum swung and the third act was revealed.

In the two years since, I have spent many more hours than I'd like tucked away in a caffeinated haze, writing, deleting, rereading, questioning what morality tale exists, and being criticized for actions already lived.

Family members have asked me not to include certain

elements, have disagreed with my interpretation of some events, have gone through periods of not speaking to me, and may never read the final product.

A few of my crucial support crew volunteers likely feel the same. They often performed thankless, menial tasks, without fail.

To both them and my family, I'll openly admit to having been an asshole (masked in the title of "man on a mission to change the world") on more than one occasion. Adding insult to injury, I write of our time together in the moment in an often skewed, selfish and self-serving way.

But still I push on.

As with any story worth telling, many moments are difficult to relive. There is death, heartbreak, misplaced priorities, failed relationships, fights, and ultimately a coming to terms with my own inherent flaws.

Such opportunities test us, shape us, give us pause, and I hope, provide an opportunity to be inspired, learn from and find our way back to relative peace.

This is the essence of *A Purpose Ridden*.

Ryan Correy

PROLOGUE

I have been hiking for hours through unending knee-deep snow. What first felt novel (an opportunity to get off the bike and rest a battered back end) has degenerated into a teeth-chattering slog over remote wilderness mountain passes. As a result, my saturated soles are now lined with painful rotting flesh – a symptom of trench foot. They signal a need to throttle back. But no, there are fresh tracks ahead.

It was in the pitch black that I encountered the last rider.

1:00 AM, JUNE 8, 2012

The burly Serge and I had separated for a short while after filling our faces at the A&W burger joint in Sparwood, British Columbia (a rare intersection with civilization). Our paths converged once again at the abandoned mining town of Corbin, just two hours later and at a decisive race decision.

Together we stood silent, our headlamps gently shining into the dark abyss. Finding solace in the hollow sounds of the industrial graveyard, Serge wisely chose to seek refuge. "Enough for one day," he said wearily. I paused for a moment, and then told him I would continue on, foolishly perhaps, alone into the dark and increasingly dangerous terrain.

The Flathead River Valley has the largest population of grizzly bears in all of North America. Many consider sleeping exposed in the woods to be an unnecessary risk – a sleeping bag alone does very little to protect you from an animal attracted to the scent of sweat and junk food. Adding further insult to the more risk-averse, I have chosen not to carry bear spray (also known as pepper spray) because of a minimalist, weight-saving approach and general lack of fear of the large animal.

Hours tick by in the darkness.

The forest service road devolves into an exhausting bush-whack through brawny coniferous trees on a steep hillside. With adrenaline fading, I stop and question the logic of continuing to grasp for slippery roots on my hands and knees. *This doesn't feel safe,* I remind my ego.

Earlier in the day, at the beginning of the race, I had relied on a line of sight to the race leaders, their muddy tracks as a backup trail of breadcrumbs. But in the dark and alone, my navigation skills appear fruitless. *Yes, I am on the highlighted* GPS *route.* The reality of an imposing rock face says otherwise, though. Worse yet, there is no obvious workaround.

Delirium encroaches as I continue pacing back and forth in search of an alternative through the thick foliage. At 3:00 a.m., I catch a hopeful glimpse of a second set of tracks in the moonlit snow. I immediately drop my bike and leap over to the exposed plateau. *Finally,* a solution to this lost wander. But *Fuck,* no, the tread pattern reveals the side by side of my own clumsy footprints. I have hiked in a complete circle.

Back on track the following afternoon, a dusting of snow crystals falls from a frozen shoe turned upside down. I place the rugged size 12 on a nearby boulder and hold up my pruned foot for closer examination. Running a thumb over the emaciated white toes, I feel the joints all pop and crack like a cheap home appliance running thin on oil.

The sound is a staunch reminder. Two years ago I found myself in a state of desperation, crawling helplessly alone across a cold tile floor, gaunt, with my vision spiralling and my heart racing. I was sure the side effects of adventure had finally caught up with me. But I never fully crossed *that* line. Instead, I lay bedridden for three months and in pain for two years, and on this day, my comeback, coming back is everything to me.

As if on cue, a light rain begins to fall from the greying sky.

I pull out a ball of cheap grocery bags from my pack, wring out my wool socks, slide them back on, wrap the plastic over top of the socks, then slip my feet back into those cold lugs. A strand of duct tape around each ankle helps create a moisture seal. This solution should keep the wind and aggravated arthritis at bay.

I stand and grit my teeth, feeling fiery nerve pain nonetheless.

Scanning back down through the drizzle, I see no riders coming up the mountain. Though there was no official start list, I'm aware of at least 100 bikepacking renegades scattered in the brutal wilderness, slowly worming their way south. Groups of similar abilities are likely working together now, pooling resources, building fires and keeping safe. *Should I indulge?*

No. Keep moving.

At 2:00 p.m., an unexpected blizzard descends on the harsh mountain. My teeth chatter uncontrollably as warm blood retreats from my extremities, which are beginning to go into hypothermic shock. I am feeling desperate. Still, forward momentum seems the logical choice.

I continue postholing through the knee-deep snowpack, shaking my head with each laboured step. *Not even fucking close.*

Many have been inspired to race the Tour Divide after watching the popular 2010 feature film *Ride the Divide*.

The camera crew failed to capture scenes like this, however. Any shots of snow looked playful, showing riders stumbling around like Chaplin in the sunshine. The brutal reality at higher elevations will therefore come as a horrendous surprise to any rider – especially one from a southern climate – who is unable to descend to the relative safety of a warm motel before nightfall.

Concern befalls.

Around a switchback, I notice multiple sets of snowed-over tracks leading downward through the flurries. With an elated yet cautious breath, my laboured push through the pack quickly transitions into a hurried step-and-slide. My bike, aptly nicknamed "The Tumbler," after Batman's black war machine, serves as a makeshift snowplow and brace.

Crunch, slide. Crunch, slide.

The onslaught of flurries begins to calm below the treeline. Out of the storm, I pause to unzip my expensive GORE-TEX jacket. A cloud of pent-up heat and perspiration comes billowing out.

Taking the minimalist approach has forced me to pay particular attention to layering, for which my clothing options are limited. There is always the concern that my inner warming layer will become saturated in sweat. When at rest, this moisture steals away precious body heat. And surprisingly, a drop in body temperature of more than a few degrees is deadly.

Get back on the bike. Keep moving.

The snowpack gives way to a muddy forest service road with veins of runoff water that criss-cross each other to form wheel-sucking rivulets. Normally, there would be no hesitation to attack. The relative safety of a one-day race (and medical crew on standby) negates such concern. But out here in the wild, there is just stupidity and death.

I proceed in a controlled slide.

Saturated earth sprays off the knobby front tire, hitting me square in the face. Instinctively, my clunky frozen hand mashes on the right brake to try and regain control. But like a car caught hydroplaning, the back wheel locks, causing the Tumbler to fishtail nervously. "Come on," I murmur, squinting through the sludge splashing up.

The sub-zero spray is a harsh reminder of the frigid mountain stream that also sloshes inside my bowels, cooling from the inside out. *Pee now, dammit!*

I dig my right heel into the ground and mash again with whatever stopping force remains. The Tumbler nervously slides to a halt at the valley floor, allowing me to unsaddle and dash into the adjacent woods.

As I run through the deadfall, instinct states the next most obvious solution: *Fuck, I need fire.*

I fumble through one of my packs for a cheap Bic lighter. With a flick, I turn up the fuel intensity to full, pointing the orange flame underneath a small pile of springy saps. The wood begins to smoke, igniting a small spark of hope, and then nothing. *It's too wet. Fuck.*

My chest and arms begin shivering violently.

I scream out loud, resorting to Plan B – exposing my withered appendage to the unforgiving wind. The simple act of relieving myself warms my core a little, but not nearly enough.

I straddle the bike again and yell out, "PLEASE!"

Tears of dwindling optimism stream down my cheeks as I reach for the emergency beacon, strapped to the top of my saddle pack. I don't want to quit the race but I'm afraid that not doing so would be "stupid," as my father would say. "And selfish," he would add, referring to the potentially fatal consequences and ensuing family fallout.

My thumb shivers indecisively over the plastic rescue button, ready to signal for a helicopter saviour, just one press away. An inch to the left, the tracking LED display flashes in my narrowed peripheral vision. It waits for forward progress, taunting my conviction to tackle the world's toughest mountain-bike race.

I have never faced a greater challenge.

"Please…"

I stare up at the dark sky, close my eyes and envision my girlfriend shuffling papers at her stuffy government job. She is distracted by the GPS signal on her computer screen, not moving, and of the few race leaders ahead. *Something is wrong*, she senses.

It is in this moment that my mind falls into a hallucination.

"Do you want me to call your mother?" a muffled voice calls out over the wind.

PART I

MANHOOD TRAINING

CHAPTER 1

CLOSE ENOUGH TO HOME

JUNE, 1996, I'M 13 YEARS OLD
Spread out around me on my carpeted bedroom floor is a riotous collage of comic books. I'm dazzled by the colour, the action, the stories and the escape. But more importantly, I'm drawn in by the superhero mythology. In particular, I enjoy the story of Bruce Wayne, the flawed (yet uniquely human) caped crusader.

The really great Batman adventures affirm all we absorb when we learn about moral codes: refusing to kill another; choosing not to grandstand through the use of one's powers; opting for personal fulfillment through selfless acts. These storied lessons have made me keenly aware of right and wrong.

Pushing character development even further, the most compelling comics also highlight the protagonist's struggle with responsibility. Extreme crisis often brings about a decision to follow a more conventional path, to hang up the cape and cowl, throw on a pair of jeans and walk among us everyday folk. But something always brings them back. That is, a sense of purpose.

The thought that the path we choose for ourselves can be both a burden and the light from which all meaning is derived intrigues me.

A heavy dream calls out for understanding. From my bedroom window, grandiose thoughts of becoming a pro hockey player drift over the prairie farmland. My daydreams rise like a storming cloud, ascending over the foothills, building in stature alongside the Rocky Mountains to the west.

Moments from last night's game play through my head. Images of gliding down the ice surface easily lend themselves to a moody orchestral soundtrack, such as *Batman Returns* or *Apollo 13*. My Walkman is warm from repeat listens.

Though my thoughts wander from end to end (and through space), in reality I rarely play any position other than defence. No matter, there is a sense of glory in responding to the more touted moves of the forward opposition. Great skill is needed for anticipating action while skating backward. Spatial awareness is key.

Other skills are apparent too. I take pride in being the fastest skater on the team. I'm also able to sustain harder efforts than most. Unfortunately, my puck handling skills have fallen behind. Hence being relegated to a defensive position. *There is plenty of time to improve,* I assure myself. All the greats had to hone their craft.

My attention turns to the posters of National Hockey League players taped to my wall. As I scan past "The Great One," Wayne Gretzky, I think of the Canadian hockey dream I share with a million other kids, and possibly more – a vague notion of fame, money and conquest on cold steel blades.

The operatic daydream is disrupted by a muffled call coming from downstairs. I remove my headphones and quickly realize it is my taskmaster of a father yelling out, "Get off your butt and come down!" *Argh, what does he want?*

Grudgingly, I shuffle his way.

It is not uncommon to have my summer fun be cut short

by chores on our acreage. Maintaining the lawn eats up at least four hours of useful time, once or twice a week. As for weeding, the prickly follow-up, my sister and I have developed a con for filling half the garbage bags with air as we tie them off. Of course, this deception only works as long as the chore sheet lists a bag requirement and not total hours.

Downstairs I find my father standing, hunched, his elbows bent on the dinner table, with a series of unfolded maps before him. I notice the sun shining on the members-only golf and country club in the Elbow River Valley, behind. Despite its proximity, there has never been a temptation to join. "A waste of a good walk," I remember my father once saying.

My approach doesn't cause him to take his gaze away from the maps. As I shuffle closer, I see him draw a line across the overlapping maps with a pink highlighter. Peering closer, I notice that the line connects the prairies, from our home on the outskirts of Calgary, across Saskatchewan, Manitoba and around the Great Lakes to Ontario.

It's finally happening.

For the last couple of years, my father has hinted at a bicycle tour across Canada. "An opportunity to toughen you up," he would say. "It's time for manhood training," he now proudly smiles, looking back over his shoulder.

I stand in shock.

He continues with a breakdown of the journey ahead and its true purpose. "I'm not going to watch you waste another summer bumming around with your friends, playing those idiot boxes [his crude description of Nintendo]. You are going to experience the country and see what it is like to do man's work." And he shall lead this grand adventure.

My father estimates the total distance from Calgary to my

aunt and uncle's cottage in Oliphant, Ontario, to be 3400 kilometres. The plan is to ride 160 kilometres each day.

Given the fact that I have never ridden farther than my friend's house down the street, I really have no frame of reference for what it takes to ride a bicycle more than halfway across the country. Naively I tell myself it will be fun. A tough reality sets in soon after.

My hands go clammy, my skin pale.

My father is a bit of a hard-ass. Twenty-two days on the road, just he and I, away from my mother (the "feudal" referee), and detached from our comfortable surroundings, *now this is an intimidating thought.*

We live in a large estate community on the outskirts of Calgary. Mansions are owned by movers and shakers in the oil industry, pro hockey players, suspected drug dealers and other established entrepreneurs. Their kids, my friends, are among a privileged new generation. "And you don't know how to get dirty," states my father.

Lexus and BMW luxury cars are common sights around the school parking lot, and it seems like every other family has season tickets to the Calgary Flames hockey team. Not surprisingly, a couple of their retired players have taken turns coaching my team. Hall of Fame captain Lanny McDonald is currently at the helm.

My parents own a used Lexus and an unimposing blue minivan with fake wood panelling. They started from the ground up, so they tell me, originally from a one-bedroom apartment in Edmonton.

With the help of their compassionate elderly neighbours (to help babysit my sister and me), and a lot of knocking on doors, they built up a successful investment advising group, the Correy Team, and a client base of a couple hundred across western Canada.

"Manhood Training" exposes what I suspect is a slight chip on my father's shoulder. He has never played the part of the millionaire, nor had the privilege of inheriting success. Seeing past the hard-ass exterior, I respect him for showing some vulnerability and for being real. "How many other fathers do you know who would do this sort of thing with their kids?" he asks.

"None," I reply.

JULY 2, 1996

We have stopped in the small agricultural town of Bassano, Alberta, just as planned. The sun now sets on day one of our cross-country bonding experience.

Moulded into a cheap plastic chair on our motel porch, I pause in deep thought. The weathered exterior of a lone grain elevator holds my attention. It is a stark contrast to the skyscraper skyline of the Stampede City no longer in sight.

Semi-trailer trucks quietly buzz by on the Trans-Canada Highway. Their windshields reflect a warm hue.

I run my fingers over my filthy skin. Exposed areas are caked with a fine layer of perspiration and sunscreen.

My soul weeps with exhaustion.

Through the open door behind me, my father towels off after a hot shower. I barely notice him pace around the musty room, unpacking. His red pannier bike bags hold maps, PowerBars, his wallet, running shoes and a set of casual clothes to walk around in. Why he would want to walk around after twelve hours of riding is beyond me. *And in this one-road, nothing town?*

I hunch forward into my hands, feeling frustrated. A solitary tear finds its way in between my fingers.

Closing my eyes, I pray that my father will come outside

and suggest we turn around, that maybe we bit off more than we can chew. Instead, I hear him unfold the maps again.

He has no intention of turning around. In fact, he's calculating the distance for the next couple of days, trying to figure out where we should stay and what amenities exist along the way. *He is oblivious.*

And then he calls out.

I don't turn around for fear he will see my eyes welling up, all puffy and red. "You know, we are still close enough to home," he says in a calming tone. "It's not too late to call your mom ... this can all be over with right now. Just say the word."

In a short couple of hours, I could be back home, showered, pillaging a well-stocked fridge, about to settle on my own supremely comfortable bed. Only I would ever be accountable for this decision. And in a few weeks' time, the sting of failure would have subsided.

Covertly, I wipe the tear from my face, playing it off as a chance to clean the grime from around my eyes. I'm not sure if my father realizes how difficult this day has been for me. He seems preoccupied with the gravity of the question somewhat lost on me.

I look back over my shoulder and take a deep breath. I realize his calming tone masks the fact that he is testing my will. "So, what is it going to be?" he smiles.

Argh, come on.

I fire back with a rebellious, half-hearted smirk, "Let's keep going."

The taskmaster nods approvingly. "Good, because I wasn't going to let you quit." *Of course you weren't.*

JULY 4, 1996

We find ourselves in a Saskatchewan headwind, pedalling over rolling, golden prairies. Civilization has all but disappeared behind. It is just us and the road and my annoyance.

Every point of contact with the bike throbs. "What the hell is there to see?" I mutter under my breath. At 15 km/h, there is very little change in scenery.

Having none of it, my father takes over the lead.

He remains in a steady rhythm, still pedalling forward with his head down. I'm not sure if he is ignoring my exhaustion or just can't hear my cries for attention. I yell into the wind, pleading for him to stop, "FUUUUUCK!"

I have never sworn out loud.

But still no change.

My tired gaze falls downward, watching my knees bob up and down like a metronome in slow procession. The sheer volume of miles weighs heavily on my mind. And at this pace it will take an eternity.

I imagine animals in a zoo, pacing back and forth. We share a similar sense of purgatory. On my right, a wheat field. On my left, a wheat field. And in front, the other, more succinctly taunting metronome. My father.

Finally, stopping without him for once, I yell, "Please! I'm tired. We have no more water!"

He surrenders.

Together we scan the horizon for signs of civilization. In unspoken understanding, my father turns to face the north as I stare in southern opposition. The wind howls in only one direction, still against us both.

A taste of blood seeps from my chapped lips. I try to swallow but find that there is no saliva to suck down. My burnt cheeks also grimace, tugging on facial muscles worn tired from chewing on stale energy bars.

He relents. "Alright, the next farmhouse we come across, let's see if they can help."

We push off again, now in sync.

As luck would have it, we come across a quaint, white-walled settlement only a couple of kilometres down the road. My father optimistically leads up the dusty driveway, walking his bike. I follow in my best Sunday smile.

As we near the house, a lean elderly man shuffles from beneath a hefty green tractor. He walks toward us, straight out of a Norman Rockwell painting, his hand extended in greeting. "Hey there! Run out of water?" he asks, seeing us holding our bottles.

My father leans in for a handshake, happy to make the acquaintance of a fellow hard worker. "Yes, do you mind if we fill up?" he asks, pointing to a dripping spigot on the front lawn.

"Nah, come on inside," the elderly farmer warmly gestures. "You're more than welcome to stay for dinner. There isn't much up the road." *Of course*, we accept.

Taking off our shoes at the front door, the farmer makes a point of also shaking my hand. Awkwardly, I notice that he is missing a couple of fingers. "Lost them in an accident with that tractor," he laughs.

I'm taken aback by how comfortable the elderly man appears, thrusting his mangled hand into mine. It makes me think about all the little quirks that kids tease each other over back at school, and how painfully boring they now appear.

We gather with the farmer and his kind wife at their dining table. The home smells of dirty boots and freshly baked pies. Handcrafted items and weathered black and white family pictures hang on the walls. There is a history here.

Over the course of a hearty homecooked meal, my father seizes the opportunity to ask about life on the farm. I quietly listen to the conversation, noting its sincerity, tone and approach. I'm not yet comfortable speaking to adults that I don't know.

The farmer's wife asks if we would like dessert. "It's apple pie," she says proudly. Apple just so happens to be my father's favourite. "And the crust is homemade," she further clarifies.

I nod, keen to devour a thick slice.

As I'm wiping the last tender crumbs away, up walks the couple's 30-year-old son from the basement – a late surprise. He has apparently been working on the computer for the last couple of hours, and "is really good with those things," his mom states.

Standing next to his elderly parents, my father and I regard the son and his parents. For me, a stark contrast takes shape. Yet, while I'm struck by the generation gap, my father picks up on something entirely different. He is intrigued by the son's intellect, honest personality and by the fact that humble and hard-working roots must run deep.

Leaving the home, my father hands the son his business card and invites him to call when we get back to Calgary (in about a month's time). "Let me know if you're looking for a job then," he offers.

THE FOLLOWING TWO WEEKS
We opt for a southern passage through the United States. The lack of services and the Saskatchewan headwinds have taken their toll.

The alternative route does not come easy, however. Soon after leaving the Trans-Canada Highway, we are faced with an unsigned network of bumpy gravel roads, flat tires, mosquitoes and accommodations atop rickety saloons.

Stopped at tiny tumbleweed cafés, I grunt responses to

my father's questions over greasy meals and map reading. My mind has numbed to the routine of eat, sleep, ride. But perhaps I'm growing stronger.

My mood begins to improve as we ride through more populated regions in North Dakota, Minnesota and Wisconsin. The increase in traffic and potential gas station breaks help take the edge off.

My go-to indulgence is Crush orange soda and Hershey's Cookies 'n' Creme chocolate bars. My father prefers the more traditional treats of Coca-Cola and chewy Fig Newtons cookies.

These sugary stops provide a sense of levity and new perspective. I had been keeping a running tally of the wooden utility poles as they ticked by, seeing only what was directly in front of me. Now I'm looking ahead, estimating that my vision extends ten kilometres toward the next gas station on the horizon.

One of those blurred shapes slowly materializes into the return customs entry for Canada. Back in the homeland, we pass through Sault Ste. Marie, Ontario, and get our first chance to visit with relatives from eastern Canada over lunch. My great-Aunt Vi and Uncle Jack are overjoyed to see us but emphasize caution on the roads head. Timely, this advice.

That afternoon my father and I are nearly side-swiped by a logging truck. The sheer force of the wind alongside the hulking vehicle blows us both into the ditch. "ASSHOLE!" my father yells out.

Shaken from the incident, I pull farther off into the ditch and collapse on the grass. My father continues staring at the semi-trailer truck with a fierce gaze, arms outstretched and in a questioning pose. *Stupid asshole.* The vehicle thunders on without a care.

Still shaking his head, he walks over with his bike and hunkers down beside me. "Complete stupidity. From now on, I'll ride behind you. That way I can protect your ass."

Though I'm not entirely sure how he'll deflect the next logging truck that encroaches onto the shoulder, there is comfort in knowing that he may be able to deliver an advance warning.

My father then starts in on a story from when he last passed through the area:

"The year was 1980. I had just finished my second degree at McMaster University in Hamilton. I had a job offer to enter the management training program at Stelco, where I had worked the past few years during the summer and winter months to put myself through school. It was a good offer and I knew a number of the management team well. However, I had doubts about spending my life in a steel company in southern Ontario, from both a health perspective and in terms of general quality of life.

"Your mom and I had been dating for several years. We met in second year at Mac, but she was a year ahead of me. We were from the same hometown of Grimsby, Ontario, but didn't really know each other in high school. After completing her BA and working for a year, mom decided to go west to the University of Alberta Faculty of Nursing to continue her studies and become a registered nurse. Without the Internet or e-mail, and given the expense of long-distance phone calls, we kept in touch by letter primarily.

"I had always wanted to see the west, but had never been west of Sault Ste. Marie. Having completed a previous bike ride from Grimsby to Prince Edward Island with a friend in Grade 12, I decided to complete the journey after graduation. At the time, I only had a three-speed bike and a used Camaro. The latter was expensive to drive and needed constant repairs. Instead, I borrowed an older friend's ten-speed bike, and with $300 in my pocket I set out to see your mom ... the best looking girl around. I was in love.

"It was another adventure and a test of whether I could do it or not. With almost no training (remember, I was in university full time and working part time), I took off in May on the borrowed bike. I had a pup tent, sleeping bag, utensils and clothes wrapped in plastic garbage bags clamped to my carrier and handlebars. The first three days were extremely hot. I headed toward London and Sarnia, which was also unknown territory. I was sweating profusely and dehydrated.

"I crossed into the United States and headed toward the Sault, where Uncle Jack and Aunt Vi live. The ride through the Upper Peninsula of Michigan was very scenic. However, the farther north I went, the more the weather changed. It got very cold and windy. In fact, when I got to the Mackinac Bridge, it was snowing. I was informed by security that I could not cross the bridge on a bike. They took me by van to the other side. It was dark and cold. I remember riding the remaining distance to the Sault half-frozen and hating every minute of it. It was a relief to cross the border and to be back on familiar ground.

"Uncle Jack picked me up on the Canadian side of the Mackinac international bridge in his small truck. By that time, it was past midnight. We went to their home and I was welcomed with open arms by Aunt Vi. She had homemade pea soup and bread ready at the kitchen table. I was starving and very appreciative. Uncle Jack gave me a rainsuit from his company, and after a couple of recovery days I headed out again. I crossed back into the United States and went along the south shore of Lake Superior (the same route we followed).

"The prairie provinces were flat and windy. I always

seemed to be fighting the prevailing westerly winds. I slept on the side of the road and at the occasional campsite. I bought food at night. After finishing my typical day, I remember sitting alone in my tent eating a whole box of Cheerios and a small bag of sugar. The prairies seemed to go on forever and I wasn't a big fan of the forever.

"But progress was being made. Every time I passed a sign for a new province, it put me closer to the lady of my life. Entering Alberta was special. I knew my journey was coming to an end and I was about to enter a new phase of my life. There was no turning back. The roads were in much better condition, although they were not paved in gold as the newspaper talked about. There was a buzz in the air. People were doing things … big things. They talked in plain language and got the job done. Coming from Ontario in the midst of a recession, it was a pleasant change of pace.

"I called your mom on the phone after I reached a motel outside of Edmonton. Of course, she wanted to come visit. I said no. I was in too bad a shape: dirt everywhere and I had lost a lot of weight. After 23 days of riding and about 3700 kilometres covered, my journey was complete.

"The next day, I rode into Edmonton and arrived at the steps of the University of Alberta Faculty of Nursing. Your mom's whole class of nurses in training was out to greet me. The head nurse at the dorm allowed me to stay downstairs, which, at the time, was highly irregular. Your mom and I have been together ever since, through thick and thin. I think you know the rest of the story," he finished.

More importantly, I see a new side to him – one of ambition and adventure. *And to think*, he courted my mom like a scene from a movie. *This man, my father.*

That night, we rest in a pair of musty motel beds watching TV. Our minds and bodies now at ease, and sharing a quiet understanding, my father hands over control of the remote. "Watch whatever you want," he tells me.

Flipping passed a barrage of commercials, my attention instantly homes in on the image of a cyclist suffering in sweltering desert heat. It is coverage of an event called the Race Across America, broadcast on the Outdoor Life Network.

Neither of us have heard of the ultra-marathon event. The announcer describes it as a dramatic coast-to-coast dash across the United States, and, apparently, "the toughest race in the world." A group of solo cyclists competes day and night to be the first to reach the Atlantic City Boardwalk in New Jersey (and come in under the 12-day cut-off). A caravan of support personnel follows closely behind.

There is something sadistic in knowing that someone is having a tougher time in the saddle than you. It's like watching a train wreck, and one that you want to see play out in dramatic fashion.

My father and I bond over the sight that is grown men falling asleep on their bikes, clinging to only a small shred of sanity. We only have to ride about one-fourth of what they cover each day, "At least 450 kilometres," the announcer says, rather matter-of-factly. *Crazy bastards*, we laugh.

THE EVENING OF JULY 23, 1996
We near our destination of Oliphant, Ontario. The process of completing an endurance event has been uniquely fulfilling and new for me. Unlike hockey, there is no scoreboard. There are no bad calls, politics or feuding parents to contend with. It's just the road and wind cutting through our spokes.

We pass a sign marked "Oliphant" on our right.

As was the case on day one, I take notice of the sunset on the western horizon. Warm rays of light now dance over the ripples on Lake Huron. They extend up our hardened legs, highlighting awkward tan lines and slightly leaner frames.

Riding out front with excitement, I lead us through the small village, down side streets and to the familiar smell of vacation lapping up from the beach. In full embrace of it, I peel back the Velcro on my sweat-stained gloves and unzip my jersey a little.

There is a welcome surprise.

Ahead, I see my mother and sister walking with their backs to us. They flew in from Calgary a few days ago to see us finish. I call out in excitement, "We're here!"

They turn to acknowledge us, then giddily jog on ahead to grab a roll of toilet paper off the ground. Curiously, they each clutch an end and string it across the road. It is a home-made banner to signify the finish at my aunt and uncle's cottage retreat. We apply our brakes and savour the moment.

Filled with elated laughter and relief, my father extends his hand to shake mine. "You did it," he says proudly.

SUMMER VACATION HAS COME TO A CLOSE
I find myself back in a rowdy classroom on the first day of Grade 7 at Springbank Middle School. I sit silent at my desk, arms folded, looking out the window.

Our curvaceous new homeroom teacher walks in and asks us all to be seated. It takes a few minutes for the class to settle.

"Welcome, everyone," she leads. "Let's begin with introductions. We'll go around the room, say your name, and something fun that you did this summer." Naturally, I sit at the back to avoid being the centre of attention. Speaking in front of groups makes me nervous.

In a cruel twist of fate, she decides to start with reject

row. I see her squinting, trying to read the folded nametag at the edge of my desk. My heart immediately begins pounding, anticipating the spotlight shift. "Okay, Ryan, why don't you share a fun story from your summer break." All eyes on me.

Palms now sweating. "I, I rode my bike."

She continues down the basic line of questioning. "Oh, that's nice. Did you go anywhere special?

"Yes."

"Where to?" She prods. Even the least interested student is staring back now.

I don't have an exit strategy. *Here goes.* "My father and I cycled for three weeks across Canada. We rode all the way to Ontario."

Heads immediately perk up around the room. Additionally, our teacher utters some intangible word of shock under her breath, which only I catch.

I should be intimidated by the attention, but I'm not.

Instead I'm reminded of the moment I told my father, "Let's keep going," on day one of our cross-country journey. I need not forget we achieved something pretty incredible: *3400 kilometres.*

I should sit up in my chair.

CHAPTER 2

CANADIANA

AUGUST 20, 1997

My father and I fly high above the Pacific Ocean en route to the foreign land of Sapporo, Japan.

Last month I was selected to be part of the Calgary Jr. Flames hockey team. Many of the top 14-year-olds from around Alberta were chosen. We travel as a team with our fathers to an international tournament hosted annually by the Japan Ice Hockey Federation. It is an incredible opportunity to build my résumé.

Initial excitement is followed by a long pause.

Rows of drowsy strangers now line my periphery. A few sit asleep, heads cocked to one side, mouths open. The bored majority remains in waking confinement, transfixed by the hum of the engine and dim aisle lighting. I let out a deep sigh.

We are cramped together at the back of the plane. Our itinerary shows the flight time as ten hours from Vancouver to Tokyo, then another hour and a half on a pondhopper to Sapporo. It's a long time, considering that these are the cheap seats. Businessmen puff disgusting-smelling cigarette smoke only a few rows away.

I try to listen to my new Discman, but my father leans in with yet another selection of sage advice. He is determined to talk strategy, despite knowing very little about the competition. My teammates assume we will dominate the smaller

Asian players with our size and speed. "That doesn't matter," my father says quietly. "You need to stand out among the guys on *this* team. You need to be a leader."

I couldn't feel further from it. Before flying from Calgary to Vancouver, the "best of the best" met for three days of team-building exercises, including on-ice practices at Father David Bauer Arena (home of the Canadian National Men's Hockey Team). Prior to the first session, we were presented with crisp replica Calgary Flames jerseys with our names embroidered on the back. Slipping them on, there soon ensued an air of entitlement. I took notice of all the gold chains, frosted tips, and loudmouth personalities.

I stood alone from the beginning. My parents dress me in the sensible styles of Eddie Bauer and the Gap. I wear "tighty whities," not boxers. I do not chew tobacco. I have never had a beer. And my attempt at bravado was laughable, winning me few friends.

What I do have is size. I'm among the tallest of the 14-year-olds, five foot eleven, stocky and pissed off when I need to be. I love nailing the opposition into the stiff wooden boards, and I'm good at it. Crushing my own teammates during practice sometimes feels more rewarding. The act has evolved into an emotional release.

AUGUST 22, 1997

There is very little time to transition into the incredibly foreign environment. Our hotel beds are a foot shorter than we are used to, the toilet in the washroom lights up, vending machines dispense colourful cans of beer, we are a minority for the first time, the menu at McDonald's doesn't make sense *and what is that smell?*

We play our first game far too soon at Makomanai Ice

Arena (where hockey was played during the 1972 Winter Olympics, hosted by Sapporo).

Before the puck drops, players on both teams are asked to skate circles to help dispel fog that hovers over the ice. (Humidity in the air condenses over the cooler surface, creating a low-lying cloud.) It is impossible to see from one end of the rink to the other without first performing the exercise.

After a short warm-up, we line up along centre ice to bow and exchange gifts. Minutes later, the puck is dropped and a swarm of crafty Koreans slice through our team of jetlagged oafs. We lose the game handily. Our best chance now is a bronze medal.

Enter, the hockey parent.

The look. It begins with our coach as we exit the ice. He shakes his head and throws a clipboard against the concrete wall. He yells in the dressing room only moments later: "What the fuck was that?!"

Expletive, expletive, expletive.

Leaving the dressing room with our heavy hockey bags of shame, we then enter the dreaded arena lobby. One by one we face a similar disapproving look on our fathers' faces. *You guys blew it.*

My father pulls me aside, red-faced. His shirt is wrinkled from squirming in the bleachers, no doubt with his arms crossed in a tight wad. "What the hell was that? You were all over the place," he says bluntly. "I'm embarrassed. You should be too."

He then turns and walks away.

I'm a million miles from happiness.

My parents pay top dollar for me to transition away from my community high school in Grade 8 to the National Sport School, also in Calgary. It is a private learning institution that caters to the unique needs of up-and-coming Olympic athletes. The first semester had already begun while I was in shameful transit back to Canada from Japan.

Mind you, a fashionably late entrance accessorizes well with the Jr. Flames tracksuit and Japanese iron-on patches. The novelty lasts only a couple of days before I realize I'm in the company of approximately 100 of Canada's top amateur athletes. They hail from many eclectic sport backgrounds, including figure skating, gymnastics and ski jumping. The brutish hockey players hold a majority stake.

A world ranking is necessary in order to be accepted into the program – in every sport except hockey, that is. Our parents need only write a hefty cheque. These payments afford regular training sessions in the mornings, either on-ice or weightlifting at the nearby University of Calgary gym.

The timeline for completing schoolwork is often negotiated (and exploited). We can borrow laptop computers when away for competition, and our teachers are accessible by e-mail. Best part of all, grazing out of desk-side coolers seems the norm, not frowned upon. Carbohydrates are our friend.

After school we have additional practices and games with our respective teams. I am now affiliated with the Calgary Royals Athletic Association in southwest Calgary. My goal, as it has been ingrained in me, is to achieve AAA status in my first year of Bantam-level hockey, and then repeat this at the Midget level over the course of the next two years.

Community-level hockey falls below the AA level and is considered to be where a career in the sport goes to die. You have two years in each category. Making AA your first year is okay. You *must* be selected for AAA the second year to remain a contender. The most talented of us reach AAA the first year and are awarded the opportunity to knock heads with predominantly older, faster players. It also raises your profile with hockey scouts.

On weekdays I drive in with my parents to their work in downtown Calgary, then take the light rail transit line to the University of Calgary. From there, it's a 15-minute walk to Father David Bauer Arena (Old Faithful) and the cold halls where legends are made. Our hockey equipment hangs in a private room, always moist with sweat and reeking from the previous practice.

SECOND SEMESTER – JANUARY 12, 1998

In the midst of an early morning session, I stand distracted by the sight of cool, condensed breath pushing through a line of helmet cages.

The school coach grabs the scruff of a player's jersey and tries to knock him off balance with a knee to the back of the leg. We are learning on-ice fighting techniques. I'll be next.

This coach enjoys using me as a practice dummy in front of the others. He believes in my ability but worries that it has not been fully realized. He tells me I need to be more aggressive, and not just when I am trying to defend myself. He and my father, they preach the same "get mean" mantra.

Standing ready, the coach pushes into me with more force than he did the player before. He has a higher standard for me, yet I fall to the ice just the same. Lying on the frozen surface, I notice him skate away with a look of disapproval. That glare stings worse than any knee. It is personal.

I fall back in line.

During the first partner drill, I smash one of my class-mates into the boards as he lunges for the puck. He immediately crumples to the ground in winded agony. I stare him in the eye for a moment, then stride away without looking back. Yesterday he made a crack about my large arms being a condition of an obsessive masturbating disorder. *Fuck you, buddy.*

Next month is my 16th birthday. I have no desire to invite the coach, the players or anyone else for that matter.

AUGUST, 1998

Following my first year of Bantam hockey, I begin touring tryout camps for Alberta Junior Hockey League teams around the province. For a 16-year-old playing hockey in Canada, this is exactly the right track to be on. The best AJHL players are drafted to play in the Western Hockey League. This talent pool then serves as a feeder for the NHL. Therefore, more camp invitation letters equals more bragging rights at the National Sport School.

My father and I attend all the tryouts we can. This requires long drives of talking about nothing other than hockey, roaming from one cold community hall to the next, gaining "learning experiences," with punctuated moments of quiet reflection in small country diners.

We criss-cross the prairies, often doubling back on the same roads we got to know during "Manhood Training," which has since spawned two additional tours. In 1997 we cycled from Prince Edward Island to my grandparents' home in Grimsby, Ontario. The following year, we ventured north from Fort Lauderdale, Florida, up the east coast of the United States, once again to the Niagara region of Ontario.

Summer bicycle tours have evolved into "a great

cross-training exercise for hockey," my father proudly proclaims. He references newspaper articles of hockey pros that ride stationary bikes in the off-season. And considering that my skating continues to be one of my strongest assets, I have no problem falling in line. In fact, I now enjoy racing my father up the occasional climb.

Still following his lead, we have experienced many new things together, including travelling through poor fishing communities along the Atlantic coast, the shock of French-speaking people and poutine in Quebec and the experience of holding minority status in those humid, predominantly black Southern states.

And there is still a lot to learn.

In South Carolina, I remember pulling up to a group of ghetto kids throwing a football. "Toss it to me," my father says, rather playfully. The kids look at each other with a kind of stunned acknowledgement that white guys don't even come through here, let alone in Spandex and on bikes. But they soon give in to their desire to play, as all kids do.

Respect for my father sways dramatically between warm moments like these in the summer and a season of cold frustration that only grows longer.

Our post-game talks teeter between hatred and appreciation (knowing he is in my corner). The end result rarely brings out the best in either of us, however. This fact is becoming more apparent.

We travel to a camp for the Olds Grizzlys AJHL team in central Alberta. While lacing up my skates with a bunch of unknowns on the "green jersey team" (we are divided into primary colours for scrimmaging), our young coach-for-the-weekend barges into the dressing room and begins arranging fights between players on the opposing squad. The parting line being, "Go out there and FUCK him up!" He then turns and spits a wad of chewing tobacco on the floor before exiting.

The following weekend, we drive east to the town of Strathmore for the Fort McMurray Oil Barons tryout. Nerves abound.

My hockey career has reached a bottleneck.

Pulling up my jockstrap and plastic protective cup, I see bruises from the previous go-round. In addition to fighting, players go out of their way to hit each other in all the tender spots, looking for any advantage possible. Hesitantly, I skate back out for another round.

But this time I have become the target of a bare-knuckle brawl.

A hulking older player starts taking cheap shots at me right from the opening whistle. He pushes me aside to try and start a fight. The referees turn a blind eye as he throttles me in the back of my helmet. Still, I stand my ground. "Screw off! I'm not fighting you!"

"Come on, pussy!" he taunts aggressively. The asshole coaches on the bench, my so-called voices of leadership, they too encourage me to indulge.

I continue to blow the situation off, hoping it will just go away. But the aggressor chops at the back of my skate (and vulnerable Achilles tendon) with his stick. A celebration of yelling and jeers follows from all directions once again. *What are you going to do, pussy?*

I feel genuinely threatened and alone. Fortunately, the last buzzer sounds to end the game.

I leave the arena in haste.

With one crisis averted, I'm about to face another: my father's likely disapproval. "Never start a fight. Just finish it," he always tells me. And in this case, I neither started nor finished. I was the *pussy*.

Choosing not to acknowledge the aggression has also highlighted my aversion to "getting mean" when it counts. And not being an all-star goal scorer, I have missed an opportunity to distinguish myself. Not to mention the three-hour drive, the expense, the energy and a future with the Oil Barons, it's all a bust.

My father is visibly frustrated and at a loss for words. We head back to the car in silence.

Inside the damned confessional, I slump down in the passenger seat, readying myself for the kind of criticism that hurts most – not of skill but of a failing in character. My heart begins beating faster.

He stares ahead with a fierce gaze, transfixed on the front door of the arena. "Fucking idiot," he murmurs. I immediately turn my head in shame, my adrenaline and emotions now swirling.

As I ready myself to receive the worst of it, he slams the car door open and starts back toward the arena. *Huh? My confrontation playbook is not familiar with this move.*

I try to anticipate the next move, now seeing my on-ice nemesis walk out of the double doors with three obnoxious friends. They're laughing, probably at my expense.

My father immediately gets in his face. Having to look up, just as I did, he begins to yell.

The thugs begin to surround him.

He continues yelling, unflinchingly, now with a finger thrust in the perpetrator's face. *Shit, come on Dad.*

They drop their equipment bags and launch into more mocking laughter. My father's pointed finger now clenches into a fist, readying to respond. But after a few more cursed stabs, the trio decide it's not worth their time and they continue on. My father stands transfixed as they brush past mockingly, his fist still locked in anger.

A group of younger kids suited in pads and running shoes walks past with their fathers, unaware. They bound into the arena with excitement while my father continues to stand in the same spot, frozen in anger.

Hockey is no longer a game.

GRADE 10 AT THE NATIONAL SPORT SCHOOL, SEPTEMBER, 1998

I have realized that this is not where I belong. The coaches and players have ruined it for me. And the parts that I cling to only satisfy my ego. But becoming a hockey player is the Canadian dream, *right?*

I continue going through the motions.

At lunch on the first day back from summer vacation, a swarm of hockey players sits around in the hallway laughing. A heavier-set teacher walks by and one player waddles behind him, mockingly. The only male figure skater in the school sits down beside us. He's always trying to fit in with the group. Someone quietly utters "fag."

The sole male gymnast in the school strolls out of the office as we are heading back to class. We rarely see him around school – he's always away competing, doing most of his schoolwork by correspondence. His name is Kyle. Some of my older skiing pals are mutual friends. We have met once or twice in passing.

Watching Kyle walk down the corridor, I'm impressed by his posture and muscle tone. He is sculpted rather than bashed and built-up. And unlike the brute force of the hockey players, his demeanour screams passion and drive. He is a champion embodied. Yet someone still utters "fag," this time a little louder. Kyle continues walking by without paying any attention.

"Hey, Kyle," I acknowledge.

With some trepidation, he nods back, "Hey, Ryan."

Five years later, Kyle Shewfelt would go on to win a gold medal for his floor routine at the 2004 Summer Olympics, in Athens, Greece. "Our Golden Hero," proclaimed the front page of the *Calgary Herald* newspaper.

OCTOBER, 1998

I fail to make AAA Midget my rookie year but manage to snag one of two coveted "call up" positions. It is an opportunity to travel with the team and suit up for action, should any players fall prey to injury. It's the best of both worlds: one foot in the AAA door and the other as an assistant captain at the AA level.

Unfortunately, the players on my team have no respect for either the captain or me. Many of them are older than us and failed to make AAA on their last chance. Out of spite, they act out for one last season before moving on to whatever it is failed hockey players do with their lives.

They hang from the rafters and swing their dicks in the locker room. Worst of all, they laugh at any attempt to convey any sense of unity on the team.

Our coach tires of their antics. Aggression resulting from this often rears its ugly head at practices following a loss. The term "getting skated" quickly becomes a rousing aftershock in the halls of the Sport School. Such practices are universally known among players for not involving pucks, just a garbage pail at centre ice for collecting vomit.

Expletive, expletive, expletive.

"Forget them, the scouts only need to see the letter on

your jersey: an *A* for Assistant Captain," my father says of the power struggle and politics. I agree but also feel a sense of failure for having become a leader that cannot lead.

AJHL scouts are at all of our important games. They can usually be spotted on their own, writing notes on a clipboard in the stands. Recognizing their presence, my father will often make a subtle lifting gesture with his two hands from behind the glass: *Pick it up.*

At this level it is common for both parents and siblings to attend every game, sometimes every practice. My mother and sister are usually in the stands, braving the cold. My father is there without fail. It is a right of passage that many hockey families share.

I thrive on cheering fans, cute smiles from the roaming "puck-bunny" section (of girlfriends and so-called sluts), making a good hit in plain sight of a scout, and receiving the approving thumbs-up gesture and nod from my father. Win or lose, however, he always has at least one criticism.

"Yes, Dad. Okay, Dad. Next time, Dad," I groan. My mother listens patiently from the passenger seat on the drive home. Her expression feigns a smile, bordering on a frown. Tension between the males is always close at hand. She is the aforementioned feudal referee.

My sister quietly stares out the window from the back seat, rarely complaining that she is not the centre of attention. Her aspiration to be a figure skater or soccer player died some time ago. I'm not really sure what she is interested in now.

CHRISTMAS, 1998
My parents make a surprise announcement to my sister and me that they are having another baby. Jokingly, my

father declares that the child will be nurtured as an artist, "not another athlete."

Where did this come from?

Aside, he softly reminds my sister and me that there may be complications. "Because of your mother's age, the chance that something might go wrong with the pregnancy increases. The baby could be born with Down syndrome, or something else. The delivery could also be very hard on her."

MARCH, 1999

The day comes when we find out the sex of the child. My parents kiss and hold hands as they share the news over dinner: "We're having a boy!" The sentiment feels awkward and surreal, a loud expression of joy in an otherwise quiet home. Even when presented with the baby's black and white outline on the cloudy ultrasound, I still feel a sense of disconnect.

My father notices a growing distance and becomes defensive of the positive aura and of my mother. He says I am being selfish, that I am rebelling for no longer being the centre of attention. *Perhaps.*

This happiness is a foreign invader. I'm also resentful toward my parents for having chosen to bring a baby into a mix of ongoing tension. I internalize the act as a chance to start over and as an admission of past parenting failures. It pisses me off that I'm the only one without any stability. *Fucking hockey.*

MAY, 1999

My Grade 11 English teacher, Miss Whiteford, challenges everyone in our class to give our first long speech in front of the class. It must be 15 minutes in length, not a minute shorter.

"So research something that you are passionate about," she encourages.

The challenge connects with me in a way no other assignment ever has. Aside, I ask Miss Whiteford if I can present a talk on a subject that might be controversial. Understandably, she inquires into the subject matter. I lay it all out on the line. After a moment of consideration, she tells me to go for it. "Ryan, I am 100 per cent behind you."

For three weeks I work on this task, tirelessly erasing and rewriting a series of poignant comments. This is the most energy that I have ever directed toward a school project. It is also the first time that my final grade is of no concern. This is real: real emotion, real action and real consequences.

On the day of the presentation, I go last. My heavy subject matter has purposely been saved for the final round. No matter, my classmates all see it coming. Quiet rumours have been swirling about the reason for my vacant nature of late.

Finally, I am asked to stand in front of the class.

My classmates and I have known each other for three years at this point. I'm shaking and nervous as hell. I take a deep breath and begin: "My speech is entitled 'Farewell to hell and welcome to new beginnings.' It is about why I am leaving the National Sport School." Ears timidly perk up.

Shaking in my delivery, I speak of an obscene abuse of school privileges, the persecution of decidedly less cool athletes, and of hockey players run wild. I'm tired of their ongoing pestering, saying that my brother will be born with Down syndrome, and also of talk of the large-arm masturbating disorder.

There is a *real* aftershock. The innocent among them silently cheer. The guilty come up to me afterwards and apologize. One of the hockey players even writes a letter of repentance to my family.

The following day I am asked to give the same talk over lunch to all the teachers, in private. A full 20 minutes passes in the staff room without a single one of them reaching for a sandwich or coffee. When I finish reading the nervously crumpled document for the second time, I gaze up to see only soft smiles and tears.

I feel a tremendous weight lifting.

CHAPTER 3

NATHAN JAMES

JANUARY 26, 2012

My mother and father have come to visit me in Tucson, Arizona. They have a rental property located three hours north in the upscale town of Carefree. I'm down in "The Old Pueblo," as Tucson is sometimes called, for a week of cycling with the team from Hammer Nutrition, makers of a line of endurance fuels and supplements for athletes. Four months ago I took on the position of Fueling Guru for the business in Canada. I also manage sales for Ontario.

The three of us are sitting alone, poolside at the Marriott on a warm afternoon. Overhead the Arizona sun creeps through the shade of an umbrella fixed to a small round table with three coffees balanced on it. Our sunglasses block out what light there is, and conceal the tension rising. My father and I sit across from each other, my mother in the middle as always.

Weighing heavily on this family reunion there sits a dark cloud. Two weeks ago I had told my parents of a book I planned to write, and of the material that would be covered in it. It quickly became apparent that Skype was not the medium to use to present such news. Nevertheless, I pushed on through increasingly tense exchanges. I felt it important that they come to terms with *it*. It has been 12 years since the passing of Nathan, my baby brother. Our last call ended rather abruptly, and in tears.

My father wastes no time: "There is something that I want to talk to you about. I'm not sure what is the best way…" He begins to choke up, then pauses.

"I want you to know that this is a deeply personal story you intend to write about. You need to understand where your mother and I were coming from at that time, that you were difficult to live with.

"You were a 17-year-old going through normal 17-year-old issues, I guess. It didn't help that I had a hard time communicating with you." I nod, choosing not to speak. There is more that he needs to get off his chest.

"Your mother and I came from nothing. Everything that we needed, we had to find a way to buy for ourselves. My father never went camping with me, never asked if I wanted to throw the ball around." My grandfather had recently cut off all ties with our family and moved out west to Vancouver Island after my grandmother passed away. The knife in the side was that he fled with our family dog, a rambunctious golden retriever named Chester.

We had started down a tangent, but I felt it was something well worth discussing. "Do you really care if you see your Dad again?" I ask him bluntly. "You never say anything nice about him. It's alright to move on." Family relationships are not as sacred to me.

My mother enters the conversation. "It is knowing that he is still out there that I think bothers your father. We don't have closure on the situation."

My father jumps back in. "We found your grandmother in a pool of blood on the floor of their home – a home that we helped build and maintain – and rushed her to the hospital, you know, when things took a turn for the worse. When I told your grandfather, he didn't rush over. He came over when it was convenient for him. And even then, he felt the need to complain about her being in the hospital, not back at home where she supposedly belonged. If it were not for us, she would have died that day from a bad fall. I did everything I possibly could to make a nice life for them the last couple of years, and he ruined it all.

"I'm telling you this so you can understand where my frustration came from. You had every opportunity in the world. We always provided for you, your sister, my parents. I did things for all of you that he never did with me. I couldn't understand why you were so difficult to live with."

Sensing a pause, I decide to share a new side of my story.

"Opportunities are all relative, Dad. It doesn't mean that I didn't have problems of my own. What you don't know about that period – playing hockey, going to the Sport School and Nathan passing – was that I seriously considered committing suicide. I became numb to everything that was going on around me. Those were my 'Fuck it' years."

We break for a coffee refill.

My father takes a deep, more relaxed breath and tells me there is one more thing he wants to say about Nathan. He intends to address the main point of contention in my writing.

"As I mentioned before, your mother and I scraped together our savings to pay for school, for our first car, for rent. Did you know that your first bed was a refurbished baby carriage? The point is, nothing came easy." He takes a sip from the paper cup, followed by another deep breath.

"Nathan was planned. We had reached a point in our lives when we could afford to do the things we wanted to, like buy new clothes for the baby, buy a new crib and spend more time. His passing was the biggest kick to the gut that we have ever been dealt. To make matters worse, I had to go back to work and inform our staff, our family and all of our friends. It took everything to keep us together during that time. Meanwhile, you were very inwardly focused. I hope you now understand why this is so difficult for us."

I promise them I would not write about the specifics surrounding Nathan's death.

SEPTEMBER, 1999

The leaves had begun to change to yellow as fall stretched over the Alberta prairies. Nathan's funeral was now more than three months behind us, still raw and rarely talked about, but enough time had now passed to slowly begin the healing process. One of those steps included transferring back to the community high school in Springbank.

This was my chance to do all the things I hadn't been able to at the Sport School: go to dances, serve on school council, take the bus and play on the football team. I was also excited to be back with old friends.

Getting away from the Sport School did not mean hockey was over and done with, however. A few weeks into the first semester of Grade 12, tryouts for AAA Midget (second year) reared their ugly head. Unfortunately, what love I had once had for the game was gone. Continuing to drive to the arena was part of a facade to satisfy my parents and anyone else who had invested any time and care in my future.

Sensing a separation, my parents remind me of potential scholarships to respected colleges in the United States that hang in the balance. "Don't throw away this great opportunity," they plead. The thought of walking the earth like Kwai Chang Caine in the movie *Kung Fu* has far greater appeal, though. This idea of mine is considerably heightened one afternoon in class while we watch a documentary on Canadian hero Terry Fox.

In 1977, six years before I was born, the fiery young athlete from Port Coquitlam, British Columbia, was diagnosed with cancer and forced to have his right leg amputated 15 centimetres above the knee. In the clutches of soul-sucking atrophy and disillusionment, Terry Fox conjured up an ambitious plan to run across Canada and raise $24-million for the Canadian Cancer Society. His fundraising goal equated to $1 from every Canadian citizen.

On April 12, 1980, Terry began with little fanfare in St. John's, Newfoundland, running the equivalent of a marathon a day on a prosthetic leg.

After 143 days and 5373 kilometres, just as Terry had begun to win over the hearts of the nation, he was prematurely forced to end his "Marathon of Hope" in Thunder Bay, Ontario. Cancer had spread to his lungs.

He died in a hospital bed just three months later.

As I watch the film, my eyes well up with a new kind of pride.

That evening I tell my parents over Chinese food that I am going to do something like Terry one day. "It would be cool to give back," I say, honestly. "I don't know how, but I'll try to do something some day." They both smile, faintly acknowledging the grand ambition, then continue in on the won ton soup.

"How are tryouts going?" my father asks.

SEPTEMBER 15, 1999

I drive up to the arena, alone and conflicted. Inside the cold musk, I lace up my skates and listen to the idiots beside me talking shit about their girlfriends, swearing and spitting tobacco on the black rubber floor.

I have no desire to converse with them. In another life, I imagine such conflicts of character would be settled by a bloody duel to the bitter end, not waiting in angst as a blood clot forms in my brain.

We line up at the metal rink gate, young morons stacked in men's armour. *Shoulders back, stand tall.* Readying for the release, I snarl and bite down on my rubber mouthguard. Soon, we'll see which asshole makes the cut.

We begin skating laps to warm up our legs. The coaches stride out of the gates last. They're in matching blue and gold jumpsuits, hair slicked back like grease balls, carrying clipboards, and showing no emotion. They will be evaluating us on every pass and play. This is an important moment.

A whistle blows and we fall in line.

We begin a tight scrimmage at the far end of the rink where tension is high. The puck drops and someone takes a cheap shot, punching me in the back of the helmet. I go slightly concussive, yet no one blinks an eye. They just wait to see if I have the balls to push on.

On the next drill, I miss a poorly timed pass. The puck bounces off my skates and flutters toward the open end. The head coach looks over at me, not in conciliation but in annoyance. He utters something under his breath and makes a note. No doubt a negative comment about "that Correy kid."

I snap. *I'm sick of these fuckers!*

I skate furiously out of line, right past his clipboard. I bang on the glass with my stick.

One of the hockey parents hastily opens the gate, asking what's wrong, but I fire straight past, jittery with adrenaline, smashing open the dressing room door.

I immediately notice that the room is silent, almost awkwardly so. I remove my helmet and stare into oblivion.

How am I going to explain this to my parents?

I just quit hockey.

OCTOBER, 1999

Only after my former AA Midget coach came calling, asking if I would consider coming back as their captain, did my parents sense that something had happened. Up until then, I had been pretending to go to practices.

I finally relent: "I'm done with hockey."

A barrage of memories and time spent working on developing my potential begin swirling down the drain. *Five years, gone.*

But my father's expression is not one of rage.

After Nathan, he lost the will to fight me on this. Now he's just hurt. And that look of sadness is far more profound than the results of any verbal punching match could be.

He no longer knows what to say.

Attempting to defuse the situation, I follow up with a plan to pursue business school. "Eventually, I would like to take over your business," I tell my parents directly and in a professional tone.

No longer will they have to sit in cold arenas and play into the politics. Now, their son is going to make something of this life.

"Please trust me," I ask them again.

They nod, still unable to speak.

CHRISTMAS, 1999

My family heads south in our oversized RV to visit my father's parents at their snowbird hideaway in Cave Creek, Arizona. It has been just over two months since that *other* departure.

Upon arriving at our destination in the Grand Canyon state, I set out on a three-hour trail run to the top of one of the neighbouring Black Mountain peaks.

Several complicated decisions plague my thoughts.

In the short term, I had defused one bomb, then quickly ignited the fuse of another: very little about my parents' financial management business interested me. They worked long hours and often appeared drained at the end of the day. And despite their success, no amount of money could justify that kind of existence, at least for me.

Running upward along a narrow path, I narrowly avoid patches of small, prickly cacti as I leap from one crumbling shale ledge to another. My chest heaves as I push the limit. I am oblivious to pain and inspired by the burn. But like all great moments, the thrill soon peaks.

Gazing over the summit edge, I recognize its allure but also accept the thin line that I now walk again. There is another train wreck forming up ahead. At 17 years old, however, hormones still cloud any reasonable foresight on my part. I just do what feels right in the moment, and breathe.

Bounding back down the mountain in a full sweat, I'm stopped in my tracks by an unfortunate sight. *Shit, what's that?* My attention immediately homes in on what looks like a wounded dog, lying in the middle of the road.

Was it hit by a car?

I cautiously step closer. It is a greying golden retriever, now convulsing.

I bend down to see how I can help the poor animal.

From behind a hedge, a woman with blonde hair in her forties appears in full gardening attire. "Don't worry, he's very sick." This is obviously not the first time a stranger has happened across the animal. She smiles and asks where my run took me.

"Up to the top of Black Mountain," I reply.

The woman appears impressed and introduces herself. "My name is Debbie," holding out her hand. I offer up my own introduction and mention that my family is visiting for Christmas. Debbie's wheels begin to turn.

"I have a daughter. You two should meet. She'll be back later this evening." Without a moment's hesitation, Debbie runs back into her cream-coloured adobe home in search of a pen. Minutes later she procures a note.

"Kelly," I read aloud, along with a phone number. Debbie smiles again and then continues with her yard work. I walk the rest of the way home, now excited by this chance encounter.

That evening, I stay in and watch a movie while the rest of my family heads out for dinner. They are somewhat skeptical about what happened earlier, yet supportive of the pursuit. They have grown worried about the lack of ladies in my life. In reality, there were very few prospects at the Sport School. And now, back at Springbank Community High School, it appears as though I am three years behind the dating curve.

The hour soon dawns when Debbie suggested that I call.

I stand in the kitchen of our rented condo, next to a phone hanging on the wall, with hopeless romantic nerves, and a sort of ambitious reasoning: there is nothing to lose. I have never called a girl out of the blue before.

I dial the numbers on the rotary wheel.

A dial tone can be heard and soon, *her* voice. "Hello, Kelly speaking."

I choose to break the nervous energy with a lighthearted comment about her mother's matchmaking. Kelly jumps to the point: "She told me I had to meet you. How about we head over to the hot tub next to the pool and tennis courts?" Hot tubs are a desert community fixture.

Um, okay. "Let's do it! See you in 15 minutes," I anxiously reply.

We meet for the first time at the locked entrance to the pool.

Seeing Kelly in the moonlight, I'm blown away. She has long blonde hair, beautiful curves and shocking green eyes. The novelty of making first contact with an all-American girl is not lost on me, either. "Hey," she flirtatiously smiles, then unlocks the gate.

We place our towels on a set of sun-bleached pool chairs and tiptoe into the bubbling hot tub. Far above, patchworks of stars dance across the desert sky. I gaze into Kelly's eyes and find myself feeling breathless. But then she smiles and I feel right at home. I'm smitten.

Towelling off, she asks if I would like to come to her New Year's party the following evening. A few of her friends are going to be there. "Nothing big. We'll watch some movies, eat some snacks, maybe play a few drinking games," she says. I refrain from telling her I have had all of one beer up until this point in my life. The Sport School ingrained a my-body-is-a-temple philosophy in its students.

"That sounds great," I blush like an amateur.

NEW YEAR'S EVE, 1999
It is the eve of the supposed Y2K meltdown.

Debbie greets me at the door while hastily applying makeup. She stops in front of a hallway mirror to make sure her white uniform is pressed properly. "Tonight is a great night to make tips," she motions at the restaurant name on her lapel. Debbie had divorced from her husband some years earlier, and now works two jobs to support her children, Kelly and younger son Brandon. Her second job involves secretarial work at her children's school.

Debbie taps me on the shoulder as she runs out the door, "Have fun tonight!"

Kelly appears and motions that the coast is clear.

She introduces me to her friends and then hands me a beer. Cracking open the cool can feels foreign, yet a welcoming deterrent for my nerves. I take a long sip of the frosty beverage and am welcomed into Kelly's circle of friends.

On this evening, I am a subtly cooler person.

Running around like buzzed fools, we set off fireworks in the front yard, yelling out, "Three, two, one, Happy New Year!" and then quiet. Looking around, we notice that the street lights have remained on. No sirens can be heard, either. It appears as though the global computer meltdown has been averted.

The all-American beauty and I lean in for a first kiss.

MARCH, 2000

Following our Christmas holidays in Arizona, I became enamoured of Coldplay's heartfelt debut album, *Parachutes*.

While the rest of North America was homing in on their first single, "Yellow," I had already moved on to the moody piano chords of "Trouble."

It was the band's televised performance on the BRIT Awards that first connected with me. Singer Chris Martin sat alone at a piano, a solo spotlight fixed on him, singing. And in an instant, their music became the soundtrack of my ambition.

MARCH, 2001

With emotions toward the all-American girl still swirling a year later, I work up the courage to ask my parents if they would pay for Kelly to fly north for my high school commencement, now just two months away.

Sensing that I have found someone truly special, they agree to help as part of my graduation present.

I anxiously present the news to Kelly during one of our weekly long-distance calls. "Best of all, your 17th birthday falls on the same day as the dance," I tell her. "It's going to be great!"

In the midst of sharing the good news, the familiar drone of an automated operator voice intrudes: "You have one more minute for this call." Thumbing my drained phone card, I anxiously await Kelly's answer.

"Of course I'll come! I can't wait to see you again," She says warmly.

And then the sound of a dial tone.

I'm in love.

MAY 18, 2001

The large ballroom sparkles.

Friends in my graduating class hold on to one another, gently swaying on the dance floor. A handful of their parents sit next to each other at the surrounding tables, arms around each other, reminiscing about another time, perhaps.

Kelly is wearing an elegant white dress that exposes her shoulders. Her skin is smooth to the touch. And those emerald eyes, *they sparkle.*

For my part, I have rented a traditional black and white tuxedo, paid for with the savings from my new $7/hr "bag boy" job at the local grocery store. The tux is an investment, worth tenfold the rental rate.

With neither of our parents around to keep a watchful eye on us, we press in close on the slow songs. During Chris de Burgh's "Lady in Red," Kelly leans in a little closer and whispers, "I wish you could come down to Arizona this summer. It would be so much fun."

Resting my forehead on hers, I present the disenchanting news, "I wish I could..." My father and I have another tour planned. This time we are headed to the lava rocks and sea breeze of Hawaii. *First World problems.*

Kelly and I continue dancing hand-in-hand, speaking only in touch.

In a few days' time, we will once again be separated by 2400 kilometres. There are also the experimental unknowns of college dorm life on the not-so-distant horizon, far removed from high school flirtation. Fortunately, I have an elaborate plan to keep the music playing.

CHAPTER 4

DETOX

JUNE 23, 2001

The school gym is unusually quiet. Any other day and it would be filled with the sound of basketballs bouncing off backboards and sneakers squeaking on the polished floor. Today, the air hovers quietly over several rows of neatly arranged metal desks and students deep in thought. The last high school exam we will ever write is now before us.

Having already walked across the commencement stage and received my diploma (over a month earlier), the process seems a little anticlimactic, even redundant. And of all the exams I could write, our instructor has scheduled the most tragic of endings: Math 30.

Mr. Nadiri failed to dissuade me from my stance that the subject is a complete waste of time. I have a hard time retaining complicated calculus equations when I know that a computer can process the information more efficiently. The follow-up argument that mathematics translates into other areas of life is lost on me.

I also rebel because numbers are often jumbled inside my head. We realized this some months back when my parents signed me up for an after-school tutoring class. Repetition is apparently the solution. Unfortunately, algebra always came second to the social experience of my final year.

Sensing the furrowed brow, I try to reassure my parents that it will all work out in the end. "As long as I get into college, that's all that really matters … I'll focus more on my grades then," I promise. What employer looks at a high school transcript, anyway? University is where you differentiate yourself.

More grumbles ensue.

As I make my way through the last couple of numbing exam pages, my black Trek 2200 road bike taunts in the periphery. It leans against the back wall, near the exit. Four frame-mounted red panniers hang along the sides of the front and rear wheels. They are loaded with roughly 60 pounds of gear, including a one-person tent, foam sleeping roll, a small cook set, gas burner and tools, as well as my riding clothes. *Everything I need.*

"Keep your eyes on the exam," Nadiri says sternly. But how can I? My mind is already a thousand miles away from here.

The evolving love story with Kelly has captured the hearts of many girls in my grade. They deem our chance meeting to be the "real deal," even going so far as to ask if I believe that she is *the One.*

At this point in our mostly over-the-phone relationship, we have yet to make any status official. Understandably, the distance is an issue with no clear resolution. And now I am headed to Hawaii with my father – another summer lost.

"That is all the time you have," Mr. Nadiri announces, tapping his wristwatch.

I take a deep breath and close my booklet.

Walking up to the front of the gym with my numerical nightmare in hand, I gently place it face down in the complete pile and acknowledge that *high school is over.*

Parting ways, Mr. Nadiri feels the need to pose one last question. "Where to?" he asks.

An instant smile comes across my face.

Rolling my fully loaded bike out to the school parking

lot, I see my booksmart friend Allison already waiting in her truck. "Are you ready to go?" She calls out, smiling.

I heave my bike into the back, then bound into the passenger side. "Most definitely!"

We drive for 45 minutes until just before a sign for the small town of Okotoks (at the south end of Calgary). Allison pulls the truck over on a quiet farm road and leaves me to unload the bike.

As I sit down in the earth to buckle my cycling shoes and helmet, she indulges in the opportunity to pet a curious steed that has trotted up to the barbed wire fence separating us. Rolling farmland accentuates the quiet frontier ahead.

Knowing my eagerness to get going, Allison walks back over and gives me a hug, "Be safe, okay?"

She stands back as I straddle the heavy frame. It holds far more weight than I have ever carried on a bike, and pulls to one side. I adjust my cook set to counterbalance some of the weight, then clip in with my left foot.

Pushing off with my right foot, I yell back and wave, "See you in a month!"

Hawaii was a white lie.

Instead, I have planned a grand gesture: to cycle 2400 kilometres to surprise Kelly in Arizona. My parents and Kelly's mom have known about this for months, and have more or less had to accept it as a lovesick reality.

Debbie is nonetheless worried. She asks that I call regularly to update her on my progress. She even mailed a phone card in advance to help with the expense.

It's just the open road now.

My first solo adventure.

Sitting down beside my bike with highway traffic passing by, I launch into a granola bar that is stashed in my warm back pocket.

Unfolding the crinkled foil, I scan through the ingredient list with great intrigue, though I am relatively oblivious as to its meaning. I proceed to chew the exposed bar in slow succession, appreciating the moment.

I begin riding again in my own time.

With no one in front to follow and match pace with, I rely on my MP3 player to help provide rhythm. The internal memory only has space for 12 songs, but my playlist is golden. Each track has a particular meaning, either for its connection to Kelly or to infuse a particular feeling. Of course, Coldplay is on the list. I have also grown particularly fond of Radiohead's *Kid A* album. The song "Everything In Its Right Place" fills my ear buds now.

Ambience-filled hours fall away.

Heading toward dawn, the familiar Rocky Mountain range begins to migrate farther from my southerly route along Highway 2, soon giving way to simple foothills and swaying prairie grass on the horizon.

As darkness sets in, I store my MP3 player away.

The occasional semi-trailer truck or distracted sedan whirls by, intrusive headlights shining.

I should find somewhere to camp.

Looking left, looking right, the farm fields remain exposed in all directions – no shelter of a forest or cover of a hill.

I keep riding out of fear.

Camping in plain sight of curious traffic doesn't feel safe. It being a Friday doesn't help matters either. "You have to watch out for the drunk idiots," my father would tell me on our tours together. "And you should never ride at night," he forewarned.

He would also tell me tales of pitching his tent in a farmer's field and being woken in the middle of the night by cranky landowners yelling at him to get off their property. And however small a possibility that scenario is for me tonight, it is nonetheless possible. So I keep on riding, my pupils now fully dilated in the dark.

My only defence is a flashing red light, clipped to the back of my Canadian-themed cycling jersey.

As I squint ahead, the moonlight helps outline the painted white line to my left and the grassy embankment, sloping down to the right. All I have to do is stay between them. Hopefully, any passing vehicles will adhere to their own rule.

What time it is, I can't say for sure. I have chosen not to wear a watch on this journey, relying instead on instinct and the inspired energy of my internal metronome. My best guess is that I am riding well after 11 o'clock. The danger in this dark hour creates a feeling that is equal parts fear and exhilaration. It propels me to get somewhere quickly.

Ahead in the distance I can make out the hue of orange overhanging lights and what appears to be a highway interchange. Taking an educated guess at the distance travelled on the day (I also chose not to bring an odometer), I figure the junction is a sign that the next town is not far off. Back in some semblance of civilization, I can regroup in the comfort of an all-night diner or gas station. My steady pace accelerates at this thought.

Having lost my sense of adventure to camp, I now wonder if any motels will still be open at this late hour. Passing under the interchange, I take a short break to consider my options under the soft island of light. Afraid to go back out into the darkness, but even more concerned about passing stares, I make the decision to push on after only a couple of minutes.

Immediately, a loud police siren sounds and flashing blue and red lights pull up behind me. I roll again to a stop, unclip both feet and grimace at what is becoming an evolving series of bad decisions. Nevertheless, I'm sure no laws have been broken. Common sense tells me that the authority figure will instruct me to in fact get some sense.

"What are you doing out here at this hour?" the officer calmly inquires. Sure enough, he is more concerned for my safety. I acknowledge our shared anxiety and tell him I will stop at the next motel.

"There are no motels open at this time. Your best bet is to head over to the Detox centre, not far up the road." He then decides for me. "I'll radio ahead to let them know you will be coming. They'll have a room waiting," he further instructs, getting back into his patrol car.

The officer hangs back to make sure I head in the right direction. Assured, he does a burnout and speeds ahead in dramatic fashion, lights again flashing. I wave to acknowledge the display of authority, slightly comforted by the fact that the most intimidating presence on the road is the guy on my side.

Cresting a short hill, streetlights from the small town of Fort Macleod soon rise out of the shadows. The Detox centre, I'm told, is at the far end of the two-road town. For fear of appearing ungrateful, I opted not to ask the officer what this "Detox centre" actually is. Perhaps it is a nickname for something.

A quiet easterly wind flows through my spokes optimistically ticking by. The southwestern town is otherwise muted. *Keep an eye out.*

I come across a small grey building that stands out among

the quaint and hard-working homes. *Is that it?* It *is* on the opposite end of town, just like the officer told me. But there is
nothing about the scene that appears inviting. The entrance
is fortified with heavy metal doors. Several security cameras
are also pointed down. Pressing the cold doorbell, I consider
making a run for it.

An intimidatingly tall man with a fierce beard opens the
door. Gazing down at me, noticing that I am unattended and
with a bike, he quickly realizes that I am the "young guy"
who was described to him over the radio. "Come on in and
set your stuff down in this room," he directs. "There is a mat
on the floor that you can lay your sleeping bag on. You'll
have the room to yourself. Once you get settled, I'm going to
lock your door, just in case." *Just in case, what?*

I spend a few minutes taking it all in.

Through my cell of surrounding glass, I watch as another
officer enters the centre, now escorting an inebriated individual into what they term "the drunk tank." There is a cordial feeling to it all. The men inside refer to each other by
name, laughing, stumbling around, drunk or high or both.
They'll stay here until the morning to detox, which I now
better understand.

I lie down on the cold floor and close my eyes. The lights
in the sterile centre remain on, never really allowing my
mind to calm. The night is further punctuated by bouts of
slurred yelling, a prolonged assault on my privileged senses.

JUNE 24, 2001
The Detox manager and I are the first to wake. My mind shut
off somewhere between four and seven o'clock this morning.
Back on guard now, I immediately begin rolling up my sleeping bag and quietly collecting the rest of what was unpacked

(and hidden under my mat). Namely, my wallet and a picture of Kelly kept close.

The detox manager tactfully ushers me outside into the fresh morning air. "Good luck," he says, breathing in a moment of sanity for himself.

I pull on my riding gloves and clip in. I feel familiar calluses forming on my palms. Pushing off, I roll up to the first stop sign, and that familiar highway headed south. From here on in, the rising sun will only grow warmer with each passing day, *bringing me closer to her*. I smile blissfully.

Not far out of town, the turnoff for an alternate highway comes into question. Inching my finger along a crisp new map, I estimate it is another 110 kilometres to the Del Bonita border crossing into Montana. But just to be sure, I backtrack to the last mileage marker and recheck my bearings. There is a sense of wanderlust in having been put to sea; I am the sole captain. Wayfaring, camping out in the wild (when I get up the nerve), interacting with strangers, travelling alone, budgeting, nutrition – it all comes down to my own decision or indecision.

Love fuels the way.

At an average speed of 22 km/h, I roll over the tail end of the wild-rose prairie in five hours, give or take a couple of 15-minute breaks to rest my sore behind and indulge in some tasty sweets. Chocolate bars, ice-cold Coke and licorice are all a constant craving. And though I have the common sense to know which sources serve as better fuel, I indulge in the freedom of being able to do what I want, when I want. A store clerk asks, "Another piece of peanut butter pie?" *Hmmm*.

Rolling up to the United States border, I notice a lone patrol officer sitting at her post. I opt to use the pay phone outside before making my way to the solitary brick building.

The priority is to call my parents and Debbie first. No doubt, they'll want to know I am alive and well (and not roadkill in the ditch).

Playing down my evening at the Detox centre, I tell them I found accommodation at a local community centre "open to thrifty travellers such as myself." Saying anything more, I know, will set off too many alarms, as I've only been on the road a short time. "And I'm doing fine, about to cross the border into Montana. I'll try and call once a day with an update."

I hang up the phone, tuck away the plastic calling card and proudly present my Canadian passport to the tightly wound border agent. It is just the two of us in the badland landscape, yet the short brunette woman blankly defaults to "Where are you going?" *Not even a "hi."*

Normally, my father handles such interactions. Alone, I try to keep the intimidation at bay. "I'm headed to Phoenix, Arizona," I say with some certainty. Hearing it out loud, I realize it is a proud announcement and one that should be said with more acclaim.

"On your bike??" She fires back. "And your parents know about this?"

Sensing the tension, I unwittingly bite my lip. "Well, yes." She then asks how long I will be gone, to which I counter, "About a month." The border agent slumps back in her chair, rather unimpressed. She pauses to consider what parent would let their child take on such a journey alone.

I stand a little bit taller, deepen my voice and quietly announce that I entered adulthood in February, four months prior. Pointing to my passport, I indicate, "You can see my birthdate right there." She looks down at the open page, then back at me. Reluctantly, she hands the passport back and motions for me to continue on. It is an emasculating first.

Enter, Big Sky Country.

There are only three hours left in the day to find an acceptable camping spot. Sixty kilometres past the border, I happen across a sheltered gravel rest area next to a stream and a rustic rocky outcropping. With what little daylight remains, I quickly assemble the tent, unroll my sleeping pad, throw on a headlamp and lock my bike to the adjoining wooden picnic table. Only a few cars pass.

Dressed in a pair of loose-fitting shorts and a warm hoodie, I kneel down by the water's edge and begin washing my face. Confident that no one is around and watching, I drop trou and sit down in the cool, flowing water. My muscle aches soon wash away. Reddened sores around my crotch are also numbed. "They're from constant friction and moist-skin irritation," I recall my father saying.

Hygiene: check.

Sitting back at the picnic table, overlooking the highway and Montana hills in relative silence, I become keenly aware of my connection to nature. My limited attention span homes in on a bug crawling into a pot of leftover macaroni and cheese. Bug-eyed, we share the simulated cheesy goodness. The sound of the babbling creek helps complete the relaxed mood.

Dinner: check.

I crawl into the tent and flop down on my back. Held up above me, and in full glow of the headlamp, I scrawl in a journal of my musings thus far. I write a promise to "savour the journey," then close my eyes and embrace my fear of sleeping exposed. Underneath my makeshift pillow of clothes, a four-inch blade remains open and at the ready.

JUNE 25, 2001

My stomach grumbles awake to the prospect of eating simulated cheesy leftovers. With the expensive metal fork that
I brought from home, I bluntly chisel off the noodle remnants from the bottom of the small pot (since abandoned by
the bug), and guzzle down a bottle of neon yellow Gatorade.
Sprawled across the rest of the table is a new map of Montana.
I make it my goal today to reach the state capital, Helena.

Because of limited road networks in the region (I infer
from the non-specific topographical tracing), and for the
sake of taking a more direct route, I make the decision to cut
east to Interstate 15, though not without an air of self-doubt.

Reaching the busy highway near the dusty small town of
Conrad, I stand back and take note of the semi-trailer trucks
roaring by. Rolling a little closer to the paved shoulder, fear
and reason once again enter my mind. I consider backtracking to a longer – albeit, safer – country road. *But that's too far.*

I begin to feel a late-afternoon urgency.

Fast-flowing traffic aside, the Interstate shoulder *is* considerably wider than the alternative. Mind you, the thought
of meeting my demise at the hand of a runaway diesel is un-
nerving. Even worse, I imagine my parents receiving the
phone call that their son has been struck down on exactly
the type of road I was taught to avoid, at night and wearing no reflective clothing. (My style has evolved from safe-
ty-conscious to more stylish, form-fitting Lycra.) "Just stupid," I hear my father say.

The sky quickly grows dark between the high peaks of
the surrounding mountains. Conflicted, I decide to take a
chance. I make it another 30 kilometres in the night, before,
regrettably, a new variable enters into the camping equation.

The shoulder is flanked by a steep cliff of crumbling rock
and soil on my right, and on my left (past the four lanes of

traffic), a drop-off into an exposed valley. Not seeing a way to navigate down, I opt to scale the cliff, one exposed root at a time. I drag the fully loaded bike behind me with my left hand, digging my heels in for leverage. For every good foothold, another fails, sending me sliding down. The shot of adrenaline helps push past feelings of frustration.

I reach the arid plateau after 20 minutes of scrambling. Standing again, I can make out only the faint outline of trees and shrubs in the moonlight. I close my eyes and try to focus my hearing. My paranoia is on the hunt for voices and any creatures that might inhabit the space. All appears quiet on the home front.

Still worried about being seen from the highway, I decide not to set up my tent. Instead, I stay low to the earth and wrap the waterproof orange material around myself. A light rain begins to fall soon thereafter. Thunder rolls in next, warding off any possibility of sleep. I lie there and feel the droplets taunt my exhaustion. And then: *clump, clump*.

I perk up at the sound of a large animal milling about in the storm. Peeking out through the deflated tent and drizzle, I see the obscured animal slowly circle about, though never coming closer. *Maybe a deer? It's not a bear, right?* I continue looking out, head cocked in a strained position, my knife at the ready.

JUNE 26, 2001
The heat of the direct sun belts down. The morning warmth sucks the moisture from my body, leaving my lips chapped, mouth dry and head pounding from dehydration. Peering out into the open, my eyes feel heavy and caked from cold sweat. I sigh, once again exhausted from a night of sleepless trepidation.

Worming out of the tent cocoon, I feel the sting of evolved saddle sores. I peer inside the Lycra and see a bevy of angry pimples forming. No doubt the skin irritation was further exacerbated from wearing soiled clothing all night. I also feel a twinge in my back from tossing and turning on the uneven, hard-packed ground.

Any fears of a large animal roaming around are quickly dashed aside when I survey the scene and catch a glimpse of the true beast. Lying in a pile of mud and dead grass, a stray brown cow stares up at me as it chews its cud. "Moooo," I yell out in annoyance. "I'm going to eat you!"

Rolling on to Helena, I dash into the first brightly coloured convenience store I come across. I'm on a mission to curb my hunger pain. But, not thinking clearly, I demolish an entire box of chocolate chip cookies before my better judgment kicks in. The ensuing food coma sends me to the back of the building, where I pass out on my foam bedroll beside a rank dumpster.

Dirty and hazy, I wake in the early afternoon and continue riding 108 kilometres to the old mining town of Butte. I'm holding out hope for cheap accommodation. However, $200 is all the cash I have on hand – part of my graduation present. One night under a roof, I find out, will cost just over half that amount.

After checking in and showering at the local Super 8 motel, I make a collect call home to my parents. Admitting partial defeat, I ask if they can deposit some more money into my savings account. My mother offers some tough love, then says she will forward the money. I can imagine my father shaking his head in the background as he takes a not-so-subtle jab at my self-assured solo-ness: "Having a tough time without your father?"

CHAPTER 5

VALLEY OVERLOOK

JUNE 27–30, 2001

The mountainous expanse of southern Montana gives way to a vast valley, channelling me toward the sprawling Mormon region of Salt Lake City. Knowing how busy this section of the Interstate is (from previous road trips with my family), I negotiate an alternate route to the east along the base of the Wasatch Range through seemingly endless stop-and-go traffic.

The sides of city streets is where all the crap ends up and where two-wheel vehicles are often relegated. The grimy brown cocktail is composed of glass, roadkill, nails, winter salt and sand. One of my skinny road tires pops on a thumbtack, just for variety. "Son of a bitch," I murmur in frustration.

Flat tires are becoming troublesome. Factors that contribute to faster-than-usual wear include long hours in the saddle, increasingly hotter (and sometimes rougher) asphalt, a heavy load and more friction. This was never a concern while touring with my father. Staying in hotels and eating out enabled us to maintain far less rolling resistance.

The puncture protocol remains the same. First, I stop as soon as possible so as not to damage the exposed metal rim. Out of the way of passing cars, I remove my pannier bags to relieve the frame of its heavy burden. Now able to manoeuvre freely, I unmount the damaged tire and tube, check and remove obstructions, repair it with a small patch and vulcanized sealant, reinstall the tube and pump back up to a pressure of 110 psi.

Unfortunately, the problem has evolved. In addition to the small pinprick, I also notice a two-inch slice along the sidewall of the worn back tire. I had, in all likelihood, been oblivious to this up until now because of my single-minded focus on traffic. I must have scraped against a larger metal object – possibly an artifact from an accident at an intersection. This type of repair is foreign to me, however. A simple patch will not suffice.

I remember hearing through the cycling rumour mill that you can temporarily repair a sidewall cut by inserting an energy bar wrapper in between the inflated tube and tire, thus creating a basic seal that will hopefully stop the tube from pushing out through the slice and pinch-flatting. Easier said than done, though. I'm fresh out of energy bars.

Now well past any commercial centre, hitchhiking seems to be the next best solution. Having never stuck out my thumb before, I consider the scene from a passerby's perspective. Walking with my bike in one hand, I strap together and distribute the four panniers over my shoulders. It should be clear that my bike had a breakdown, that I am a clean-cut individual and that I am at least trying to get somewhere, instead of appearing helpless, unmotivated and lost in time.

Not long after I begin walking, an older blue pickup truck with two bearded gentlemen in their late twenties inside stops and they offer to give me a hand. "Got a problem with your bike?" the man in the passenger seat sticks his head out the window and asks.

"Yeah, it's something that I can't repair on my own," I reply, trying to hold a friendly smile.

"Hop in," the driver says. "We'll give you a ride to the next town."

I slide across the dusty back seat and introduce myself. After 30 minutes of friendly banter, the conversation delves deep. Roger and Dave are disgruntled Mormons, recently excommunicated from a fundamentalist sect in northern Arizona. A couple of my high school friends were Mormons, but of the softer, non-threatening variety. Roger and Dave speak of a "leader," of being incessantly preached to and what they term a "backward" community.

Roger speaks over his shoulder while turning down a quieter, two-lane highway. "You get sucked in, you don't know anything else. We still believe in the religion. We just had to get away from the crazy fucker standing at the podium." The talk of faith reignites the question of my own, or lack thereof.

Nathan's passing brought the question of mortality into our home. Each of us internalized it in our own way. My mother and father grew up going to church but stopped in their teen years. Their feelings seemed to straddle a line between a brutal reality on one side and sunshine in heavenly pastures on the other. Nathan was not an elderly family member who had come to the end of a long life. He was their child and was never given a chance. His death made us ask *Why?*

My sister delved much deeper into faith. Her more supportive friends encouraged her to come along to church with them on Sundays. I would often hear of her attending youth group social events, like movies and prayer sessions. I quietly scoffed at each invite. My religious cynicism was no secret.

I saw Nathan's death as proof that there was *no* god. Further aggravated by my hockey problems, and alone with my thoughts in the back ravine, I'd contemplate how to end my life – part of the "Fuck it" phase. Through those suicidal doldrums, I witnessed *no* divine presence attempt to pull me back. There was just my own cowardly nature.

My cynicism grew darker when I saw people preaching to my parents, trying to perpetuate the holy myth. I wanted my mother and father to deal with the pain head on, rather than grow complacent and perhaps trust in the divine. *Why can't we talk about this without the world crashing down?*

I took on a new view to calm my mind: that the world needs imbalances, and that death should not be considered such a bad thing. Great moments only feel good because we know the sting of shitty ones. Of course, I kept these thoughts to myself.

A year later, the wound of Nathan's passing was still very fresh for my parents. Listening to the two Mormon men describe their fall from fundamentalist ideals was just the comfort I needed. I appreciated knowing that even the most devout could find balance and realize the difference between real spirituality and covering your problems with holy water.

The truck pulls up to a ragged-looking tool shop in the next town. Waving goodbye, the two guys speed off down a lonesome main street, headed back home to their wives in a desolate corner of southern Utah. Whether or not the number of partners is plural for each, it didn't feel right to ask. *The world needs imbalances,* including odd numbers.

I walk inside the faded wooden building. Among the clutter and aged knick-knacks, a grizzly old shopkeeper greets me. Assessing my problem, he quickly scrounges out a new tire that just happens to fit. He smiles as I walk back out into the daylight, ever so thankful.

JULY 1, 2001

In the late afternoon heat, I pass through the town of Kanab and soon roll up to a bright milestone. Leaning my bike up against the red and yellow state sign, I stand back and admire the feat of cycling through southern Alberta, Montana and Utah, mainly under my own power. The final stretch through Arizona was now at hand.

Travelling along an arid plateau, I come across a windswept campground off on its own. There are only a few sites taken. After I briefly mention my quest for love, the owners invite me into their Airstream trailer for dinner. "Tell us about your journey so far," they ask, with cool drinks in hand. I sip my own, then delve into the odyssey that begins with a wounded dog and a phone number.

Twilight is replaced by a few patio lights, then darkness in the great beyond. I lie on a picnic table with my dinner belly extended and arms outstretched. Far above, the starry expanse revels in grandeur. Watching for small satellites crossing the night sky, I wonder if Kelly is looking up at the same sight.

She is probably wondering how the tour with my father is going. The Hawaii lie is holding strong.

The last time I spoke with her was from an Internet café in northern Utah. I mentioned to her, "You might be able to hear the waves of the ocean in the background ... I'm sitting at a little bar right now, eating homemade potato soup." The soup wasn't a lie. It was damn tasty.

"I wish I could be there with you now," she answered with a sigh.

JULY 2, 2001

Stuffing away my gear the next morning, I jump back at the unruly sight of hairy tarantula legs crawling out of my pannier bag. I'm reminded that, yes, these menacing-looking creatures do exist outside of insect exhibits at the zoo.

After calming those arachnophobic nerves, I grab my disposable camera off the picnic table and snap a close-up. Judging by its size, the tarantula must just be a baby. I run to tell the campground hosts of my encounter. "The little ones are called 'spiderlings' – they're harmless," they tell me.

On the way out of the campground, I make sure to stop and thank the elderly pair for their hospitality.

The first ten minutes on the bike always seem the most painful. It takes some time before cold joints begin rotating through viscous fluid and for muscle fibres to stretch freely. Once the first bead of sweat starts rolling down my brow, I know I'm ready. It is at this point that my body finds a rhythm.

Alone on a quiet road, with nothing but the wind to mix things up, I begin to notice my wonky left knee. I spend 20 minutes focusing on correcting my heel from rotating outward on the downstroke (which causes my quadriceps to graze the top tube on each revolution). I have never received any instruction on biomechanics. I just do what I think makes sense.

Thousands of pedal revolutions prove a worthy testing ground. Ten days into my journey and I now have a pretty good idea, within a millimetre or two, of what height to adjust my seat to, which angle to point my handlebars and how much float (angle of rotation) I need in order to allow my shoes to pivot. The devil is truly in the details.

Black storm clouds crackle in the distance.

I try to outrun the weather. The visibility inside passing cars (with rain hitting their windshields) is no doubt reduced. I keep in mind that I am a foreign entity on these roads. Country travellers don't check their mirrors and blind spots the way city drivers are expected to. I dare not make any assumptions.

I make camp atop a high plateau among tall cedars and intermittent shelter from the drizzle.

The warden at a neighbouring campground asks if I would like a pass to stay there for the evening. I ask him what the difference is between paying for an official site versus riding down the road and pulling off into my own private hideaway. "There really isn't any difference," he replies. "Some people just like the peace of mind that comes with staying at a campground." Sensitive to that fact, I thank him but continue on down the road anyway.

My attitude toward camping has evolved since the Detox centre. Each successive night proved to be an interesting challenge, as desperation arose from having little money. I became familiar with all sorts of improvised lodging, including sneaking into the backyard of a house under construction.

A few miles down from the warden's office, I hike out of sight and farther into the woods. Before setting up my tent, I swap out my cycling shoes for runners, lightly cover my gear with tree branches and backtrack to a small gas station across from the park campground. With a huge grin, I purchase as much as I can carry with two hands.

Walking back toward my campsite, I peer through the trees to see if I can spot my gear. Confident that I am well hidden, I build up a small fire from fallen tree limbs and a cache of dry pine needles. I proceed to chow down on six hot dogs, half a loaf of bread and a gallon of milk. I bury the remaining food in a frosty dirt hole. The food will keep, since the evening air is cooler at higher elevations.

I let out a loud belch. *Brilliance.*

My gas station combo tastes just as great the following morning. The fatty indulgence reminds me of family camping trips long past. Only gooey white marshmallows are missing.

The warm morning light shines through the tall cedars in strands, highlighting specks of gently floating particles in the forest lull. I'm inclined to take in the enchantment, and continue with my packing only after the moment has faded.

The forested plateau snakes and rises for a couple more kilometres before descending sharply toward a crew of four grizzled men filling potholes with steaming asphalt. It has become customary for me to nod and often receive a similar gesture of respect back. *Hello.*

The scent of boiling tar hits my senses.

Passing the workmen, I immediately round a blind corner into a new realm. An incredible desert valley landscape comes into view. I stop to catch my breath and gaze for miles in every direction. Only a small stretch of pavement separates the road from the frontier below. Overhead, a lone eagle circles in the blinding sun.

The sound of Thom Yorke's melodic "Motion Picture Soundtrack" now fills my MP3's earbuds. In times of great introspection, Radiohead always fits best. Coldplay is reserved for feelings of love and all the rest.

My Mormon saviours had mentioned yesterday that this area was settled by John D. Lee in 1871. He and his wife Emma Lee French (one of 19 wives) were directed by the Church of Jesus Christ of Latter-day Saints (the epicentre of Mormon fundamentalism at the time) to manage a cable ferry crossing on the Colorado River. This is the northern tip of the Grand Canyon.

Riding down along the lonely stretch of black asphalt,

I soon feel an oppressive heat radiating upwards. Since I had spent the past couple of nights at higher elevations, this Arizona reality had yet to make an appearance. I stare, dazed and dry-mouthed, into (what now feels like) an apocalyptic landscape of desolate cacti.

My bike is the first to wave the white flag. The Trek surrenders with the sound of one tire popping, then another and then one more. Every 15 minutes I stop to repair another slow leak. It is apparent that the combination of a hot road surface, balding tires and a heavy load are conspiring against me. Five kilometres away from any type of services, my only option is to get off and walk. It's 75 sweltering minutes to the village of Lees Ferry.

Collapsing on the step of a dusty Chevron gas station, I hunch over a delectable bounty of snacks. Feeling heavy, I notice, between my sweaty legs, a fly staggering along the dusty ground. I flip my head back and take another gulp of sweet orange Gatorade. A second bottle stands at the ready, sweating condensation. Nothing can be done for the fly.

Looking ahead, the road is adorned with but a few aged motels and a gift shop. *You fly away, to what?* There are no bike shops, and zero chance of new rubber.

What now? I lean down between my legs and pour a sip of the fluorescent drink next to the floundering fly. The insect stops, stumbles some more, then tips over and rattles a silent death cry. The quiet moment invokes a lost sense of pity in me.

The sound of a hissing radiator refocuses my attention.

In front of me, a trendy couple in their thirties have stopped for gas. The boyfriend is wearing a baseball cap with art deco-style letters that spell RAGE. Having been a fan since junior high, I instantly recognize that it refers to the band Rage Against the Machine. I smile at the couple, "Their latest album rocks, hey?"

Pleasantly caught off guard, the boyfriend walks over and begins chatting. We bond over the album *Renegades* while their tank fills.

The young couple then asks where I am riding to. "To Phoenix, to surprise my girlfriend. I've got just one more day, and a long day at that. I need new tires, though," I reply.

They're intrigued to learn more about the story. "Hop in the car with us," the girlfriend waves me over. "We can give you a ride to Flagstaff. That's where we live."

I side with reason and accept the friendly offer. Admittedly, I feel a little ashamed to be giving in so easy, but also grateful. From the air-conditioned backseat view, I soon realize that this is the most desolate stretch of the entire journey. I'm not sure I would have made it on my own.

By the time we ascend again to a higher elevation at Flagstaff, the couple has made plans to take me out for a pasta dinner as well as provide a couch to sleep on. "Anything we can do to help on your last leg," they beam. The love story has caught hold.

JULY 4, 2001

My last day on the road begins before sunrise. All that stands between Kelly and me is 211 kilometres and about 13 hours on the road. My new companions have provided all I need to finish, including new tires and a pack full of snacks.

Feverish anticipation easily gets me up and out the door. I begin to slip away just as my hosts are waking, bleary-eyed, to a timed coffee pot. "Be safe," the boyfriend says. We shake hands and acknowledge our chance encounter. As with so many other people I have met along the way, I know we will probably never see each other again. We exchange phone numbers nevertheless.

"Thank you for everything," I whisper.

Enter, the morning darkness.

Sprinklers spit water on manicured lawns, a jogger runs past in soft new sneakers and but a few lonely cars are heard. It is the Independence Day holiday in the United States.

The patriotic sight of red, white and blue American flags disappears as I depart the mountain town on Interstate 17, headed south. Walls of ponderosa pine soon give way to another desert valley expanse and a steady descent for the next hour.

Listening to my MP3 player, I blast Coldplay's "Yellow" in unison with the sunrise. The low light heightens all the colours around me, providing a rich texture. The oranges and browns of the rolling valley look like savoury cinnamon rolls. My stomach is clamouring for McDonald's.

Reaching the valley floor, the heat climbs 15 degrees without blinking an eye. The cool rush I felt while descending is replaced by sweltering, sun-dried winds. Behind squinting eyes, the cinnamon rolls now appear scorched. But this place has character, I'll give it that.

I'm thrust into an old western movie.

Feeling each kilometre bringing me closer to *her*, I fend off the sun and find my rhythm. My head bobs up and down like a cowboy, my feet circling around the dedicated steed, *again and again*. The brim of my helmet casts only a small shadow.

I think of what I will say when I first see her.

I'm coming for you, Kelly.

I arrive at a more modern Chevron gas station at the edge of Cave Creek, Arizona. With what few minutes remain on my calling card, I dial Kelly's home number.

Ring, ring.

Expecting my call, Debbie answers right away. She's elated to hear that I have arrived safe and sound but continues speaking in a whisper. "How do you want to do this?"

"Ask Kelly to join you for some grocery shopping," I suggest. "I will meet you at the end of the street. Look for the Canadian flag jersey!"

I mount my bike for the last time and pedal over to our meeting spot. My heart is racing as I think about the long-awaited moment.

Peeking around the corner, I see Kelly's car pull onto the street. Debbie points ahead and feathers the brake. Kelly immediately gets out and stumbles toward me, her hands over her mouth in shock. She comes closer, shaking and crying. "What, I don't get it, I thought you were in Hawaii...!"

Debbie stands back to snap a picture of our reunion.

Holding Kelly close, I grin, "We lied."

CHAPTER 6

DRASTIC TIMES

JULY 25, 2001

Three weeks had passed since my surprise arrival in Cave Creek, Arizona. I think fondly of holding Kelly's hand, of all the matinee movies we saw, of jet skiing on nearby Bartlett Lake, of hiking in Sedona, and laughing as we nearly got flung off a sand dune buggy at Rocky Point, just across the border in Mexico.

It was the perfect summer vacation.

Sitting alone now in a row of hard plastic chairs in Toronto's Pearson International Airport, on my way home, I replay my most cherished memory again and again: over breakfast after a desert camping trip with new friends, Kelly finally referred to herself as my girlfriend.

I hold on to this warm feeling, clutching my pannier bags beside me. My bike is packed in a cardboard box, flying somewhere high above without me.

Earlier that afternoon I was denied access to my connecting flight home. Reason being, I was not dressed appropriately. "Pardon?!" I question at the check-in counter. "I'm wearing a clean shirt, shorts and sandals – what's wrong with that?" But, having snagged a "Buddy Pass" (a greatly discounted ticket) from my friend's father, a pilot, I was apparently required to dress more formally.

"You are representing the airline. Your friend should have told you this," I'm instructed. The lady at the check-in counter then suggests I catch a bus into Toronto and buy some new clothes. The next flight won't be until tomorrow, though. *So where do I sleep?*

A worker in a blue jumpsuit walks a few feet ahead. He appears to be transfixed by his own thoughts, just barely gripping his floor waxer, slowly swaying from side to side. The airport is quiet at this late hour.

I squirm and shift my weight onto my other side, feeling the hard edges of the plastic seat uncomfortably dig into my back.

At 2:30 a.m. the gentleman makes a second pass with the waxer, humming to himself. I turn the other way and try to block out the view of the blurry concourse lights by holding my bags in front of me, still grasping them tightly. As I do this, I'm reminded of the nights I chained my bike to my tent, of the restless sleeps and of the strangers at the Detox centre.

You're almost home.

AUGUST 5, 2001

I'm back to working a few shifts per week at a nearby grocery store, bagging and carrying out items to people's cars. It is a menial task.

One of my fellow baggers is mentally challenged. The other is 60 years old. Daydreaming in their presence, I begin to strongly consider whether my energy can be better utilized somewhere else. *But doing what?* I am a high school graduate with no clear direction.

Over dinner I boldly tell my parents that I have no interest in carrying on their business. "It would be good to take a year off and consider my options," I reason.

My parents are infuriated. They tell me that I am "pissing"

away my summer and barely working. My slags against long hours and stress at their job only fan the flames higher.

Several tense exchanges ensue, and not just between my father and me. My mother also is visibly distressed.

Chairs slam as we depart from the table in anger.

I retreat in haste to my bedroom and glowing computer screen. *Why can't they just fucking understand?*

Shut off in my room, I begin a formal Internet search into worldly inspiration. I'm desperate to plot my uncharted passion, that *something else.*

My solo tour down to Arizona has ignited a sense of wanderlust in me. I have to believe there is more to life than a job without passion, or material possession for that matter. This is a clear rebellion against my comfortable surroundings.

The movie *Fight Club* has made a particular impression on me in this regard. I want to believe in Brad Pitt's gospel: "The things you own end up owning you." And just like his character, Tyler Durden, I want to hit rock bottom. I want to live as a nomadic gladiator.

Shivering on my bike seems to have far more potential than investing in the cozy corporate ladder, whether it be for my parents or for someone else. But from the outside looking in, my wandering plight appears as lazy, hormonal self-destruction.

I do only the bare minimum to keep our family waters from boiling over. But I'm apathetic toward everything outside of *the search.*

AUGUST 18, 2001

It is a warm summer weekend. My mother is upstairs making lunch with my sister while my father grunts around outside, doing yard work. I'm in my room again.

Before my sister has a chance to call everyone together for lunch, my father barges through the back door and begins yelling in frustration. I can't hear exactly what he is saying at first, only that he is addressing my mother. My not voluntarily coming out to help is a huge piss-off. "Tell him to get his ass out here," he grumbles, then slams the door behind himself.

Any other day and I would crumble in obedience, but not today. "FUCK that!" I yell out. I sit on my bed and wait for what comes next.

My father storms back in 15 minutes later.

He immediately charges down toward my room, then bursts in, red-faced, and grabs my T-shirt collar. The polyester stretches as it balls up in his fist, pulling me close. He stares me right in the eye and yells, "Get your fucking ass up there!"

I retaliate.

I grab his shirt with both hands and begin pushing back. The two of us are finally caught in that hockey fight, trying to find the balanced upper hand. The only difference is that this is not a game.

We push up against a wall like angry titans.

Intense pulling turns to shoving, first across the chest and then higher. Open palms angrily morph into closed fists, then hatred.

In a moment that is very much a blur and feels like an eternity, my mother throws herself between us, crying, "Stop it, please!" She grabs my father's hand and pulls him back upstairs.

Impulse leads me to the bedroom closet.

I reach for my backpack and hockey equipment bag, emptying out the useless contents. I quickly separate out what matters onto my bedroom floor. *What do I need to pack?*

Clothes are the only essential item. Books, CDs, the bike, my computer, hair gel, they all get left behind.

Where I'm going, I don't know. No matter, *I'm getting the hell out of here.*

I head straight for the back door as soon as my father is out of range. Seeing the two bulging bags, my mother's heart breaks in two. She pleads for me to stay. But no, "I need to get away from him. Please don't worry," I assure her, exiting quickly with the heavy load.

Shaking and in tears, I begin walking along the highway shoulder toward Calgary.

The closest refuge is Jack Astor's Bar and Grill. My good friend Chris works there as a server in the evenings. *I'll wait outside on the patio until he arrives.*

I store my vagrant luggage to the side, so as not to draw the attention of the cute blonde waitress. With what little cash I have in hand, I buy a watered-down Coke from the young lady and sip it slowly. I have a couple of hours to kill.

Chris arrives in time to catch a long sigh from me. Halfway through his shift and a hundred or so cracked peanut shells later, I work up the courage to tell him about the fight with my father. "I need a place to say," I ask, ashamed. Without hesitation, he says I can share his bedroom. I only need to ask his father for permission. Coincidentally, he's on his way in for happy hour.

Chris's father, Garth, sits down for dinner. Chris gives him the heads up, then I fill in the gaps and make the final plea. Without giving the situation much thought, I tell them both that it will only be for a week or two. Like Chris, Garth responds warmly, "No problem."

I let out another long sigh, this time in relief.

Chris and his father live on the other side of Calgary. Their hillside condo overlooks downtown and the Bow River.

The Colpittses graciously share their food and their living space, and never ask for a dime of rent money. We eat steak dinners and watch TV together. The atmosphere is relaxed.

Chris and I share late-night conversations about babes and our hopes for the future. Inspired by the movie *Cocktail*, Chris wants to become a bartender like Tom Cruise's character in the film. He practises "flaring" with hard plastic bottles in our shared bedroom. Watching him hone his craft, I'm reminded of when he and I used to play baseball. Chris was the star pitcher; me, the roving talent. My father coached us back then.

A week passes and I begin to wonder, *How are they holding up? Have they moved on? Do they think of me?* I'm troubled by the thought that my mother and sister may still be crying through sleepless nights. I consider phoning but pull back.

When I can afford a new calling card, I connect with Kelly and refocus my attention on the all-American dream. She tells me about possibly going to post-secondary school at DeVry Technical Institute. The next day, I pay to write the entrance exam at a local affiliate. I'm still holding out hope that we can go to school together in the United States – while completely brushing off the foreign student costs. Debbie persuades me not to make any impulsive moves, and to stay put for now. "Alright," I concede.

The hour-long bus commute to my job at the grocery store is growing tiresome. Chris convinces me to switch jobs and work at the restaurant with him. That way I can catch a ride in and stop taking public transit. "And besides, you'll make way more money with tips," he tells me. Without a second thought, I hand in my notice and thank the grocery store manager for the experience.

As expected, I start at the bottom at Jack Astor's. I'm busing tables, cleaning off greasy plates, resetting the paper table covering and crayons (a novelty to keep customers occupied between services) and helping the servers in any way possible.

I'm entitled to a percentage of the tips brought in, plus extra if the servers see fit. Each night before going to bed, Chris (also a busboy) and I sit cross-legged on our beds and count the night's take. Chris aspires to purchase a new car and sets his sights on attaining an engineering degree at the University of Calgary. My own coin rolls sit in savings, patiently waiting for the all-American escape.

I buy Kelly an expensive promise ring and am a shameful penny-pincher on everything else. Chris is often the first to pay for drinks when we go out, as well as for cab fare and groceries when we need them. He is a good friend, my best friend.

I decide to take on another job, something within walking distance of Chris's condo. I apply at a downtown Italian restaurant.

The job is prep work, portioning ingredients for meals to be cooked later. It requires that I be up and out the door by 4:30 a.m.

I'm a walking zombie for the first week. Still half asleep, I struggle to memorize procedures and complete tasks on time. My nimble female trainer shakes her head, discouraged, sensing that I am a lost cause. Even I know it. *This is fucking brutal.*

SEPTEMBER 11, 2001

I wake for work at 4:00 a.m. after only four hours of sleep. The night before, I'd helped close at Jack Astor's – and missed the last bus. On a whim, I decide to walk home. The ensuing journey across town takes three hours.

Partway through the next day's prep shift, my managers call me into their office. "This might not be a great fit for you," they tell me. The message rings loud and clear. *I have to get my shit together.*

Standing at my solitary station in the kitchen, I continue chopping, weighing and portioning ingredients for the day's lunch service. There is a part of me that wants to earn back the managers' respect. I also think about how to run away from the situation. I am getting good at that.

Distracting me from the moment, the head cook suddenly calls into the back room of the kitchen, "You guys gotta come see this!" Four of us huddle around a TV at the bar. CNN news is on. They are reporting that a plane might have hit one of the World Trade Center buildings in New York. At the time, the size of the aircraft was unknown. We all assumed that it was something small, and an accident.

The footage then cuts to a harbour view of Manhattan. The two towers stand like iron giants high above the crowded city scene. Smoke billows out of one of them as if from a chimney.

And then, screaming.

From out of nowhere a second plane hits. The tone of the reporter's voice changes in an instant. And for the first time in my life, the term "terrorist attack" is uttered in the present tense. The act of aggression is unlike anything I have seen before.

I finish my shift and head home in the early morning sun. All around me, business people walk throughout downtown

Calgary stunned, not knowing how to process the severity of this moment. All sense of time has stopped.

Back at the condo, I glue myself to the news and nothing else. Amateur video covers the drama from all angles and is refreshed on the hour. The scene is now of office paper floating to the ground and flames consuming the upper floors. An estimated 200 people trapped high above begin jumping to their death.

At 9:59 a.m. the South Tower collapses, followed by the North Tower, at 10:28 a.m. Dust and debris shoot into the sky as if out of a cannon. We see images of scared New Yorkers running away, their bodies covered in white ash and bright red blood. They scream, "Oh, my God!"

Then, cut to black.

A sudden urgency hits me. *It's time to move on.*

NOVEMBER, 2001 – JANUARY, 2002

I nervously set up a lunch meeting with my parents. We haven't seen or spoken to each other in three months.

The reunion is met with awkward smiles and no talk of the incident that led to my abrupt departure. We instead chat on more cordial terms about reuniting for a Christmas trip down to Arizona. Of course, I smile at that thought. My father grins back, "You look good."

That Christmas, we rent the same home in Cave Creek. Half the time, I stay with Kelly, her brother Brandon and Debbie. On Christmas morning, I share time between both homes, like a foster child. The gift highlights include my first digital video camera from my parents – movies have been a long-held passion, and filmmaking a bubbling interest – and a book on cyclist Lance Armstrong from Debbie, called *It's Not About the Bike: My Journey Back to Life.*

I give the promise ring to Kelly atop Black Mountain at sunrise. Holding her hand, I promise to be a friend forever. We kiss. Soon thereafter, Kelly stands in tears at the end of the driveway as our motorhome departs once again. I look back at her out the side window. In a moment she disappears, taken away again.

I delve into Lance's story on the drive home. I'm only vaguely aware that he is the cyclist who recovered from cancer to win the Tour de France – now three times over, beginning in 1999. Like the story of Terry Fox, this is a man who stared death in the face and decided to make a difference.

I feel inspired once again.

Loving thoughts of Kelly mix with an urgency brought on by the September 11 attacks. These combine with inspired ideals of the one-legged runner and the cycling god. I begin to outline a roadmap for turning my passion into purpose.

I devise a plan to cycle 14,000 kilometres across Canada and around the perimeter of the United States to raise $1-million for cancer charities. Having cycled most of Canada and up the US eastern seaboard from Florida, the circumnavigation feels like a natural progression. The charitable inclusion *just feels right*.

I call it Ride for Life.

CHAPTER 7

MARATHON OF HOPE

JANUARY – MARCH, 2002

Following our family Christmas trip to Arizona, my parents and I begin meeting more regularly for lunch near their office. We are all anxious to move on.

They offer me a job with the Correy Investment Team. The exchange is honest and sincere but backhanded by a question of whether I miss my "cozy little cave." I take it on the chin and feign a smile. *How soon we forget the boxing match that transpired only six months ago.*

Whatever. The job appears to be a positive move for all involved. I appreciate the opportunity to step away from dish cleaning, cooking and my duties as a busboy. I have become a jack-of-all-trades at Jack Astor's. Not so much at my other job, though.

Before the Italian restaurant has a chance to fire me, I drop off a wordy letter with the hostess, and then split. It states that I must leave immediately to be by my girlfriend's side in Arizona. "She has been in a terrible car accident," I write. Feeding off a post-9/11 panic, I expect that no questions will be asked. In truth, Kelly is in perfect health. I'm just ashamed to admit defeat out loud.

There is a partial truth to the letter, however. *I am* concerned for Kelly's safety. Taking the job with my parents is an opportunity to make a more substantial income and help bring her to Canada.

Sensationalized news reports now have us wondering, *What target is next?* The Palo Verde Nuclear Generating Station (the largest in the United States) is located only 80 kilometres due west of downtown Phoenix. "We need to get her out of there," I tell my parents. They agree.

I trade my starched white cooking uniform and colourful Jack Astor's T-shirts for black leather shoes, dress pants, pressed button-up shirts and a tie. My father pulls me aside at work the first day, leans in and cleans up the knot a little. "There, much better," he gleams.

My parents are proud to have me working alongside them, and to tell their clients that the family business has grown by one. Seeing them smile, it's nice to see that living apart has helped purge our anger. *It's time.*

For fear of overstaying my welcome at Chris's, and realizing that I may already have done so, I timidly transport my belongings back home while my parents are away on vacation. Chris and his father are at work when I leave one afternoon. I didn't give either of them any notice. Like ripping off a Band-Aid, *there's just no easy way to do it.*

APRIL, 2002

My family and friends all know now that I am determined to cycle around North America for charity. Surprisingly, the biggest challenge early on is finding a cause that I can name.

Retired volunteers on the other end of my phone inquiries cringe when I tell them about my ambitious plan and my age. They are concerned about how it will look if something happens to me on the road: mishandled donations, a car accident or worse. I'm stunned by how difficult it is to receive an endorsement, and after several tries I give up, frustrated.

This is what I get for being too afraid to call up the one

charity that matters to me: the Terry Fox Foundation. I'm so inspired by the legacy that I'm petrified of drawing any attention away from it. But after having explored every option for cancer charity on the Internet, I decide to give them a call.

I leave a message after hours. Nervous, I tell them how Terry inspired me to follow a dream.

The next day, Terry's brother Darrell calls and leaves me a voice mail. Darrell is the national director for the charity. Back in 1980 he was part of the small support crew driving behind the one-legged runner on the Marathon of Hope.

Press 1 to hear your message. "Unfortunately, Ryan, as you know, the run, which is now an annual fundraiser around the world, is our big event. I am not going to be able to endorse your ride. What I can do is wish you the best of luck. Have a great time out there!"

I'm shaking as I listen to him politely decline my offer. This is the closest I will ever get to Terry and arguably the closest I will ever get to one of the most important moments in Canadian history. He inspires me to keep fighting the good fight.

I finally reach an agreement with two charities: the Lance Armstrong Foundation (LAF), in the United States, and the Childhood Cancer Canada Foundation, out of Toronto. I focus in on kids because of my brother Nathan. The connection to cancer is thanks to the inspiration of Terry and Lance.

Lance's profile is growing in North America. He is a regular feature in all the cycling publications and frequently on the cover of *Sports Illustrated*. Seeing the image of his lean frame, his square jaw and his cool blue United States Postal Service-sponsored cycling kit (and matching Trek bike), I'm star-struck. He personifies the superhero myth.

In mid-April I book a discount flight down to Austin,

Texas, to take part in Lance's Ride for the Roses hometown event. Since I am unable to afford a hotel room, the kind folks at the Lance Armstrong Foundation arrange a homestay for me with a local participant. The weekend's main draw is a 160-kilometre century ride. I have never ridden with so many people before. There are thousands.

Gazing around at the Lycra-clad Lance hysteria, I feel like I have entered into a circle of cool, though I haven't yet earned a place there. Other riders have raised thousands of dollars for the charity. I overhear several speaking about "their companies." They are big shots. I have only contributed the bare minimum of US$250 – every last penny from my savings account.

Comedic actor (and cycling enthusiast) Robin Williams rallies the crowd with jokes about being the hairiest guy to ever wear Spandex. His pal Lance finally shows up with a wagon full of photographers, literally. A sea of cyclists strains to catch a glance of the legend. I have never seen such envy and admiration. And admittedly, I'm caught up in the fever.

Despite claims by the announcer that this is not a race, Lance shoots off the start with a few hundred of the fastest. My ego tries to keep up, but bonks not even halfway through. My skin goes clammy, my muscles weak. Apparently, two bowls of sugary cereal is not a proper breakfast fuel.

A SAG wagon, a support vehicle that picks up ailing riders, pulls up beside me and they ask if I would like to be shuttled to the finish. "No, thank you," I tell them, waving, too prideful to accept. I then ride up beside an older gentleman. Next to him rides an overweight woman, neither trying to impress the other. I'm humbled and slightly embarrassed to be at the back of the pack. And I realize: *I need to start training.*

I reason with my parents to allow me time off in Arizona. My body is hockey heavy and bulky, weighing over 180 pounds. If I learned anything from the ride in Austin, it's that I am not currently built for sustained climbs on skinny tires.

I plan the trip south as an opportunity to engage in long stretches of desert pavement, focus in on Ride for Life logistics and, most importantly, feed off the energy that Kelly gives me.

Debbie has arranged for me to stay with Kelly's grandparents in the barren countryside. Left to focus on the task at hand, I stock up on pasta and try to immerse myself in a daily riding routine. Kelly is still in school, now finishing up Grade 12. I have no other choice but to ride.

It is well known that my priority is training. Nevertheless, it feels odd to be near Kelly but spending so little time together. Sometimes when I get home from a ride and there are no messages waiting, I wonder if there is a problem. This idle time plays tricks on my mind.

Returning from one of my rides in the hot sun, I hear my adopted grandparents on the phone with Debbie. Quietly, I unbuckle my shoes and head to the kitchen for a glass of water – it is midday and I have been sweating profusely. On the other end of the line, Kelly's mom shares the unfortunate news that the family dog has suddenly taken a turn for the worse. *Shit.*

I try to connect with Kelly, but she is sad and understandably scattered with her emotions. Alone in bed that night, I think about meeting the dog, Brandy, on the road for the first time, about how sick the dog appeared then and how that chance encounter led to Kelly and I meeting.

A day goes by. No news and no contact with Kelly. On the second day, we receive word that Brandy has passed away, yet there is still no contact with my girlfriend. Selfishly, I feel a little hurt that she does not seek me out for comfort. "She just needs some time alone," my adopted grandparents reason.

My own retreat ensues.

I continue going on rides, now in the early morning hours to avoid the encroaching summer heat. My attention homes in on sponsorship plans during the free time that remains. Then one day, I no longer wait by the phone for Kelly's call. *Am I resentful? Or do I just need this more?*

Unfortunately, Ride for Life is only a month away and I still do not have a support vehicle, a driver or money to pay for day-to-day expenses. But a sense of purpose has awakened within me. I am now singularly focused and determined to make my dream a reality. I cannot imagine a more important task.

Kelly's high school graduation takes place a few nights before I head home. As one might expect from a big American school, they hold the diploma ceremony on a brightly lit football field with plenty of pomp and praise. It's nice to see the family smiling again, but something is different.

After the ceremony, the graduating class and their guests pile into a row of yellow school buses, laughing, and head to an amusement park celebration in east Phoenix. Seated next to Kelly, there are a few awkward pauses before I find a way to articulate my thoughts among the rambunctious atmosphere.

Am I an asshole? For reasons I do not fully understand, I have become disconnected from our blind love. Feeling the need to seize a crucial life moment (and closeness), I softly explain to Kelly that my feelings have been inspired to serve a greater good. "What do you mean?" she asks, stunned.

"I think … you should be with someone who can give you their full attention," I say with a sigh, looking down. She then turns her head to gaze out at the moonlight shining through the window of the bus. I see her wipe away a tear, and notice the promise ring sparkle one last time. We are no longer boyfriend and girlfriend, just friends.

LATE MAY, 2002

My parents hold their annual dinner for 100 local clients in Edmonton, Alberta. This year it is taking place at the luxurious Fairmont Hotel Macdonald, a historic seven-storey château overlooking the North Saskatchewan River valley.

As per tradition, they invite a representative from a worthy cause to come and speak. My parents will often match any donations that their clients contribute. Last year they highlighted the efforts of firefighters working at Ground Zero in New York City. This year I have been granted an opportunity to speak about Ride for Life, along with a representative from the Childhood Cancer Canada Foundation.

We raise an impressive $12,000. The catch, of course, is that half of this amount has been pledged by my parents. Noticing me shy away from the handing over of a cheque, they step in and proudly assure me that "it's for a good cause." At 19 years old, I have only a vague grasp of what this amount of money represents to them.

A partner business that has helped sponsor the evening then hands me a $1,000 cheque for expenses. The representative in the tailored suit does so without blinking. Watching my reaction once again, my father reminds me that this is but a tiny contribution for those in the investment business. "Learn how to make *the ask*," he advises.

Asking strangers for money is not my forte. Having

experienced how challenging it is to earn minimum wage at the grocery store, I shy away from soliciting for more than a couple hundred dollars from potential sponsors. The hard reality is that my expenses for the 14,000-kilometre Ride for Life will run to several thousand dollars. Gas, food and accommodation: it adds up quickly. I budget $240 per day.

As the start date looms closer, my parents continue to ask if the sponsorship situation has improved. Each day I try a new strategy, even going so far as to fax a one-page proposal to every logical phone number I find in the Yellow Pages directory. It's time-consuming, slightly embarrassing and yields no results.

With frustration mounting, my parents step in again and offer up their green Chevy Tahoe as a support vehicle. Of course, I accept. Finding a vehicle has been the most complicated *ask*.

It's not an easy acceptance, however. I would prefer to make it all come together on my own, to prove that the venture mattered to someone other than those directly related to me. But the lesson I am quickly learning is that just because Ride for Life is for charity, it doesn't mean others should automatically care.

Of those businesses that do take the time to hear me out, the question I am most often asked is, "Who else is sponsoring you?" They all seem to be waiting for a credible name to come on board. I pound my fists. *Someone has to be first.*

During a particularly bitter patch, I paint over the Trek decals on my bike after receiving a rejection letter from the famed Wisconsin company, the sponsor of Lance Armstrong and the U.S. Postal Service Pro Cycling Team. It is just another stab in a long string of generic refusal letters that begin with the word, "Unfortunately."

As disheartening as this process often is, it is also teaching me plenty. I'm learning about the importance of a groomed image, the power of perception and about being direct. I have become better about approaching businesses in person instead of relying on faxes and e-mails to make a connection. On days when I'm not working with my parents downtown, I drive up and down Calgary's commercial Macleod Trail, stopping in at businesses to make *the ask*.

Following the sting of another rejection, I walk across the street to a Subway restaurant for lunch. Midway through my meatball sandwich, the owner and I get to chatting about what I am up to. He slips me a couple of extra stamps for my loyalty card. "Every little bit helps," he says. That evening, I upload a large Subway logo to the sponsor section on my newly created website, www.ryansdream.com. *It's time to work smarter.*

I approach an event management group to help attract more sponsorship and media attention. Considering the cause, and that the owner's mother has had a recent bout of cancer, they offer their services pro bono. "You'll be a media darling," they say, excited, while also being careful not to make any sponsorship promises. To my surprise, within the first week they secure a laptop from Sony (so that I can update my website while on the road) and sunglasses from Smith Optics. They also begin hearing back from interview inquiries with Calgary media.

Walking back to the car after another meeting, I stumble across a small window sign for a design firm and decide to introduce myself. Speaking with the receptionist, I provide a brief overview of my journey, then make the vague segue, "I'm not really sure why I'm here, but maybe you can help. I have a website, and it would be cool if I could have a logo to put on the main page. Do you guys do that sort of thing?" The lady smiles and nods, then calls in one of the designers.

Like my favourite superheroes, I appreciate the importance of having a symbol to stand behind. The designer directs me to a dimly lit, fashionable office, and asks about the journey. Like many who take the time, he becomes curious about my ambition. "Don't worry, we won't charge you," he interrupts. He then gives me a piece of homework. "This evening, I want you to go home and put together some design elements that inspire you."

Late into the night, and after several hours spent in deep thought, I e-mail a rough compilation of jpeg images. The concept is a Canadian and American flag, separated in the middle by a cyclist. A few days later, the designer and I meet to review his initial pass. The first logo is wordy, brown and reeks of a needy cause. The second is much simpler, with few words, strong curves and masked in bold primary colours. "That's the one," I point.

With a logo and website in hand, I now have the foundation to develop an online presence. But seeing it all together for the first time, I immediately notice that a piece is still missing. I pause to consider a potentially deeper meaning behind Ryan's Dream (instead of just a splash page for Ride for Life). I realize now that there may be more to the grand vision than what I see in front of me. But the message remains hidden.

My discount web developer builds the site as a resource for the ride, including journal entries, pictures, sponsor logos and an expensive animated banner at the top. Many hours are spent wondering whether blue or yellow is the best colour for *that* button, and should it flash or pulse? The micromanagement doesn't feel like the best use of my time, but it is nonetheless intriguing. I like having input and an understanding of every aspect.

Soon I learn that anyone can have a website; the challenge

is attracting visitors. To that end, the event management group coordinates a feature interview with A-Channel for their evening news, part of a weekly segment called "The People We Meet." The evening it airs, my family excitedly converge around the basement television. *Here we go.*

"Yellow" by Coldplay (a personal request) warms the room as I speak about being inspired by Terry Fox and Lance Armstrong. Cut to a shot of me sweating away on a stationary bike in our cramped furnace room, a map of the route superimposed and then a plea for support. It is dramatic and purposeful, and a push at just the right time. Watching my parents, transfixed from a distance, I notice that they seem encouraged, proud even. *Could it be?* I'm winning over my toughest critics.

JUNE 1, 2002

I'm still without a support driver. I chat up the opportunity with everyone I know. "It will be the adventure of a lifetime!" I reason. "Three months on the road, supporting a good cause, with paid accommodation and all your meals covered. You just need to drive behind me (with all of our gear) and accept donations – the same simple setup that Terry Fox had. And that seemed to work out all right."

The responses from extended family and friends generally fall into two categories: either "how much can you pay?" or "I can't take that much time off work." Understandably, many people I ask are in college or have a full-time job to consider.

Days fall off the calendar without any progress.

Finally I shoot for the stars and call up a childhood friend from Edmonton (where I was born). It has been almost six years since I have spoken with Adam. He and his fraternal twin grew up in the house next to ours. We were inseparable until that fateful day when my father got a job offer in Calgary.

I've got first-date jitters, not really sure how to phrase my offer over the phone. His voice mail picks up, then the beep. I hesitate for a moment, then start in on the proposal. "Hey, Adam, it's your old friend Ryan in Calgary … been a while. Next week I plan to cycle around North America to raise funds for cancer research. I need someone to drive a support vehicle. You game?" I hang up and wait anxiously.

The next day I see there is one missed call on my phone. It's from Adam. "Hey, Ryan," the message begins. "Good to hear from you," he says, laughing. "I just quit my job. Come pick me up … let's do this! Crazy. Alright, talk to you soon."

JUNE 7, 2002
The event management group arranges for the send-off to be at Fort Calgary. One cameraman responds to the media release.

Together and reacquainted, Adam and I stand with my parents and a few family friends. A group of seniors pass us on their way to visit the pioneer attraction, looking confused. Any signs of uneasiness I brush off with a smile. I remind everyone that "Terry Fox began his journey without anyone knowing who he was, either."

The hour of our departure strikes. I hug my mom and sister and shake my father's hand. Adam hops in the truck and switches on his walkie-talkie. I turn on mine, "Check, check." He gives me a thumbs-up out the window. "Let's do this," I call back. With one last wave, we pull onto the city street and begin rolling.

A block down, we hit a pesky red light. I wave again to

the group: *Bye, see ya!* The next block, we hit rush hour traffic coming out of downtown. The group is still in plain sight, including the lone cameraman, fixed on our inaction. *Jesus, this is embarrassing.*

We continue through stop-and-go traffic. Four lanes of idling cars stare at me from all angles, trying to make sense of the decaled truck and my stake to the centre lane. After an hour and a half of riding through the tailgate fumes, we reach the eastern edge of the city, the tail end of the bottleneck, and the beginning of the Trans-Canada Highway.

The shoulder widens and we begin to pick up speed. The wind increases too, making it difficult to hear Adam through the small receiver in my right ear. He soon adopts a method of driving up beside me and yelling through the passenger window instead. "How far behind you should I drive?" he calmly inquires.

I'm not really sure. This is new to me too. "Far enough that you won't run me over if you sneeze and accidentally press on the accelerator," I reply with a semi-serious smirk. Two car lengths should be appropriate.

We settle into a somewhat familiar rhythm. Every now and again, I look back to see if my father is there. Instead, I only see Adam slowly cruising, his eyes hidden behind a pair of dark sunglasses. His attention is caught up in the great yonder.

An hour out of Calgary, back among the open prairies, an overweight gentleman in a beat-up sedan waves us over. I slow down to see what he has to say. Rolling to a stop, he extends his hand to shake mine. "I heard about you on CJAY 92." CJAY 92 is a local rock station in Calgary. "Good luck!" He then passes Adam a crumpled $20 donation through the passenger window. "It's not much, sorry." *But it means everything.*

Adam and I stop at the large provincial sign welcoming travellers to Manitoba. Saskatchewan, before this, was the same as I had remembered it: quiet and unpopulated. Our donation tally remains at one.

Competition is a factor. During the last week and a half, we have come across a variety of inspired athletes who are running, rollerblading, skateboarding or hopscotching their way across Canada – all for charity. *What separates us from the rest?*

Cars rush by without much of a clue as to what we are doing. Large decals on the side of the truck read: "Ride for Life: Uniting People in the Fight against Cancer." There is also a small logo on the back window (right above our donation bin). Unfortunately, both are impossible to decipher at highway speed.

Frustrated, I load my bike into the back of the truck and drive with Adam to the closest business that makes signs. Two hours later, we mount a large plastic banner on the tailgate with bungee cords, rope and duct tape. In bold black and white lettering, our mission is now unmistakable: "CAUTION! BIKE TOUR IN PROGRESS, 14,000 km For Cancer Research, Donations Kindly Accepted Here."

Still no one stops.

We reach the steps of the Canadian Shield and enter into more forested lands, then soon into Ontario. Passing by the vast waters of Lake Superior, we happen across a turnoff for the Terry Fox memorial (on a high hill overlooking the town of Thunder Bay). I remember now, *This is where Terry was forced to end his Marathon of Hope.* My eyes tear up as I gaze at the bronze statue in full stride. I am in complete awe and humbled to be in the presence of this historic moment long since past. My quest appears so little in comparison.

Back at the truck, Adam chats with a kindergarten teacher who has taken notice of our cause. Pointed in my direction, she walks over and asks if I would be willing to speak with her students. The tykes in the group of 20 or so sit cross-legged, happily eating lunch on the grass. A few chase each other around the monument. They have only a faint understanding of the shadow that nips at their feet.

Thirteen days on the road and this is the first time anyone has acknowledged our ride. "It would be great if you could chat with the kids about how Terry has inspired you," the teacher says. *Of course.* I embrace the opportunity.

Standing in front of the young crowd, I smile again, "Do any of you know how Terry lost his leg?" One hand shyly reaches upward.

The engagement thrusts my mind back into the cause. I switch gears from feeling the need to collect donations to something equally as important – that is, building awareness.

For the next two days, rolling Precambrian hills and sunshine nourish this thought further. Not even the pesky blackflies distract me.

I'm excited to reach the city of Barrie, just north of Toronto. The Childhood Cancer Canada Foundation has organized a fun ride with kids from the region whom they have helped, along with their parents. It is my first real connection to the cause.

Arriving at the boardwalk along Lake Simcoe, I'm greeted by a group of youngsters on tricycles. Up close, the cancer reality hits like a freight train. Many of the kids are still bald from chemotherapy treatments. It doesn't stop them from laughing, though.

I pretend to be a leader in their presence.

A father comes up to shake my hand. "Thank you so much for all your hard work," he tells me sincerely. I stand speechless and in utter shock at it all. The kids, *they are so small.*

RIDE FOR LIFE HEADS DOWN THE EAST COAST, 2002

The rubble site of Ground Zero in New York City represents the first-quarter completion of Ride for Life. Adam and I walk by sombre flower arrangements and posters for missing family members overlooking the crater of wreckage, still being excavated nearly a year later.

From the Big Apple, we turn south and head down the east coast, passing by the Liberty Bell in Philadelphia, the White House in Washington, DC, old plantations in the Carolinas, all the way to the warm beaches and retirement homes in Florida.

Still no donations.

Jacksonville, Florida, is the halfway point of our journey. Coincidentally, Adam and I end up staying at the same oceanfront Best Western that my father and I stopped at on our tour north from Fort Lauderdale to Ontario in 1998. Over a couple of beers and seafood that evening, I'm thrust back into a memory of that time, and a feeling of failure now. After 7000 kilometres, we have only raised a few hundred dollars.

Adam and I wake up the next morning hung over. The sour stench of crustacean vomit wafts thought the white-walled room, escaping out through our open balcony window to an impressive view. Looking out at the ocean sunrise, I choose to not feel any shame for the odour. *We both needed to cut loose.*

Adam packs up the truck while I ready my bike and check out. He tries to hide the events of last night behind those dark sunglasses, but his groggy body language says it all. I watch him heave a cooler into the trunk, then immediately hunch over, ready to vomit again. Something about his unflinching loyalty, especially in light of his current struggle, makes me grin. He is a good friend.

RIDE FOR LIFE HEADS WEST ACROSS THE SOUTHERN STATES, 2002

Our route west parallels Interstate 10 through Alabama, Mississippi, Louisiana, Texas, New Mexico, Arizona and on to the beaches of California. Back in the planning stages, I had expected the southern portion of the ride to be the most difficult.

The heat and humidity do not disappoint.

I step outside our air-conditioned truck after a break near the Gulf of Mexico wetlands at Biloxi, only to be saturated in perspiration after a few minutes of riding. Taking after Lance, I stop wearing my helmet to allow for better airflow. I'm also keen to emulate the grandeur of his determination: he's currently riding toward a fourth Tour de France victory. *USA Today* keeps me abreast of all the mountaintop drama in the Pyrenees.

But that action seems so far removed from here.

Old shipping vessels and stilted wooden shacks line the Mississippi River Delta up ahead.

Stopped on the outskirts of New Orleans, we're drawn in by a pair of thick accents at a McDonald's: a group of older black men telling stories of shrimp fishing and the way things once were. Bicycle racing and Lycra have yet to enter their lexicon.

We reach Texas and head straight for the familiar state capital of Austin, home of the Lance Armstrong Foundation.

The evening before a scheduled tour with the foundation, a news crew shows up at our hotel to do a story about the journey. Savouring this brief flicker of attention, I slick back my hair, put on the cool shades and parade around in front of the camera. Adam stays back in the room.

To my wonderment, an attractive blonde woman pulls me aside after seeing the display. We get to talking in the pool later on, and when the coast is clear, she pulls me up to her room. Without any reservation, she then slowly strips off her slim bathing suit and motions for me to come closer. *My first groupie.*

I'm not sure what has come over me. *And her breath*, it tastes like cigarettes.

I pause to consider the irony of trying to raise funds and awareness for cancer research and sleeping with a girl who smokes. But it feels good. It is a far cry from daily reason and routine, and an embrace of my teenage hormones.

I'm channelling Lance's celebrity.

The next morning, I meet with an employee of the Lance Armstrong Foundation to get a tour of LAF headquarters. The offices are located in a historic wood home, painted an innocent white. Inside the tasteful, cozy space hang several of Lance's yellow Tour de France jerseys framed on the wall, along with a multitude of other memorabilia.

I ask the tall redhead if she happened to catch my interview on the news last night. "No, I'm sorry," she politely responds in an English accent. There is much fanfare with Lance still in the lead. My tour is but a tiny footprint within their multi-million-dollar fundraising efforts. She soon ushers me back out. "Have a nice ride," as if to say *Who are you, again?*

Adam and I reach the smog of Hollywood, California. As per normal routine at the end of a long day of riding, my partner in crime begins unpacking while I check in to the hotel.

It has been an especially taxing afternoon. Coordinating our navigation through large cities (in this case, Los Angeles) is often tense and filled with more wrong turns than right.

While signing my name on the credit card receipt, Adam timidly approaches the office. "What's up?" I ask, already sensing a problem. With his head down, he tells me he accidentally dropped the sponsored laptop on some stairs.

The computer is destroyed.

Motioning to the door, I tell him I'm going for a walk to clear my head.

I stroll for a half hour until I stumble upon a Kinko's copy shop that also houses computers. The recent incident at the hotel makes me think I ought to review our online bank account, which I see has now dwindled to a couple hundred dollars. When I check my e-mail, I see that a promising new sponsor has stopped responding to funding requests.

Reason takes hold.

In view of a glorious California sunset, I walk confidently back to the hotel and ask Adam if we can chat over a meal at the diner downstairs.

He sits down at a booth, concerned and rightly defensive that I might lay into him about the computer. Instead, I look him in the eye and explain that I have come to an important decision.

"We have run out of money. This is all that we have left," I say, handing him an envelope. "I need you to drive back up to Calgary tomorrow morning, the shortest route possible. I also need to borrow your backpack. I'm going to continue on alone, up the west coast, and finish what we started. No more hotels, extra meals or expensive gas. No more scrounging for media, failed press releases or wasted fundraising efforts. Ride for Life as we know it is over."

Adam nods, somewhat relieved.

CHAPTER 8

LEAVING HOLLYWOOD

RIDE FOR LIFE, DAY 62

The bedside alarm begins buzzing. Next, an automated call rings in: "Your 3:00 a.m. wakeup call." I get up without needing to be coaxed.

Propped next to the bed is a small red backpack, jam-packed with only the essentials. The rest of our gear (save for Adam's toothbrush and a change of clothes) has already been stuffed away in the truck. After our diner conversation last night, there was nothing left to do but prepare. *Why delay this any longer?*

Adam will soon be headed on a more direct path north through Nevada, Utah and Montana. My route up the Pacific Coast Highway remains true to the original plan. "I'm going to finish what we started," I say again to my childhood friend.

Outside the hotel, the two of us hug in the early morning stillness. It is the first time we have done so. Stepping back after the embrace, he bounces the keys in his hand, smiles, hops in the truck and then slowly pulls onto the quiet street. He waves back and I watch the Ride for Life banner pull away for the last time.

And then, there was just one.

I take a moment to find my bearings.

Early morning traffic buzzes along Highway 101. To the east, high above on the hills overlooking Los Angeles, the infamous HOLLYWOOD sign shines brightly. *How ironic,* I have spent probably a third of my young adult life in a theatre. I love movies. But now, cycling through the heart of the American movie industry without all the glitz, I must accept a certain failure, and break from reality.

I think back to riding through the desert oasis of Palm Springs a couple of days ago. The morning before a scheduled media interview at our hotel, I happened across a replica U.S. Postal Service Pro Cycling Team jersey – the same royal blue that Lance is wearing in *le Tour* – and decided to buy it. As I'm spinning back through town, a group of Hispanic construction workers thrusts fists into the air and yell, "Go Lance, Go!" as I pass by. They have no clue. Nevertheless, I give a slight wave and allow my conflicted ego to again pick up steam.

Idiot. The Hollywood sign passes into my periphery and I'm left in unfamiliar darkness on the freeway shoulder. Each time a car screams by, I'm frighteningly reminded that I shouldn't be travelling this route, that I'm not allowed. Pedestrians and bikes are forbidden on most major highways. Unfortunately, packing a city map was overlooked last night. This situation that I am in right now, *I deserve it.*

Squinting into the darkness, my poor planning is rewarded with an abrupt encounter with a storm drain. Its metal teeth immediately catch my front wheel and cause the skinny tire to burst. *Fuck.*

Caught between a retaining wall and the deadly stream of traffic, I begin the tense process of changing the bastard. My composure is promptly tested as I realize that no spare tubes made it into the backpack either, only a patch kit. Even at the best of times, repairing a small puncture can be a challenge. I remember a trick my father taught me.

I turn away from the traffic. If I'm going to get hit by a car, it's going to happen whether I'm looking or not. Facing away allows me to focus my other senses on the task at hand.

First, I close my eyes and press my lips against the tube (after having pumped it up a little). Moving the rubber past the sensitive skin in small increments, I feel for the faintest bit of air seeping out. I soon sense the spot but also notice that the bead hook is bent inward. With a splintered chunk of wood I find lying near the drain, I try to pry it back into shape. But the rim doesn't budge. I only manage to scrape the polished surface.

The sunrise will soon expose me. I'm afraid that a news helicopter might also home in: "*We have an interesting new development. There is a homeless man on the 101 Freeway, leading out of downtown...*" I continue walking in search of sanctuary. Of course, there are no off-ramps nearby.

The creeping sun warms the hovering smog. In clear view, speeding sports cars, stares and the intoxicating smell of gas now flood my vulnerable senses. Like a stray dog, I grow jittery and insecure.

Ring, ring. I jump. My cellphone impatiently calls out from the red backpack – my parents, no doubt. They are just finding out about my decision to continue alone. I reach back. WHEEW, WHEEW. I'm interrupted by the sound of a police siren behind me. Looking over my shoulder, I take stock of an unimpressed police officer. He dismounts his beefy motorbike and walks toward me with an intent to educate. I drop the cellphone back into its pocket. *Okay, yeah, I know.*

He escorts me off the highway with a stern warning and then continues on.

I have no idea where I am. Trusting my instinct, I roll on through a patchwork of affluent San Fernando Valley neighbourhoods on a westerly bearing (staying left of Highway 101, which eventually intersects the coast). I figure that sooner or later a bottleneck will push me out onto the infamous Pacific Coast Highway.

Not even six months before, I looked at a map of California and imagined that this would be the highlight of the tour. I had grand delusions that the Golden State would become well acquainted with Ride for Life, and our cause. In reality, I navigate through a series of communities and strip malls in complete anonymity.

On the outskirts of Calabasas, I happen across a group of cyclists riding together in formation. *My people.* They tell me to hop on the back and follow them the rest of the way. But since I'm still a rookie with peloton protocol, I hang back a few extra feet so as not to insult the elegant echelon.

All is well until my front tire punctures as a result of the bent rim protruding inward. I decide not to yell ahead and draw further attention to my hopelessness. Instead, I'll walk the rest of the way, up and over the coastal mountain range. The pack disappears around a steep corner.

Catching up in elevation, I see *it* for myself. The late morning sun sparkles on Pacific waves gently rolling in. And for all my problems, I can't think of any at this moment. Below is a tiny oasis lined with sports cars, surfing, prime real estate and smiling people. This most definitely is Malibu.

I hate the idea of hitchhiking, but there hasn't been a single bike shop along my path. *Decision made.*

I stick out my thumb. Within minutes, a Volkswagen Westfalia (complete with surfboards, cook stove and the Beach Boys blaring from the stereo) pulls over. Inside the can of nostalgia, a laid-back guy in his thirties extends his hand to shake mine.

His grip catches me in a moment of déjà vu. I remember

entering a cruise ship talent contest (while on a family vacation as a child) and lip-synching "Surfin' Safari" to a crowd of intoxicated and overfed seniors. And now I'm in it:

We're loading up our woody
With my bike inside.

Apparently there is a bike shop just ten minutes down the road. "Do you mind if we stop by my house first?" the friendly surf bum asks. *Of course not.* I'm just a little surprised that he owns anything besides the van.

The dude pulls up to a gated community, punches in a number on a keypad, then continues up a pristine street to a large home, complete with an oceanside boat dock and palm tree landscaping. "I sold my software business to 'the man' for a pile of money," he laughs, noticing the surprised look on my face.

We continue on to the bike shop, where my new friend asks the owner to "hook him [me] up." He then disappears with a stoned smile, back into stranger never-never land.

A stout mechanic promptly bends my wheel into better form. "There, that should get you home." He extends a ritual fist, "Good luck, bro."

Never having been one for extravagant handshakes and shorthand, I defer to a polite Canadian nod and a "thank you."

Next to the bike shop is an expensive looking organic supermarket. My stomach grumbles. *Argh, food.*

I splurge on chocolate milk, Gatorade and a large macadamia nut cookie. At the checkout, a well-dressed lady notices the web address on the back of my Ride for Life T-shirt (in place of the U.S. Postal Service Pro Cycling Team farce) and asks, "What is Ryan's Dream?" I tell her the same story I'd shared with the surfer. Without blinking, she reaches into her purse and hands me a wad of American bills. "For you," she says kindly. I keep my hand closed and smile as she walks back out to the parking lot and her Mercedes.

The shiny black luxury sedan pulls onto the warm Pacific Coast Highway and drives away. Alone, I sit down on the concrete curb to refuel and count the crisp green bills. *Holy shit*, it's $300.

I'm caught in a dilemma as to how the funds should be used. She never really specified. I could easily keep the money for myself and use it to cover food and accommodation for the next three days. But I also have a sense that her generosity was drawn out by something more meaningful than tacos and cheap motels.

I stare at the wealth before me and consider the man that I want to be.

RIDE FOR LIFE, DAY 65

A thick layer of fog hangs over the coast in the morning. I wear a thin red rain jacket over my T-shirt for warmth. Inside the back pocket, I feel my cellphone vibrate again. Another new voice mail.

Deciding to listen now, I recognize an underlying tone of panic in my mother's voice. There is also a message from the event management group. Everyone wants to know if I need help and if they should send money. I call them all back and plead, "Please don't. This is the way it needs to be."

I pass a turnoff for the Hearst Castle, a gaudy monolith, high above. Soon the road narrows and begins a windy ascent of the rocky coast. My attention flows around the next blind corner. There is no shoulder to wander onto.

At lunch I prop my bike up against a rock wall overlooking the ocean. The view is mesmerizing. Unwrapping a tuna sub from a nearby market, I cherish the little moments: biting into the warm bread, tasting the ocean catch and unscrewing the cap off a bottle of cold Coke. I listen to the sound of the tide below, the wind blowing along the narrow coastal cliff and tourists walking by.

My body relaxes as I take a deep breath. No longer do I feel the need to puff out my chest.

I consider the stark difference between venturing out on my own, and creating a public display. The latter requires a degree of attention and planning that took away from the spontaneity, the rawness, and worst of all, turned me against myself.

I'm now on the path of repentance.

RIDE FOR LIFE, DAY 67

My route follows California State Route 9 north from Santa Cruz on the coast, up and over rolling, forested mountains and smooth, wet pavement. The scene is straight out of a theatrical car commercial.

The lush green curtain opens to a sprawling view of San Francisco and the surrounding bay area.

After checking into a hostel overlooking the frigid waters, I find out I will be sharing a "mixed-private" room. Two of the bunk beds are reserved for three young women from Denmark. The hostel manager asks if that is a problem. *Duh, no.*

Knocking on the door, I'm greeted with *"Gooddag"* (hello) by the blondes, all close in age. The girls and I become instant touring buddies, nothing more.

They are visiting California after a work exchange on the east coast fell apart.

For two days we hike up and down the steep streets, taking pictures and dining on back alley Chinese cuisine.

They are a giggly bunch, and a welcome break from deeper thoughts. As far as they know, I'm on a solo tour.

Arriving back at the hostel on our last evening, we happen across a fistfight between a scantily clad hooker and her abusive pimp. He brutally pummels her slim frame without recourse. *What the hell?!*

Instinct kicks in as I run to make the tackle. I'm quickly joined by another bystander while the Danish girls dash inside and call for help. Soon the police arrive, their sirens and flashing lights echoing off the Victorian row houses. The pimp continues to yell incoherently, arms flailing.

The next morning, I'm still vibrating.

Seeing me off after a flavourful Starbucks breakfast, the girls assemble for a group hug and wish me luck in their broken English. Waving back, I roll on toward the misty Golden Gate Bridge, alone.

RIDE FOR LIFE, DAY 70

I arrive in the evening at a quaint coastal hostel in the small salmon fishing village of Klamath, California, about 500 kilometres north of the San Francisco Bay area.

While boiling water for Kraft Dinner, I befriend a young surfer who is walking the length of the state in search of hidden surf spots. He displays his hand-built fibreglass board with pride.

That evening, a group of us misfit travellers staying at the Redwood Retreat assemble in the musty, yet cozy living room for an impromptu sharing circle. "What's your story?" asks the wiry caretaker.

Standing in front of a colourful wall map of North America, I trace a large rectangle with my index finger and state, "I have cycled over 12,000 kilometres to get to this point." I dare not embellish any further. They tell me I should be proud.

Over a hearty porridge breakfast the next morning, I happen across news that Lance won *le Tour* over two weeks ago. *Bravo.* I used to check the paper religiously for updates on the fourth attempt. It appears to be an afterthought now.

I shoulder my bike, say goodbye to the hostel patrons and walk down a few sets of wooden stairs to the Pacific Coast Highway, which is bathed in ocean fog.

Back in the car commercial, I steeply ascend through the forest giants of Del Norte Coast Redwoods State Park. Cool air collects with perspiration from my brow, condensing into salty droplets. The dew collects in the red beard now growing on my face.

If only Adam could see me now. Sweat stains cover the neckline and underarms of my Ride for Life T-shirt. My shoulder and neck muscles have grown toned and stiff, more accustomed to the weight of the backpack shifting side to side. I'm a mountain man.

RIDE FOR LIFE: HOME STRETCH

I reach the Canadian border crossing at White Rock, British Columbia. The Peace Arch customs agent asks for my story, so I explain, "I have been on the road for two and a half months, cycling throughout North America in support of cancer research." I then remove my backpack to expose the web address on the back of my stained T-shirt. "Please consider making a donation." He waves me on through.

Back on home turf, only 944 kilometres left.

The last leg of my journey takes me along the Trans-Canada Highway, up and over the Rocky Mountains, through the fertile lands of the Interior, over Rogers Pass, all the way to the familiar tourist destination of Banff, Alberta. I arrive on August 29 at the Hostelling International Banff Alpine Centre, an elaborate hostel perched high above the mountain town.

The event management group (having kept in strained communication with me) pays for a fancy steak dinner at a local connection. Even after I deviated from the original plan and didn't become the media darling, they still choose to honour my efforts. I sit in the corner of the restaurant so as not to draw attention to my sandals, shorts and spare T-shirt (my only change of clothes). The meal is exquisite.

Later that evening, I befriend a group of Brits back at the hostel. They are headed out on a pub-crawl with a couple other travellers. They taunt me and I give in all too easily. "Sure, I'll come along!" I'm not a drinker but I consider the celebration earned.

Seated at the first tavern, I boisterously proclaim I will outdrink the pot-bellied foreigners. My conquest ends far short of this goal, though, with my having to ask a cab driver to pull over so that I may vomit. I throw up once more while stumbling to the shared accommodation.

All the next day, I lie in an agonized fetal position. I don't want to move. I can't. I tell myself that drinking is horrible and I will never do it again to excess and I will be the first person to ever hold true to that commitment.

RIDE FOR LIFE, DAY 86

I emerge into the crisp mountain air, still hung over but ready to complete my trek around North America.

Coasting down Tunnel Mountain Road, I feel a certain sense of trepidation. I look back toward the west and consider what tomorrow would look like if I kept on going – to forgo everyday responsibilities and continue living this life of exploration (no matter the expense). But I have a responsibility to finish. *I said that I would.*

The morning carries on with a quiet satisfaction. Soon after leaving Banff, I pass the town of Canmore and exit the Rocky Mountains. Ahead are those familiar foothills and the finish in Calgary, not far now.

I roll past the turnoff for my junior high school and consider, *What strange dream is this?*

At the Calgary city limits, I happen upon a cyclist who has fallen over at a stoplight. He is still attached to his expensive bike – apparently somewhat new to clipless pedals. As is usually the case, the rider had come to a complete stop before realizing that his feet were still attached. I roll up and tell him it's alright, "We've all been there."

A moment of embarrassment is quickly replaced by astonishment when he asks where I am headed. "I have friends and family waiting at Eau Claire Plaza downtown," I tell him. "I'm just about to complete a 14,000-kilometre trek around North America."

"Seriously?" he questions, somewhat skeptical.

"No word of a lie. You'll probably see it on the news tonight," I reply. He asks if we can chat some more.

The man and I roll on to a popular smoothie establishment near the plaza finish. While sipping on a complimentary sorbet blend, I tell him of my adventures and a dream gone awry. He listens intently.

When the planned completion hour approaches, he hands me a cheque for $1,000 and says, "Again, well done." For a moment, I stare at the cheque and think about how things would have worked out differently had this money arrived before Hollywood. But it didn't. Maybe it wasn't meant to.

I straddle my bike for the last time.

Up ahead, I see a group of family and friends in Ride for Life T-shirts. They are holding up a white finish banner underneath the Olympic columns at Eau Claire Plaza. They smile, clap and take pictures as I approach.

The banner catches on my chest and drags along with me. As I pull it aside and give my mother a hug, the same lone cameraman who was also at the send-off is the first to ask, "So, how does it feel to be at the end of your journey?"

I look down at the banner, which, I notice, has not ripped. I think about my promise to raise $1-million for charity and how I came nowhere close: I raised a total of $14,000.

Instinctively I respond, "This is just the beginning."

Back at home that night, I unload my backpack and find the $300 contribution that the lady in California gave me at the organic market. Not giving it another thought, I put the crumpled bills into the Ziploc bag with all the other donations.

Now *it's time to shave.*

CHAPTER 9

JUST THE BEGINNING

SEPTEMBER 15, 2002

Sitting at a picnic table outside the entrance to the University of Calgary, I people-watch while waiting for a meeting with Kurt Innes, head of the National Cycling Centre, which is housed at the Olympic Oval. The Canadian Cycling Association, the governing body for the sport in Canada, suggested that we meet. Along with the two charities, the CCA had endorsed Ride for Life early on as a means of adding credibility to my plight. I'm now encouraged to explore their racer development program.

It has been a month since I finished my 14,000-kilometre tour around North America. Following the banner finish, I recall sitting around an outdoor pub table with my support team in Eau Claire Plaza, scruffy and laughing.

Driving home from the finish line, I asked my mother to stop off at a record store so that I could buy the new Coldplay album, *A Rush of Blood to the Head*. Later that night, I listen intently to the inspired album with my headphones in bed. In particular, I'm drawn to the triumphant "Clocks," which I listen to on repeat.

Kurt walks up and apologizes, "Sorry I'm late." We immediately begin with the base mileage I've logged over the last three months. "It's impressive," Kurt says. "It's right up there with what any professional is doing. Not many racers your age have those kinds of miles in their legs. We would definitely like you to join our program. I believe we can help develop your speed and technical…" Before he can finish that thought, a woman with curly red hair comes up and taps him on the shoulder.

Her name is Clara. Kurt introduces me and mentions that I just got back from touring around North America. Clara shines a bright toothy smile and begins asking me all about the trip. She and her husband just got back from a bike tour in the Yukon. "It was great cross-training," she says.

Little do I know that the woman in front of me is Clara Hughes, the only athlete to ever win medals in both the winter and summer Olympics. She is also a regular at the Olympic Oval. On any given day, she'll likely warm up on a stationary bike, then complete a series of sprint intervals on the speed skating track. The two sports complement each other well.

A wave of admiration comes over me as she leaves for practice. "She's just a regular person like you and me," I say to Kurt, aside. The chance meeting is a perfect introduction to the endurance community. It also feels like a complete 180-degree turn from hockey. "Count me in," I tell him.

I train with the Olympic Oval program through the fall.

WINTER, 2002 – SPRING, 2003

At Christmas my parents buy me my first matching team kit, complete with cycling shorts, jersey and a winter riding jacket.

For my birthday in February, they help me to purchase a shiny new Project One Trek road bike. It is custom-painted in Oval team yellow and includes a black decal along the top tube: "Ryan's Dream." The money comes from a savings account my grandmother had started for my sister and me that was probably meant for schooling. She is now in a home suffering from dementia.

I tell my parents I am going to be a professional bike racer and that my hockey training will complement this new path. They are cautiously optimistic about the transition.

Olympic organizations like the Oval program have more faith. Bobsled athletes are often approached to run track and field. Hockey players are sought after for speed skating. And I'm somewhere in the middle: an amalgamation of a powerful sprint and numerous miles. The Oval coaches persuade me to try track cycling because of my larger muscle mass.

I proceed with some hesitation.

The Tour de France and the open road have served as my cycling muse. In contrast, racing around a concrete velodrome is a seemingly flat expression of my two-wheeled passion. But this is where opportunity is at the moment: Canada has some of the top track cyclists in the world, and funds the sport accordingly. We have never fielded a Tour de France team, though.

I'm now determined: track cycling is my future.

My parents express concern that speeding blindly ahead toward such a vague goal is not intelligent, nor *balanced*. They remind me of how I loved Kelly, of how I thought she was the one, and then not. They remind me how I played hockey for all those years and then just gave it up without talking it over with anyone. They remind me of all the things I tend to start but do not finish. "You are twenty years old now. It's time to commit to something," they say sternly, meaning something more grounded.

A college acceptance letter keeps the frustration at bay.

I enter into a two-year university transfer program at Mount Royal College, beginning in the spring of 2003. My course load will help satisfy entry requirements for business school at the University of Calgary, while also leaving enough time for training. *Balance.*

Unfortunately, economics and calculus classes do not compute. Complex numbers and homework feel counterintuitive to me when I could be spending time training. I begin to ponder, *What holy hell is this?*

In the midst of writing a mid-term exam, I drop my pencil and walk out of the large class, frustrated. The next morning, I skip going altogether. I decide instead to meet with a representative from the college administration. I ask to be withdrawn from my classes. They try to persuade me otherwise. "No, I unfortunately do not have any desire to stick it out," I say, self-assured.

I am a college dropout.

As with the hockey debacle, I withhold the news from my parents. Instead, I reignite the conversation I've had with them before: that business school may not be for me.

Feeling the weight of additional misplaced hope, my parents become proactive in helping me find an alternative through the college haze. As long as I continue going to school, that's the new priority.

Over dinner they tell me about a unique program a client's daughter has recently entered. They hand me a colourful brochure. On the front, in bold lettering, it reads, "Bachelor of Applied Ecotourism & Outdoor Leadership (ETOL)." The brochure is filled with youthful people rock climbing, mountain biking, rafting, hiking and smiling. It is a far cry from the madding crowd of professionals in buttoned-down suits.

I decide to give college a second try.

My ecotourism studies begin. It is the first time in a long while that I agree with my parents about the path I am on. "And I promise, I'll stick with it!"

The small class consists of a range of ages, facial hair and mountain types. I stand out in a collared shirt (in honour of a new start). My peers are more loosely kempt, in jeans and T-shirts. The tone is laid-back. Offhandedly, someone jokingly refers to the ETOL program as "hippie gym."

We all come to the program with a similar love for the outdoors. Some plan to channel that energy into being a guide. Some hope to be park rangers. Most are unsure, though, like any other college student.

It is clear that I am the only one with a strong entrepreneurial drive. My leading thought is that the ETOL degree will add a level of credibility to my vague cycling passion and perhaps reveal a new piece to the elusive career mould. It also just sounds like fun.

Our first assignment is a leadership game, stationed outside in the school courtyard. We assemble next to a ten-foot brick wall and are challenged by our instructor to find a way to get everyone on top of it. Meanwhile, the attention of onlooking classes is pulled our way. I look back at their intrigued faces, seemingly caught in glassed purgatory. *Don't give it a second thought.*

"I'll go on the bottom," I volunteer.

I'm determined to show that I can get dirty. With me and two other gents forming the base of a pyramid, the remaining sweaty feet stand united on our backs and shoulders (and my white-collared shirt). Then, one at a time, each student reaches up and over.

We succeed, but not without injury.

Nearing the end of the exercise, the shortest girl in the

group falls and breaks her arm. She continues on, however, determined not to let the group down. This is my introduction to fear-based learning: that which is learned from dangling off the edge, not just from a book.

Though I lack much of the backpacking experience the others have, my conditioning is better than average. Physical challenges like the wall allow my strength to shine. I am also adept at learning new skills quickly.

I begin to sit in the front row.

SPRING COLLEGE TERM, 2004

It is rare that I do not have an opinion or engage in discussion about something. Learning about the outdoors and sustainability has hit the right nerve. And because of my new forthright nature, my peers often choose me to lead class projects.

The commanding power inflates my ego.

I stand at the front of the room and tell the group what I think we should do and who should fill what role. Naturally, a quiet rebellion forms. One person even goes so far as to refer to me as Hitler in anonymous feedback.

Our instructor shares this information with me.

Reading over some of the more critical notes from my classmates, he suggests that I not become emotionally defensive, and instead learn from the experience. "The best leaders are calm, pretty even-keel," he encourages. I appreciate that he sees my potential. I also understand that my leadership style needs to change.

Following an outdoor leadership day for a local high school (which we organized), our ecotourism class meets for a routine debrief. Knowing there is a strong contingent of ill will toward me, I opt to listen rather than add any opinion that may fuel the fire. Furthermore, I apologize.

I promise to be more democratic with my leadership from here on in, and to facilitate group communication rather than dictate group direction. Those on the fence seem to appreciate my candour. And thankfully, tension – for the most part – calms.

I'm learning.

On my first winter camping excursion, I lead the charge up to a secluded mountain site in Bow Valley Provincial Park. As night falls, my sweaty clothes get the best of me. Soon helpless and shivering, I become entirely dependent on my tentmates for shelter and warmth.

I stumble along at the back of the group the following day, exhausted from near hypothermia.

Our next class debrief centres on the fact that even the most physically capable can falter in the outdoors with poor preparation (and improper clothing choices). It is a humbling exposé of my stubbornness and the importance of the group dynamic.

WINTER COLLEGE TERM, 2004

Later in the program, I once again have the opportunity to test my winter camping skills. The class is called "Wilderness Survival Skills." Part of our final mark includes hiking into a remote mountain area in Spray Valley Provincial Park, camping overnight on our own (without the regular comforts of a tent, sleeping bag, stove etc.), then executing emergency retrieval methods on the trek back out.

We spend weeks learning about and preparing homemade survival kits, understanding how to build snow shelters, how to insulate our bodies from the cold, what berries you can eat and how to construct traps to catch small animals.

I ask our instructor if I can go without my survival kit and snowshoes and simply hike into the woods in my jeans on the day. "That's how I would normally be dressed," I tell him. "And I would never have all these survival supplies on hand."

He scratches his chin.

"Okay, but I'm going to make you take snowshoes," he tells me. There has been a lot of snowfall in the valley where we are headed, and he doesn't want the group to have to wait up while I posthole through the snow. Whatever supplies I decide to take with me for the night alone, that is my decision.

The evening of the practical exam, I huddle alone beside a smoky campfire that is slowly inching down through the melting snowpack. Behind me, mockingly, sits an abandoned attempt at a frigid snow shelter (a.k.a. "the ice box"). Above, a blanket of cool stars can be seen through the tall pine forest. And once again I'm shivering.

Every 20 minutes I must trudge back through knee-deep snow to find more dry kindling and moss to burn. The measly fire is barely worth the cold hunt, however. My eyebrows are singed from hovering so close to what small flames do manage to flicker.

The frigid air keeps me awake all night.

I watch the moon trace a path across the sky. Below in an open valley, I can hear some of my peers grouped together, laughing over a fire – they have obviously abandoned the intended solo nature of the task. I tell myself that *I will stick it out*.

Time passes, minute after minute, hour upon agonizing hour. And then the sun begins to peek over the horizon. Bleary-eyed, I stretch out my palms toward the rays shining through.

Coughing to one side, I vomit out a dark, phlegmy mess (from inhaling smoke all night). "Longest night of my life," I say in a raspy voice, reaching for my water bottle. Little twigs and sediment swirl around in the last gulp.

On arriving back at the Drake pub in Canmore, I waste no time in ordering a larger Angus burger and plate of greasy fries. My instructor pulls me aside and congratulates me for making it through the night without calling out for his help. "You probably gained more from this lesson than anyone else," he tells me. I'm given high marks for "Survival." Considerably lower marks are awarded for my shelter.

SPRING COLLEGE TERM, 2005

We are required to take on a Directed Field Study (DFS) after our second year in the program. The goal is for students to gain practical experience in the ecotourism industry. Many of my peers choose to work for guiding businesses near their home-towns. Living near the Rockies, the opportunities are vast.

The thought of directing my energy to help build some-one else's business feels counterproductive, though. I ask my instructor if I can instead engage my entrepreneurial yearn-ings. Naturally, he inquires as to how I will fulfill the DFS program objectives.

I tell him that I will plan another cycling adventure.

"How is that work-related?" he probes. I tell him I would have to find sponsorship, coordinate route logistics, create an emergency action plan and look after many other crucial tasks. The learning outcomes are definitely there. He perks up and agrees to be my mentor.

But what is the next adventure?

Late into the night, I sit in front of my computer and read cycling travel blogs in search of an inspired route. Unfortunately, most are short in length and located primarily in North America. By this point, I feel like I have seen all that there is to see in Canada and the United States. *I need something different, something unique.*

By chance, I happen across a blog by an Italian gentleman who cycled from Prudhoe Bay, Alaska, to Ushuaia, Argentina, in 140 days in 2000 and claimed a new world record. The total distance was 25,000 kilometres along a route called the Pan-American Highway. Upon further reading, I learn that the "highway" is actually a series of interconnected roads – the longest in the world.

I'm immediately drawn to it.

Imagine, passing through 14 countries and two hemispheres in one college semester. The possibility of achieving a new world record also adds a new dimension to the professional side of things. I consider how it can be used as a tool to attract sponsors and media interest and to fuel what still feels like a necessary promotional beast.

The decision is made.

Determined to better balance my ego this go-round, I approach the Make-A-Wish Foundation of Canada about supporting the wishes of children with life-threatening illnesses. I ask them to connect me with a family so I can get to better know the cause, to live it. I'm reminded of the kids I met in Barrie during Ride for Life.

DANA

I walk up to the door of the selected family and introduce myself. Their son, Dana, has a brain tumour. Shaking his hand for the first time, I'm struck by the 15-year-old's swollen face. His mother quickly reiterates that the enlargement is a side effect of the drug treatments. They show me a picture of him before the illness. He's an athletic and rebellious kid, like any other.

The family is aware that I am considering filming a documentary about my impending journey from Alaska to Argentina, and that I would like to film Dana's story in order to have some supplementary footage. There is a parallel in our stories, I'm sure. Mine is figurative, of trying to establish purpose. Dana is faced with something much more literal.

The camera is held on standby.

Over the winter, I meet with the family weekly in an effort to get to know them better. For my 22nd birthday, in February, I invite Dana out for a movie and pizza. Chewing on a thick, cheesy slice, just the two of us, we get to talking about our respective journeys. I promise Dana I will find a way to reach Argentina. He says he will do his best to beat the cancer. I feel a friendship forming.

Dana's wish to see monkeys in Costa Rica is granted a couple weeks later. I ask the family to take along a small video camera to record their fun adventure.

Reviewing the tape, I watch as Dana points to howler monkeys in the jungle canopy and crocodiles along a river's edge. Cut to him lounging in the pool with his brother and sister, joking with his father and enjoying the sun. I'm happy to see the family laughing and supportive.

Shortly after their return, I get *the call*. Dana has fallen ill and is in the Alberta Children's Hospital. I leave class early and race over.

Quietly entering his room, I notice that Dana's parents are visibly upset. His father gets up to shake my hand as I walk over. His mother offers a hug. And Dana, despite being extremely weak and hooked up to all sorts of foreign machines, still manages to say, "Hey."

I visit a couple more times over the next two weeks, often just quietly chatting with Dana's mom while he lies on the bed watching cartoons. *Family Guy* is his favourite.

Another call comes late one evening while I'm at home with my parents. Dana has fallen into a coma and has been brought home to rest. The family does not know how much longer their little man can hold on. "You're welcome to come over. Just know that this is probably it … he is completely unresponsive," his mother calmly explains, in between tears.

Dana lies on a hospital bed in the living room. His eyes are shut, his breathing heavy. I try to keep my composure around the family and their friends, pretending like I know how to deal with these sorts of situations. But I don't. *Who does?*

I'm handed a book of lined paper and a pen to write either a memory or a message for the kid, otherwise known as "Dude." I think back to the night he and I went out for pizza on my birthday and decide to write my promise: that I will find a way to finish no matter what. I look at his still body as I write.

Dana took his last breath the following morning. His emotional funeral was held on April 24, 2005.

JUNE, 2005

By this time, I had managed to acquire most of the resources I would need to begin my Pan-American adventure. The sponsorship ball began rolling in early April, when I convinced Guru Cycles, out of Montreal, to sponsor two frames. (It is too long a journey to place hope in just one.) I still needed to supply the components, though (wheels, shifters, cables etc.).

I accomplished this task by selling my expensive yellow Trek through an online classified, and using the resulting funds to buy two sets of parts. The gentleman who purchased my bike inquired about "Ryan's Dream" (the top tube decal). "I'm cycling to the end of the world," I declare.

Sensing my need for additional funds, the gentleman suggests I come to the next board meeting of his downtown business and present my story.

A week later, I stand in front of several suits at the end of a long mahogany table. They stare at me, expressionless.

Make the ask. I tell them of a dream to cycle the longest road in the world and why that should matter. They stand to shake my hand, then usher me to the door. I'm not exactly sure what to make of the formal encounter.

A few days later I get a call from the man who bought my bike. "You conveyed your message well," he tells me. "I was using that presentation as a test to see how you might do in front of my friends with money. You passed!" He plans to make some calls on my behalf. I anxiously await the ripple effect.

One e-mail comes in, then another. "I heard about your crazy ride. Count me in for $1,000." A third message arrives from a businessman with several designations under his signature. "Let's meet for coffee, see how I can help," he says in what is becoming familiar BlackBerry shorthand.

I have entered an influential network. My father is familiar with some of the names on the list. Many of them send a cheque without ever requesting a meeting or talking on the phone – just a simple e-mail. And surprisingly, each of them appears to have a bigger connection than the last.

Over coffee with the third gentleman, I'm put in touch with a higher-up at Precision Drilling to see if they will sponsor a new truck to go the distance. I have already purchased a used camper to fit on the hoped-for four-wheel drive.

I push the elevator button for the top floor of a skyscraper in downtown Calgary. On the way up, I nervously adjust my tie and check to see that the proposal is in order. Since finding out about this meeting a week ago, I have been memorizing my notes as best I can. I'm learning to be more concise with *the ask*.

I'm escorted through locked security doors and into a large, windowed office overlooking a city of ants below. There is an air of importance that is intimidating.

A burly gentleman with the look of a beastly cattle rancher walks over and introduces himself. He has a much firmer grip than mine. "So, how can I help?" he asks directly.

I begin my proposal: "This summer I'm going to…"

"What do you *need*?" he interjects.

"A four-wheel drive truck," I ask shyly.

"Done," he shakes my hand again. "You can pick the vehicle up this weekend in Edmonton. My guys will have it ready for you."

Riding the elevator back down to reality, I ask myself whether the oilman felt I deserved a truck and no further explanation was needed. Or perhaps this was a nothing decision, a feel-good opportunity that served as a momentary breath in his day. In any case, I'm incredibly grateful.

In a few short months, I have amassed approximately $100,000 in equipment and funding. Only one piece of the puzzle remains: who will be my support driver?

Like Ride for Life, I need someone to help cook meals, drive our home on two wheels, help with navigation, ensure the validity of the record attempt and, of course, provide an added sense of security. It is not an easy role.

Honouring the right of first refusal, I call up Adam to see if he has any interest in returning. He and I haven't spoken much since our departure in Hollywood. I brace for a decidedly less enthusiastic response (compared to his blind voice mail acceptance three years ago). He goes on to tell me that university is his focus now. "Totally understand," I reply.

I move quickly to set up interviews with interested students at Mount Royal College. After some informal chit-chat, I start in on the meat of the conversation. "How would your parents feel if you were abducted in Colombia? How do you feel about living in a camper for four and a half months?" And, "What is the greatest interpersonal conflict you have had to deal with?"

They pause to consider the harsh realities of being on the road for so long, often under challenging circumstances.

None commit to a second interview.

One month before my early July departure, I am still without a comrade but continue with preparations as though everything is in place. "The missing support driver" becomes a go-to punchline for friends and family, *again*.

In late 2004 I set up a non-profit organization, the Ryan Correy Inspired Entertainment Foundation, to account for the charitable arm of my rides. I applied for funding from the Wild Rose Foundation to purchase filmmaking equipment for the Dana/Pan-American Highway documentary. The good-news column grew longer when a cheque for $6,000 showed up unexpectedly. I had been successful in my bid to the Wild Rose Foundation. One hundred per cent of the proceeds from the documentary will go to Make-A-Wish® Southern Alberta.

I make the trip to a high-end camera store the same day the cheque arrives. As I'm standing in line to pay for my new Apple laptop and Sony HD video camera, a tattooed man in his thirties (who turns out to be a camera specialist) approaches and casually asks about the documentary project. His attention perks up when I tell him of the long road to Argentina, and the wondrous filmmaking potential. His name is Mark.

That weekend, Mark and I meet for dinner at a Greek restaurant near his work. He is interested in the support driver position, and smiles as I ask the tough questions. Seeing this as an opportunity to develop his photography skills and feed the adrenaline junkie within, he meets my final commitment inquiry with a resounding "Hell, yeah. I'm in."

Two weeks before the send-off, I hold a press conference at the Famous Players cinema at Chinook Centre. The theatre is a fitting venue to promote the journey, complete with a large movie screen to emphasize the global scale projected. The manager has also graciously agreed to show my documentary once it is completed, in early 2006.

I stand in silhouette against a backdrop of our planned route down through the Americas, microphone in hand. The theatre manager and a representative from Make-A-Wish® Southern Alberta wait patiently by the entrance, ready to greet any reporters. It's a world record announcement. *Of course they'll come.*

The seats remain empty.

JULY 2, 2005

I awake in the camper to a misting of raindrops running down the reinforced windows. For my last night in Calgary, I thought it wise to break in our mildew haven.

Suited up in my Lycra Canada jersey and shorts, I ride over to Bow Cycle on my road bike to begin setting up for the send-off. Mark will drive the truck over. The shop has become an integral partner on this trip, providing clothing, spare parts, tools, a mountain bike for unpaved sections of the route, and promotion on their website.

Within the hour, I'm joined by my family and my best friend and former roommate, Chris, as well as a few chums from my Ecotourism program and some of the mysterious donor elite.

Dana's mom makes an unexpected appearance. Seeing her standing shyly on the outskirts of our group, I step aside to speak with her alone. Dana passed away only a couple weeks ago.

She speaks softly, saying it is important that a representative from the family see me off. Then, tearing up, she hands me a small plaster disk. "Before Dana passed away, we made imprints of his thumb to give to family and close friends." My eyes begin to well up once I realize the significance of the gift.

We hug and I tell her I will carry it in my jersey pocket always.

PART II

LONGEST ROAD

CHAPTER 10

MIDNIGHT SUN

DRIVING TO PRUDHOE BAY, ALASKA

The gravity of our situation sucks all the air out of the truck cab. I'm caught in a moment of deep reflection.

I stare out the window as Mark drives. He has a large stack of CDs on rotation and prefers the methodical, hard-hitting likes of Tool. I've got Coldplay's latest album, *X&Y* (picked up on our way out of Calgary), on heavy rotation. Our different taste in music is the first point of contention between us.

We drive all day and through the night. Prudhoe Bay, Alaska, is 4043 kilometres to the north. Many signs remind us of this fact.

You are leaving the Calgary city limits.

Welcome to Edmonton, City of Champions.

Welcome to Beautiful British Columbia.

Welcome to the Yukon, Larger Than Life.

Alaska – 300 km.

After a day and a half, we find ourselves farther north than either of us has ever travelled. There are no skyscrapers on the horizon. Out here, low-lying spruce trees dominate the landscape.

There are but a few lonely highways. Semi-trailer trucks carrying raw materials loom large among the wildlife. Bear and moose have long since replaced the sight of dainty deer and mountain goats in Alberta.

We stop only for gas, snacks, pee breaks and the occasional

photo opportunity. Standing in the wilderness, overlooking a lake with mountains reflected, Mark seizes the opportunity to test his new camera. He explains shutter speed, aperture – expressed in f-stop numbers – and other differences between my consumer camera and his single-lens reflex with detachable lens and polarizing filter.

Mark rarely asks to be in front of the camera and only takes pictures of landmarks, such as border signs, if I feel they are crucial to our record-keeping. (Guinness World Records requires you to supply evidence of your world record attempt, such as pictures, video and statements signed by local notaries.) Given the choice, though, Mark would much rather focus his lens on blossoming purple fireweed now in abundance.

Goofing off in front of the camera is an entirely different conversation. Mark is a champion of all things jackassian.

My introduction to this behaviour was on the eve of our departure. Mark and his like-minded buddy built a potato gun for shits and giggles. Now, watching him massage a large welt on his chest, I'm happy to have abstained.

On the second day of driving, we come across a large black bear searching for berries on the side of the highway. Mark sees an opportunity to lighten the mood and get his adrenaline fix. "Let's see how close we can get," he says, grinning. Cabin fever has set in and I'm more inclined to side with his extreme sensibilities.

We hop out of the truck in our flip-flops, cameras in hand. Sneaking up, the bear sees us approach but continues munching without much care. Mark inches closer. The bear shoots a glaring look. Then, not thinking, I move in for a better picture. The beast immediately turns to give chase!

Our adrenaline skyrockets. Mark and I sprint back toward the truck (parked on the far side of the highway).

The bear is only a few furious steps behind as we stumble through knee-high brush in our ill-conceived footwear. A few tourists have now stopped to watch the scene unfold.

We reach the pavement and turn in relief to find that the bear has stopped at the grassy edge. The animal appears to be aware of the RV and semi-trailer truck traffic hazard. *Thank god*, it's the only thing that saves us from getting mauled. "Ha ha, that was fucking close!" Mark laughs. I nod and try to catch my breath. Still laughing, he lights up a cigarette.

I step back from the situation.

My initial thought is to cringe. We are raising awareness for the Make-A-Wish Foundation. The boy I had befriended died from a life-threatening brain tumour. *How could you?*

Having gotten to know Mark over the last month, I understand the extent to which smoking really is an addiction. I know he wants to quit and appreciate that he never lights up near me. He is always conscious of my well-being. And now that I think about it, I've yet to catch a whiff of the toxic fumes.

He catches me staring judgmentally.

That night, he confides in me that he wants to quit, for good this time. I tell him I want to make sure he is doing it for the right reasons. We have a long journey ahead of us. "I'm prepared to accept the smoking and the occasional drink at night," I tell him. "As long as you are fit to help the next morning, that's all I care about."

The give-and-take is important, especially in a volunteer situation. I'm only able to pay for Mark's rent while he is away. I need to keep his unwavering commitment in mind. *Remember*, there was a long list of failed interviewees before him.

Moving on, we begin to discuss strategy once the record attempt begins. The plan is for Mark to leapfrog throughout the day, prepare meals, take pictures, shoot video and help make sure my bikes are ready to go. I still need to go over general maintenance with him, such as how to fix a flat tire and lube a chain properly.

I'm tasked with making executive decisions, keeping up with communications (weekly blog entries, e-mail inquiries with notaries ahead etc.) and deciding on the route. The Guinness rules stipulate only where we must start and finish. Deciding how to allocate our limited cash supply, and how to manage the 25,000-kilometre gap between Alaska and Argentina, that falls on us. And there is more than one route south.

I print out a table with the previous record holder's daily mileage (from his website) and post it on the wall inside the camper. The core task is very simple: take it one day at a time, beat the Italian's mileage and hold true to much the same route, as interpreted from pictures he posted. Next to his mileage, I add a column for my daily distance. There are 140 blank rows.

On day one, the Italian rode 100 kilometres. Early on, I was confident that similar daily totals would be easily surpassed. My opinion soon changes on the drive north of Fairbanks, Alaska.

We are now in true wild territory. Some 640 kilometres of the infamous Dalton Highway lie ahead. Its washboard gravel surface begins to rattle the truck from the start, quickly covering the exterior in mud and large insect entrails. On the horizon, wildfires spew smoke in all directions. We're forced to roll up the windows and recirculate our own sweaty air.

The massive Trans-Alaska Pipeline runs parallel to the road on an elevated platform (so as not to freeze underground). Connected to one of the largest oil fields in the world, the pipe runs 1290 kilometres south to Valdez, Alaska. Surprisingly, very few services exist between Fairbanks and Prudhoe Bay. We will have to be self-sufficient for the next week.

Intermittent pipeline service vehicles and dust-spewing tankers are the only traffic, save for a couple of fully loaded touring cyclists. We pull over for each of them, offering up a Coke and friendly conversation.

The first has just begun his journey to Argentina. The slender Japanese man is not entirely confident in his abilities but plans to take the next two years to try and make his dream happen. We converse in scattered English, exchange e-mail addresses, take a group picture and wish each other well. I'll likely catch up to him in a few days' time.

Nearing the outskirts of desolate Prudhoe Bay, we pull up to a bearded Spaniard who is just moments away from finishing a two-and-a-half-year journey north from Argentina. *What a coincidence!* Here we are, about to begin our own trek south the next morning. Unfortunately, the conversation does not go as I had hoped.

His perspective is hardened from many days alone on the road. He tells me that racing the route will take away from the beauty of it all. *How could you say something like that, especially on the eve of our departure?* I explain that our path is *different*, not necessarily better or worse.

A little stunned by the standoffish conversation, Mark and I get back in the truck and continue on to the gathering of portable units and oil field operations that is Prudhoe Bay. First thing tomorrow morning, the stopwatch begins.

We wake in the morning to rain and dreary skies. From the top bunk in the camper, I look out a window to see churned mud outside. There is scarce wildlife and vegetation, just this guck and a grouping of portable units. The one beside us is a makeshift motel for oil workers and ambitious Beaufort Sea tourists. Breakfast inside is $30 a plate. I decide to splurge.

A small buffet of pancakes, eggs and stale sausage withers away under a row of heat lamps. The dining room is empty, except for Mark and me. We stare at the fake wood interior and choke our breakfast down in silence. There is really no reason to stay. "Let's just get out there and do it," I reason. Bleary-eyed, we get up and make our way back into the northern discomfort.

I begin dressing in every layer of cycling clothing that I have with me, including a balaclava and two winter jackets. Mark unloads my mountain bike and readies the video camera on his tripod. A cool wind howls outside.

The Guinness rules state that I must start from the gates of the oil company installation at the end of the Dalton Highway. Mark parks 20 metres away, far enough to catch me riding up.

Mark is still new to the video equipment. He zooms in just in time to see a security guard jump out of the booth (at the gated entrance) to demand that I come inside. Following timidly, I catch a glimpse of Mark throwing his hands up in the air. *What the fuck?!*

Inside the security booth, video surveillance screens and men in uniform surround me. One of them asks for my passport. I try to tell him what we are doing but am cut short. He then looks me straight in the eye and orders, "If you do not get out of here in the next five minutes, I'm going to call the FBI." I have obviously underestimated the nature of their operations.

Straddling the mountain bike once again, I check the time on my watch. It's 9:05 a.m. *And go.*

I clip into the pedals and begin riding back down the muddy gravel road toward Mark. As I pass by the camera, he asks what the hell happened. Shaking with adrenaline and shivers from the wind, I laugh, "Yeah, we need to get out of here."

Mud splatters up my back as I exit Prudhoe Bay onto the rough Dalton Highway. With the balaclava material pressed firmly against my face, I'm much more aware of my deep breathing and of air trying to push through. Mark passes me on my right and yells out the window to see if I need anything. He is visibly excited. I give him the thumbs up. *Thanks, I'm okay.*

He speeds on ahead to a ridge along the barren horizon.

A group of caribou passes on my left. The herd huddles together for warmth. Learning alongside them, I hunch a little lower in the saddle and try to limit the extent to which my torso is exposed.

I also keep my elbows bent, to brace for baby-head rocks and divots along the way. Unlike the smooth shoulder of the Pacific Coast Highway, this stretch of road requires my full attention. I zigzag from one side to the other, looking for worn vehicle tracks to follow. There doesn't seem to be any consistency to it. *Steady,* deep breaths.

As I power up the ridge, Mark waves and yells out, "Fuckin' right!" from behind the camera. And though I'm not thrilled about him swearing on tape, I'd be a stooge not to embrace his enthusiasm. I smile inside the mask.

Hours grind by on the tough gravel surface.

A truck driver tells us that paving the Dalton Highway is

out of the question. Asphalt would never hold up in the winter weather. The lowest recorded temperature was −52°C, in 1989.

Day one comes to a close at 11:00 p.m.

In the land of the midnight sun, it still feels very much like dusk – one of the main reasons why I chose to start at this time of the year was to have more riding hours in a day. In the upcoming winter months, it can remain dark for upwards of 54 days in a row. A July departure also accounts for the changing seasons in the southern hemisphere. The inversion is the main reason it takes slower, fully loaded touring cyclists so long to complete the trek. They have to wait out the seasons.

Collapsing on the truck tailgate (at the entrance to the camper), I feel my palms and neck throbbing from the unrelenting washboard. "How far have we gone on the day?" I wearily ask, massaging my aching muscles.

"Almost 160 kilometres exactly", Mark replies. I hoist my limp, muddy body into the camper and proceed to mark a difference of 60 kilometres in the first row of our mileage tracker. Under normal conditions I could cover that distance in half the time it took today. *C'est la vie.*

"Are we done?" Mark asks, also feeling a strain.

"Yep, let's pack it in."

PAN-AMERICAN HIGHWAY, DAY 2
Breakfast the next morning is oatmeal with canned fruit. Mark prepares the meal on a small portable stove in the camper. "It gives me something to do," he says, sensing that I would likely appreciate the extra time to read. "Thanks, man," I respond with sincerity.

On the go right now is *Between a Rock and a Hard Place,*

the story of adventurer Aron Ralston. Two years before, in 2003, he made the life-or-death decision to cut off his own right forearm after becoming trapped under a canyon boulder in southern Utah. The ordeal lasted 127 hours.

In a week or two, I'll break out *Walking the Big Wild*, Karsten Heuer's chronicle of his ambitious 18-month conservation walk from Yellowstone National Park to the Yukon. The wildlife biologist and park warden was on a mission to educate locals on the importance of their Y to Y Wildlife Corridor.

The Ecotourism program has inspired me to read these types of stories. My favourite so far is *Into The Wild*, by Jon Krakauer (of *Into Thin Air* fame). The desperate Alaskan account of Christopher McCandless fell into my lap through a book review assignment. At the time, I was on a week-long paddling and hiking expedition through the Kootenay mountain range in British Columbia.

Included in the Pan-Am stack of reading was a wrapped Bible my sister managed to sneak into one of the drawers of the camper. She and I rarely discuss anything of depth. Even so, I think we share many of the same feelings about Nathan's death and the problems I have had with my father. I'll look past the religious undertones and keep this Bible as a protective totem. I think that's what she meant it for.

I finish the hearty breakfast and push off.

The Dalton quietly climbs through grey skies, up and over the Brooks mountain range, and descends to a pioneer restaurant at Coldfoot. Our raspy waitress tells stories of how semi-trailer trucks link up in the winter, forming trains to push each other up and over the icy ridge. Historical pictures hang on the wall as proof.

Intermittent improvements in the road tease with my road bike sensibilities from here on in. On day four I manage 220 kilometres on graded gravel to the Yukon River, arriving well after midnight. Unfortunately, unrelenting swarms of mosquitoes and a cold drizzle cut our celebration short.

After 670 kilometres, the Dalton connects with the Alaska Highway, and dedicated asphalt. A smile comes across my face as the first few hours tick by with ease. I have to travel a daily average of 200 kilometres until I cross the finish line in Ushuaia. It is a heavy expectation, as there are no planned rest days, though I've budgeted for a swath of unforeseen stops.

· Our first shower, restock and chance to communicate with the outside world is on day six in Fairbanks, Alaska. Skimming through the local paper, I read that my idol, Lance Armstrong, is on the hunt for a historic seventh Tour de France victory. That news is second only to our experience of regional bear aggression.

A challenge of another sort finds us in week two.

East of the Yukon capital, we stop for a quick lunch break at a cozy highway pit stop. While I finish up a bowl of warm soup, Mark exits the restaurant to fuel the truck. Not long after, a cold wave of terror hits as I realize where my bike is parked, and that Mark probably forgot. Too late, I hear the carbon-fibre frame crack under the weight of the front bumper as he pulls ahead. I run outside to see my companion standing over the carnage, pale white and in shock.

The bike is completely destroyed. I take a deep breath and think of the next logical step.

We need to backtrack to Whitehorse to order new parts and ready my spare road bike. Mark nods with his head down, telling me that he will pay me back. "Don't worry about it, man. It was a mistake," I say in my own irreverent haze.

PAN-AMERICAN HIGHWAY, DAY 26

My parents and sister make a special trip west to visit Mark and me as we pass through the small town of Cache Creek, British Columbia. It has been over four weeks since we hugged and parted ways in Calgary.

They flag us down at the driveway of a hotel on the south edge of town. "We thought you would never make it!" my mother excitedly yells out, referring to the fact that we have arrived two hours later than expected. Cell and e-mail communication is spotty in the mountainous northern region.

Dad gives me the customary man-to-man handshake after my mother and sister have finished with their own tight embraces. "We got you guys a room. Let us buy dinner," he says with respect, and a look that asks, *How are things going?*

Spaghetti and meatballs are on the menu at the hotel restaurant. Even though Mark has done a great job of preparing meals with limited means, it's nice to be able to choose from a larger selection (and to give him a break).

As we chow down, my family delves into a long list of questions about all that they have been reading in my blog entries, posted to the Guru Cycles website. One of them makes an offhand comment about the bike that was accidentally run over: "How did you guys manage that??" Mark recoils in his seat.

I try to brush off the incident with an awkward laugh.

My family is eager to begin the long drive home after dinner. Waving goodbye, I'm surprised by how much I'll miss them. It's hard not to follow them, to open up the floodgates on how difficult the trip has become and to call it quits.

And then it's just the two of us again. Mark mentions with a blank face that he's going out for a drink.

Although I'm sympathetic to his downtrodden state, part of me wants him to stew in it just a little longer. It maintains an asshole power in our relationship and my ability to control his more rambunctious tendencies. Still, I don't question his desire to be alone. "As long as you are good to go in the morning," I remind him.

When I wake up in the comfy hotel bed the next morning, Mark is nowhere to be seen. The sheets on his bed are still neatly folded, the same as they were when we first arrived. A chocolate mint rests on his pillow. *Where the hell are you?*

Deciding to trust that he will be back at the truck on time, I move ahead with getting ready like any other day. Loading our expensive camera gear back in the truck, I hear Mark rustle awake in the camper. I grit my teeth.

He tells me he had a couple of drinks and hooked up with a girl at a nearby bar. "We went back to her place…"

"Let's just go," I stop him short. I'm frustrated by this new loner side of his personality, that he went beyond what I consider to be acceptable fun and that he did not embrace my parents' generosity by staying in the room.

I don't really want to talk any further.

The first few morning exchanges of food and leapfrog support are met with grunts from my end. "Yeah, fuck you too," he defiantly smiles back.

I'm fuming inside. All I can think about is delivering a sharp response, and that I can't do it. I have no choice but to calm the situation down. We're not that far into the trip, and I fear Mark will hop on a Greyhound bus and leave me holding the reins alone. *But he hasn't ditched yet. He very well could have.*

PAN-AMERICAN HIGHWAY, DAY 39

The green coastal mountains open to a warming view of the Golden Gate Bridge. This time around, I'm fortunate enough to still have my support driver in the game. Mark has driven ahead to take pictures from the popular vistas of the Marin Headlands, part of the Golden Gate National Recreation Area. The plan is to meet up in a couple of hours at an address downtown.

One of my sponsors in Calgary has arranged for me to meet with a representative from Thomas Weisel Partners, a wealth management firm in San Francisco that is a supporter of Lance Armstrong.

Back in 1999, when Lance was coming back from cancer, Thomas Weisel was one of the few businessmen to get behind the underdog athlete and help finance the U.S. Postal Service Pro Cycling Team with Lance as the lead. It was a gamble that paid off – big time. The Texan and his team once again ride as victors along the Champs Élysées, in Paris.

A junior partner at the firm escorts me to the top floor of a swanky office tower. My Lycra noticeably clashes with his fine suit, but he's a bike guy. He gets it.

Exiting the elevator, I'm presented with a luxurious view of the San Francisco Bay Area. The company has found success not only in backing Lance but also with the acquisitions advisory arm of their business, especially in the technology sector. The walls of the office are lined with framed yellow jerseys. The "maillot jaune," as it is known, is awarded to the leader of the Tour de France at each stage of the race. Lance has racked up a total of 83 of them.

I'm awestruck. With one season of racing under my belt, I now have a better appreciation of what it must take to reach Lance's level. He is a god among us mere mortals on the bike. And his contributions to the cycling and cancer communities are impressive.

Two-wheeled fanatics around North America are feeding off the positive energy and buying bikes in droves. Nike also crafted a yellow rubber band as a fundraiser for Lance's new LIVESTRONG Foundation (formerly called the Lance Armstrong Foundation). The unique accessory, which most people wear as a wrist bracelet, has become a viral hit and raised millions of dollars for the fight against cancer. It is this ripple effect that intrigues me the most.

Allegations of blood doping aside, I'm inspired to once again ask the question *How do you create change?*

The junior partner shakes my hand and offers up a U.S. Postal Service Team riding cap as a parting gift. I fall back to reality on the elevator ride down.

Mark pulls up streetside and asks, "How was it?"

"Do you ever get the feeling that you are meant to do something more with your life?" I question. He patiently drives on as I ponder this deep thought further. We make our way back to the Pacific Coast Highway, away from the bustle of city traffic.

In view of the glorious blue ocean, Mark helps me unload my road bike from inside the camper. I take a moment to reprioritize my thoughts before pushing off again.

We have fallen behind record pace. Our journey has been marred by several delays, the destroyed bike near Whitehorse being only the first. Wrong turns, time-consuming errands, pointless squabbling and losing sight of the urgency have also played a part. And now, forgotten hours that seemed inconsequential at the time have become a tiresome burden of lost days to shoulder.

I look to Mark and tell him with a renewed enthusiasm, "We need to get back on track and crush this record."

He shakes my hand. "Let's do it!"

PAN-AMERICAN HIGHWAY, DAY 44

The afternoon sun blares down. Ahead is the dusty, gunslinger border crossing into Mexicali, Mexico.

Having departed this morning from the beautiful California coast and palm trees of San Diego, I'm finding the desert, the dusty desolation and the Spanish accents are all a little jarring. I tell Mark to stay close from here on in – no more leapfrogging. We can't afford to take any chances in foreign territory.

We present our passports to a grizzled border agent with a mean mustache. He looks at the two of us with a blank stare, then at our passports, then back at our smiling faces. He motions us through without saying a word or asking to check inside the camper. We are now on Mexican soil.

Ahead is a sea of low-lying beige shacks and small businesses. In its centre, the golden "M" of a McDonald's restaurant stands noticeably high above the sandbox. Mark and I nod to one another, not yet ready to accept the Spanish unknown, and set a course for the colourful refuge.

Outside the restaurant, I dust off my *Complete Idiot's Guide to Learning Spanish* reference book. Neither of us knows the language.

My blood pressure rises as I try to piece together the sentence *"Dos conos de helado, por favor"* (two ice cream cones, please) in the mind-numbing heat. Mark stands with the video camera focused on me all the while. *How stupid this must look.*

After the savoury air-conditioned break, we head east toward a two-lane highway with no name. Signage is sparse, and not easily interpreted. Our route should parallel the United States border for the next week, then turn south after we round the Gulf of California.

The other option was to travel down the Baja Peninsula. We decided against this because of what we hear is an unreliable ferry crossing from the southern tip (at La Paz) to mainland Mazatlán. A couple of blogs have mentioned that the boat schedule is sporadic and rarely reliable. We cannot afford to wait around for more than a day.

We rely on a gut feeling.

That evening, we pull off the road and hide behind a bluff on a quiet stretch. The two of us lie in our bunks, sweating, listening to the sound of cars passing.

PAN-AMERICAN HIGHWAY, DAY 45

Day two through northern Mexico, Mark holds back in the afternoon to fill up on gas. Alone on the straight two-lane highway, the shoulder abruptly ends, and I feel danger quickly squeeze in. The passing drivers are not familiar with cyclists, nor do they care, especially for a gringo.

I can't stop. We'll lose too much time.

The familiar sound of a police car pulls up in my panic. The officers are concerned for my safety, though are unable to understand my motions signalling that I am meeting Mark up ahead. They escort me to the back of their cruiser, load my bike in the trunk and speed ahead much farther than I could have travelled on my own.

Fuck, fuck, fuck.

I plead for them to stop at the next impoverished road-side cantina. They oblige, finally sensing that I am waiting for "*mi amigo.*"

Standing at the edge of the highway, I sit on the frame of my bike and pray that Mark will find me. I have no money, nor means to communicate with him. And with the sun setting, hope now dwindles too.

The headlights of the truck appear three hours later.

Mark is understandably distraught, having searched in all directions. We collapse at the small bar, relieved. I quickly point to the menu: "*Pollo y cerveza, por favor*" (chicken and beer, please). The waitress motions insistently to a younger girl (her daughter?), suggesting a side blow job.

Mark laughs. *What a day.*

PAN-AMERICAN HIGHWAY, DAY 46

There is a ring of salty perspiration around the neckline of my jersey. Mark pulls up beside me and cracks the driver side window just enough to pass me a new bottle. Conversing about the road ahead, he yells over the air conditioning that blasts inside.

Every other hour, I indulge in an opportunity to cool my core temperature. Feeling the truck fans blow chilly air across my radiating skin, there is a moment when I wonder how long the vehicle can keep up with this output. It is a blistering 42°C outside in the desert sun.

Mark is much better versed in automobile mechanics. "We should be okay," he tells me. Faith is placed in the fact that the truck was brand new when I picked it up. It should be able to handle us driving it into the ground in the short term.

Outside, my bike leans against the truck on the shady

side. The black rubber tires do not hold up very well in the intense heat, especially for extended periods of time. They become pliable and more susceptible to flats. The shade created by the truck is a temporary haven.

But the drinking water remains warm.

There is nowhere to buy ice, so I don't bother making a fuss. We treat our parched mouths at sparsely located cantinas along the highway. They often serve cold soda and have a couple of rickety fans blowing. As for a washroom, it is often more hygienic to piss or squat behind the building. There is rarely any running water.

We stop at a rundown place near the town of Sonoyta, in the northern Mexican state of Sonora. Next to us at the bar are a couple of tired hombres slumped over Tecate beers. As has been the case for the last couple of days, we go out of our way to say *"Hola"* and start in on small talk with what other Spanish we have acquired. Most locals appreciate that we make an effort, though there is some initial resistance.

Simple gestures and the sight of my unimposing bike often dilute any tension that exists. The United States border (and a First World nation) is less than five kilometres to the north. Black helicopters searching for border jumpers circle high above.

With heavy eyes, we finish our drinks and accept once again that it is time to head back out into the oppressive heat. I drop some coins on the bar, saying *"Gracias."*

Mark and I are both exhausted from the furnace outside and nights spent sweating rather than sleeping. The evening before, we had been in our bunks (on top of the sleeping bags), panting, with sweat dripping down. Sleeping outside in the exposed air feels like a security hazard. So our sweatbox remains locked.

Mark heads to the vehicle while I walk around back to

take a leak. "*Hola,*" I say again, nodding to one of our bar mates crouched in the number two position.

Stumbling back around, my rubbery body feels like Gumby, fresh out of the microwave. I round the front of the shack, just in time to catch Mark manoeuvring out of his parking spot.

Wait, WHAT?! Instantly, my attention homes in on my bike leaning against the shady side of the truck. It falls over as he turns the wheel. *Oh shit.*

Running to try to stop him, I watch again in horror as the bike is sucked under the vehicle and trampled by the heavy rear wheels.

Mark sees me running and yelling.

He immediately realizes what has happened, gets out, surveys the damage and begins pacing frantically. "Fuck … sorry … goddamn it!" He assumes he has ruined the trip. Only my mountain bike is left, and there is no way that any records are going to be beaten on that hulk of metal.

Mark looks at me with sullen eyes. "What are we going to do?" he asks.

Surveying the map, I say to him, direct and composed, "We need to pack up what's left of the bike and find a pay phone. I have some important calls to make."

We're headed back.

CHAPTER 11

GRINGO

"Say something, anything!" Mark pleads.

"Let's just keep driving." We head toward the border crossing at Sonoyta, then north. "I'll call my ex-girlfriend, Kelly, once we get to Phoenix. I have kept on good terms with her and her mom, Debbie. Hopefully we can stay with her while I order a new frame from Guru Cycles." I feel it necessary to honour that sponsorship, no matter the cost.

Are we being dared to end this?

Back in my flip-flops and shorts, I prop my legs up on the dash and try to read into Mark's thoughts as we drive on. I'm curious to see whether he will bail or push on through the challenge. He is mostly expressionless, however, his thoughts lost in some realm of dwindling optimism.

I take this time to write our sixth blog entry on the laptop, including an update on our travel statistics. *Total kilometres ridden = 7505. Total calories burned = 288,000 (82 pounds). Number of totalled Guru Cycles bikes = 2.* "If only you could understand the heat and pressure ... Mark didn't mean to do it," I write.

In trying to take the high road, I unintentionally belittle him. Though no one reading the blog posts would understand anything to that effect, he worries that the public will only remember him as the idiot that tried to sabotage this journey. In particular, he is concerned with how his family and co-workers in Calgary will view the accident.

And he is becoming more defensive. I am too.

A tense interpersonal dynamic is emerging. The darker side of my personality sees the damaged bikes as a leverage point. This story can easily be altered to offer a harsher perspective. I'm also aware that I have established a level of trust with my blog followers (including media) that Mark has not.

Even though I'm more concerned about getting back on track, I can't look past the fact that Mark also has a voice. *He could say that I am controlling, that I am not the hotshot cyclist some believe me to be.*

I have read about team members on expeditions turning on each other, fighting over the rights to video and pictures, cheating on spouses and disclaiming the leader's boastful media claims. This is the darker side of that team picture – the one where everyone is smiling, holding up a sponsor flag on some mountain summit.

Just breathe.

Mark's vulnerability has manifested into something far more concerning than a potential battle of words. He rarely takes pictures anymore, and spends far less time outside the vehicle. He is also smoking again, which is perhaps the most discouraging sign of all.

I watch him from the passenger seat and notice his eyes welling up behind those dark sunglasses. The last time that I saw a grown man cry was my father, at Nathan's funeral, now six years past. *I've got to bring this back around.*

"I'm not mad at you, Mark. It sucks that this happened. I wish it hadn't … this is going to be an expensive fix. Let's just keep our heads up and shake it off."

We cross the American border into Arizona, back into the arms of relative safety and First World amenities.

I quickly find a pay phone and call Kelly. Her family has always been supportive, even after the breakup. "You're welcome to stay with me as long as you need," she says. "Also, my mom is going to pick up some Chinese food tonight, any suggestions?" I smile with relief. This kind of gesture means the world right now.

My second call is to Guru Cycles in Montreal. "Can you ship a new frame down to Phoenix? I'll pay for it, whatever you have in my size," I plead. I'm determined to show my commitment and to honour their support, even if it means waiting a couple of days. *I fought too damn hard for that sponsorship.*

Mark hears me making these calls.

He plans to stay in the camper while we are in Phoenix. "Are you sure??" I cringe. The average temperature for August is 34°C. Yet, the last thing he wants is for anyone I know to look at him judgingly. "At least take some of our cash, go see some movies, explore a little," I offer. With sunken shoulders and eyes down, he nods.

Four hours after the incident at the desert cantina, we reach Kelly's apartment building in the sprawling city. Mark drops me off at her door, then drives away. This is our first break from each other in over a month and a half.

I spend the next couple of days working away in a coffee shop around the corner. Blog update, *check*. New frame ordered from Guru Cycles, *check*. Progress report for my Directed Field Study, *check*. Answering e-mails that question Mark's involvement in the trip, *check*.

With a cool head, I find myself being more defensive of Mark. The more I think about it, I begin to question the absurd. *Are we becoming unlikely friends?*

A local Guru dealer helps to exchange the few undamaged components from the trashed bike to the new frame (some of which even survived the first incident), bending others back into shape, and making up the difference in shiny new Shimano. The repair costs $2,000.

The afternoon that my Frankenstein bike comes back to life, the heavens open up and I learn that Coldplay is performing a concert at the Cricket Pavilion later that evening. On a whim, I buy two tickets as a way to thank Kelly for letting me crash at her place, and to help reignite those inspired thoughts of cycling.

That evening, we sit on a blanket and watch Chris Martin belt out "X&Y" to a sea of adoring fans bathed in amber light. The last time Kelly and I had seen the band perform live, I was holding her in a loving embrace in floor seats at the Calgary Saddledome only four years ago. Now our hands are separated by a few defining inches.

PAN-AMERICAN HIGHWAY, DAY 50
Mark waits in the distance as I hug Kelly goodbye the following morning. Turning to walk toward him, I pull my shoulders back and embrace the challenge ahead, "Ready?" I ask. He nods, looking more refreshed.

Two days prior to this, my one ask of Mark was to write a blog entry detailing his side of the incident, and to move on. Here's what he wrote:

> Well, everybody, it's Mark for the first time on the e-mails, if only it could have been under better circumstances. Yes it's happened, Ryan is without a road bike and we are just starting our leg through Mexico. There really is nobody to blame but myself in this ordeal due to acting without thinking. I

don't know where to begin; in a rush I moved the truck whilst the bike was against it. I am having a difficult time wrapping my head around the situation for many different factors but the level head Ryan has and the resources he has worked so hard to get seems to be getting the two of us through thick and thin. I have the utmost respect for Ryan and his outstanding ability of keeping cool under fire and his forward thinking! All apologies go to those this has caused a direct or indirect inconvenience to. It has hit me like a ton of bricks as well. All the best and hopefully everyone is well.

He shakes my hand. *Here's to a fresh start.*

We drive back to the border at Sonoyta, back to watchful eyes and miles of desert sagebrush, back to that same fateful cantina. We have been transported to another time.

I suit up and ask Mark to record the moment on video.

Reaching into my back pocket, I hold the Ziploc bag with Dana's plaster thumbprint inside. "We have a big challenge ahead of us. The record is slipping away. Mark and I are going to try our best to get back out in front." We are now 2000 kilometres behind record pace.

I push off.

We are back to leapfrog support. It is safer this way, especially since there is no shoulder on the highway. I'm also feeling more accustomed to it all – the stares, the language, the uncertainty. Having the vehicle follow directly behind me draws unneeded attention.

Our direction of travel turns south down the mainland of Mexico (through the heart of Sonora state), past the dust bowl of Santa Ana. Soon after, we unexpectedly come across what appears to be a second border crossing. The Mexican border agents are much more persistent this time around. They want to see proof that the vehicle is mine. *But it's not.* And they most certainly do not understand the concept of sponsorship.

Apparently, Mexico has strict guidelines about vehicle importation. While there is a so-called Free Zone extending 20 kilometres inside the Mexican border (a government initiative to stimulate tourism), you are required to have a vehicle permit beyond that point. We have been travelling within the slim border zone for the past week, oblivious to this fact.

I process my thoughts aloud with Mark in confidence. "Okay, they want a signed document in Spanish from Precision Drilling (our truck sponsor). It cannot be a photocopy or fax. It must be an original. Obviously, that is not going to happen in the next day or two. Let's drive back to Santa Ana. I have an idea."

We speed back to town with dusk on our heels.

With the windows rolled down, we scan the streets for the nearest Internet café. These crude hole-in-the-wall providers have sprouted up to respond to the bubbling intrigue about all things online. Since many people cannot afford a home computer, these businesses eliminate that barrier.

"There's one!" I frantically point to an Internet Explorer logo, painted on a white alley wall. "And it looks like it's still open!" Mark lets me out.

Inside, I'm presented with a row of outdated computers that are hooked into a modem dial-up connection. Above, a fluorescent light bulb flickers. The connection is brutally slow.

I double click on the Microsoft Paint program and size the canvas to 8.5 × 11 inches. Next, I click open the Internet browser and lift a logo from the Precision Drilling website. Third, I track down an automated online translation service and type in a formal letter. I copy all of these items back into the Paint document, press print, then borrow a pen to forge the signature of *El Presidente*.

Adrenaline accelerates us back to the border crossing before it closes for the evening. The same impatient guard is there, waiting.

I run up and shake his hand, then motion like I understand what he needs. *I must have forgotten this document in the camper, señor.* I hand over the forged letter in a sealed plastic sheet. He looks it over once, then looks back at me. My poker face is holding strong. He takes one last look and then waves us on, farther into Mexican hell.

PAN-AMERICAN HIGHWAY, DAY 57

Sprawled across the back seat of the truck in just a swimsuit (in place of unkempt underwear), I am keenly aware of my pasty mouth and cracked lips. A film of sweat and dust is caked on my skin. All the doors are wide open.

The morning sun warms my forehead.

I try not to think about the restless sleep I just had. It is impossible to find a comfortable position in the camper with this heat circulating inside. Thinking about it makes me thirsty.

I'm in a dehydrated daze.

I focus in on a floating particle in the corner of my eye, and watch it swim across my field of vision. *How does it always stay one step ahead? It looks like a bean.*

I think about the refried beans and broken nacho chips we have waiting for breakfast. Indigestion doesn't seem to be a problem anymore.

Then, rather suddenly, a silhouetted plump figure steps behind me, obscuring the sun shining down. I see him from the waist up and he has a pistol in his hand. *What the…?!*

I jump upright and realize it is a *Federales* officer with the Mexican national police. He yells something at me in Spanish, then turns to survey the sagebrush and barren highway shoulder. He continues yelling in Spanish. I have no idea what he is saying. But he doesn't look so much mad, as concerned.

I slip on my running shoes and hop down out of the cab. I try to remedy the situation: "*Yo solo sé un poco de Español*" (I only know a little bit of Spanish). He grunts. Pointing to the desert, the officer waves his finger at me: "You go BANG BANG!"

I hear Mark rustle awake in the camper. He pokes his head out, and to the side. We exchange a quizzical look.

The officer calms down a little. "*Mal hombre* (bad men). You go BANG BANG!" He points to the highway.

I yell over to Mark, "I think that he wants us to leave."

Mi amigo jumps down off the tailgate in his boxers and says, "Agreed."

Half naked, we waste no time backtracking to a nearby cantina. There we find out that the Sonora natives do not take kindly to *gringos* sleeping on the side of the highway. They have killed some in the past, we're told. *And here I was*, sprawled out on the back seat, doors and drawers wide open to the world.

"We need to re-evaluate our camping strategy," I tell Mark. Parking away from civilization is perhaps more dangerous than we originally thought. "Maybe we should consider hiding in plain sight." I have not decaled the vehicle with sponsor logos for this very reason. That being said, our white skin tone and shiny truck exterior are not easily concealed among the earth tones that are prevalent here.

We decide to stop washing the truck. Also, recognizing that it is now commonplace to see gas stations guarded by young militia with guns, we adopt both a new nightly camping scenario and a security routine.

After topping up the tank each evening, we buy the watchful eyes a round of drinks and then break into casual conversation. When the mood is set, we ask for their help watching our vehicle overnight. Holding up their beers, they often nod, *No problem.*

Moments like these give me a new appreciation for what Mark brings to the table. He is a little rough around the edges but he embraces the opportunity to converse with these guys – thankfully, as I am the outsider. They jabber away amid tobacco puffs and tattoo tales.

Thinking back to all the neatly kept individuals that I interviewed for the position, Mark seems the perfect fit now. I write on my blog that I am lucky to have him.

PAN-AMERICAN HIGHWAY, DAY 58

Mark honks the horn, signalling for me to pull over. He gets out of the truck and starts in on a rant about how some guys in a car claimed he rear-ended them. "Well, did you??" I ask.

It becomes apparent that the answer does not matter. Mark's unimpressed new friends pull up in front. One flashes a badge and says he is a cop. The other two stand with their arms crossed. They want money.

In a naive moment, I ask that we exchange insurance

information. They laugh. In Mexico, cash is king. "We go with you to *el banco*," they tell me.

Surrounded at the nearest ATM machine, I withdraw $200. The cop looks at me. "No, I think $100 more." I do as he requests, because we are outnumbered and I have no witnesses to corroborate the story. *I feel sick.*

That night, I make a plea to my sponsors for more cash: "Otherwise, we will have to turn back." The unforeseen expenses are adding up. We no longer have any cash, just credit, and not every gang takes plastic. Three of my sponsors graciously wire more funds. One stops returning my e-mails.

As long as we have the means to keep going, we do.

PAN-AMERICAN HIGHWAY, DAY 60

Passing through the tourist destination of Mazatlán, Mark and I get lost from each other again, this time for an entire day. I'm forced to drink stagnant water from a well to quench my thirst. In return, I'm rewarded with two days of diarrhea and headaches. Mark and I sweat it out in a crummy motel room, watching the cheerleader comedy *Bring It On* in Spanish.

"Okay, no more leapfrogging," I suggest.

PAN-AMERICAN HIGHWAY, DAY 71

After taking my daily malaria pill, I head out on a straight road, with the awareness that Mark will soon catch up after he washes our breakfast dishes, another menial task that he long since volunteered to take on. An hour passes, then another, and one more. *Where the hell is he!? We just talked about this.*

A semi-trailer truck pulls up behind me and blares on the

horn. The driver could easily pass around me but doesn't. He's trying to make a point. So, I point back with my middle finger. No translation needed.

The semi revs its engine and hastily pulls around. Ahead of me, the driver screeches on his brakes, forcing the tail end of the heavy load to fishtail. And now, smelling the smoke from the screeching tires, I realize that this situation has escalated from a simple annoyance to altercation status. *Oh, fuck.*

Stopped in the middle of the road, the husky driver smashes his door open and jumps down. Wasting no time, I run into the dense forest of palm trees along the road. My nemesis surveys the foliage with his fists clenched. He's not willing to give chase over tougher terrain, though, so he concedes defeat and continues on.

My heart is racing.

I reach into my back pocket to turn off my MP3 player. My fingers brush across a pair of keys: the truck keys. *Son of a bitch.*

In an instant, I realize that I am just as capable of making simple, mystifyingly stupid mistakes. *Mark is going to get a kick out of this,* I laugh to myself.

I walk back out of the jungle when the coast is clear.

Not willing to concede more time to riding back, I barter my way on to a passing chicken bus and hitchhike back to the place where we last camped. The truck is still there, of course, with Mark suntanning outside. "Okay, that one was my fault," I yell out, fully ready to accept my comeuppance.

"Let's get going," Mark says, trying to remain humble, but sneaking in his own shit-eating grin, I notice.

We drive ahead 90 kilometres to where I first encountered the semi, laughing at first, and then retreating back to a loss of empathy and frustration. *Another several hours lost.*

During a bologna lunch break parked next to a shack in the middle of nowhere, we bear witness to a father teaching his daughter an important life lesson: how to cook a chicken. *Grab chicken, break neck, slit throat with knife, hang upside down, drain blood, pluck feathers and then boil.*

I look down the desolate highway, toward nothing in every direction. There is no opportunity here, nothing beautiful to strive for. And in the words of my faithful travel companion, I reiterate: "Mexico is a piece of shit."

PAN-AMERICAN HIGHWAY, DAY 75

After almost a straight month of hair pulling and sweating it out in Mexico, we reach the Guatemala boundary at Tapachula. As we roll up to the border crossing, several young kids grab on to the vehicle and surround me on the bike. "Mister, mister. We help you get across. Very cheap."

We wave them aside. "No, *gracias.*"

Inside a building with national flags and a presidential picture hanging on the walls, we are told by an official in uniform that we must pay a $100 permit fee. She then tells us to cross the street to a neighbouring building. An official there will sign off on the permit. That person asks us to pay another fee.

On the other side, the kids laugh, "You not need to pay, ha ha."

Welcome to Guatemala.

CHAPTER 12

LIGHTNING STRIKES

Neither of us has the desire to backtrack through Mexico with our heads hung low. Extreme heat, hostile encounters and sparse resources are not so much of a concern, though, as they are now habitual challenges in our day-to-day.

Our minds react in a similar way, in that they learn to adapt to painful stimuli. Sitting alone with Mark in the camper one night, I say again, "If the means to keep going are there, we will."

PAN-AMERICAN HIGHWAY – GUATEMALA
Guatemala greets us with a blanket of warm rain, rich soil and lush green mountains. The new colour palette is greatly appreciated, as is the moisture.

The village locals do not seem to look at me with such awe and bewilderment anymore. There are more bikes on the road here, which makes perfect sense. Resources are not as spread out as they were in the Mexican desert. People live closer together here, well within riding distance of each other.

Bicycles are still very much a luxury, however. It is not un-common to see groups of kids and/or adults sharing the saddle or even the frame space. On first glance, I wonder how the bikes do not buckle under the weight. But these bikes are built of heavy, rigid metal (as opposed to carbon fibre) and are pretty much bombproof in most regards. They can support the extra weight. Mind you, the average Guatemalan is half my size.

They ride their bikes to work, to deliver goods (from bushels of hay to car parts), to and from open-air schools, and back home again. I have yet to encounter gridlock, and mostly everyone smiles a disjointed white toothy grin as I pass. Still, I give a little extra space to the rural people that appear out of the jungle, often walking with a machete in hand.

My grade school geography and social studies are meshing together in the most wonderful educational environment possible. I see how a fertile land can elevate people out of extreme poverty, or at least better provide for those in rural regions.

My studies in the Ecotourism program help me to make the sustainability connection. In Mexico, the only profitability that I encountered was in the resort towns. The money that those businesses make rarely trickles down the food chain to neighbouring suppliers, however. The problem is further compounded by foreign ownership, which creates economic leakage.

It comes as a surprise when I learn that Mexico has a much stronger economy than Guatemala. Mexico has a modern industrial sector that deals in automotive, electronic and mineral resources. The Guatemalan economy, by contrast, relies on more basic exports like coffee, sugar and bananas. They are also hindered by a lack of infrastructure and educational resources, and the crime rate is high.

If only the world could see beyond the beach resorts, nightclubs and commonly visited ruins in Mexico. It is a much harsher place than what I see before me now.

The resourcefulness of the Guatemalan people is shared

with us in little flashes of brilliance throughout the days. A man in a dark shack replaces a broken spoke on my front wheel. I'm slightly embarrassed, having never done this myself. The repair is second nature to him.

Stopped for a meal of boiled pork and rice from a street vendor, I don't even think twice about where the ingredients originated, just that they are cooked and taste delicious. My gut has evolved into an unwavering digestion machine.

Our snacking mainstays have evolved from stale energy bars from 7-Eleven convenience stores to freshly baked bread, jam and packaged cookies from small markets. My water bottles contain only that: water. And, if available, we try to purchase the 19-litre water-cooler jug. "*Agua*" (water) is our lifeline. Bottled soda is the backup.

We sample all that the street vendors have to offer. The food is often fresher, cheaper and less time-consuming than cooking for ourselves on the go. This is a good thing, too, as it is becoming increasingly difficult to find the right gas cylinders for our camp stove.

Freshly squeezed orange juice and *ceviche* (raw fish marinated in lemon or lime) are my personal favourites. Mark eats much the same fare, though far less than me. Riding more than 200 kilometres a day requires that I try to consume at least 6,000 calories per day. On the bike, I burn an average of 500 calories per hour. My resting metabolism has also increased.

Food is much more a part of the culture here – not just a means to an end as we are accustomed to in North America. You honour the exchange with payment, conversation and a greater appreciation of the labour put forth. Everything is homemade. Microwaves are an anomaly.

Honouring tradition is important, too. Religious tradition (many Guatemalans are Christians), breaks from work in the afternoon, communal tea and coffee, soccer (if something rolls, there is a kid who will kick it) and regular family gatherings are ingrained in the culture.

If a smile and a few simple words of Spanish do not help to bridge the gap, pointing to my chest and saying "*Canadiense*" helps. There is often an advantage in making this distinction. *No, we are not American.*

We interact with street vendors, pedestrians, kids begging for money, farmers tending their crops, motel owners and a smattering of surfers in search of the next great wave.

It has been almost a month since we saw another *gringo*, or spoke English outside of our two-man bubble. Even the regular tourist traps are dominated by Spanish-speaking tourists. They come for the cooler climate, of which bursts of rain are a regular feature.

My palms are white with moisture blisters, torn open from rubbing against the cork handlebar grips. Mark takes a picture of the top skin layer melting away. It looks like a painful chemical burn.

We agree to decrease my exposure to the elements. Rainy periods can instead be used for naps and recovery.

I enjoy the quiet time to read. Mark and I have started to swap books once we are finished reading them. Most recently, he handed me a memoir by humorist David Sedaris called *Dress Your Family in Corduroy and Denim*. The melodramatic comedy is a nice break from tales of survival.

The thought of taking the time to write my own story has come up once or twice. But truthfully, I'm a little intimidated by the idea. My short 22-year history lacks an arc of conflict and clear resolution. *How do I explain what I do? What is my purpose with cycling? Why should others care?*

Anonymous blog commenters laugh at this introspection. Some attack my credibility, while others claim they could ride faster. And although they are but a few lonely haters, their criticism hangs heavy and ultimately dissuades me from putting pen to paper.

PAN-AMERICAN HIGHWAY, DAY 79

Enter, El Salvador. A gang of grubby-faced kids runs along-side us, once again pestering us to let them help us across the border, for a nominal fee.

Having lost our patience at the Mexico–Guatemala border, we welcome a new approach. One of the ten-year-old boys rides with us in the truck to a nearby bank and suggests we take out cash (in United States currency) for whatever dealings await us. Feeling out his intentions, we share a pizza on the way back.

The young entrepreneur ushers us over to one of the border agents. Laughing, the two exchange some of that all-too-familiar Spanish shorthand. "Pay him," the boy then instructs me. He guides us to another agent, who inspects the vehicle. "Pay him," he instructs me, again. Mark and I look at each other. *Jesus Christ*, the situation reeks of bribery.

Six hours later we finally cross into the smallest country in Central America. The boy holds out his hand upon our departure, expecting payment. Mark kicks him a soccer ball instead.

We reach the quiet border of Honduras by nightfall. Instead of proceeding with another round of bribes, especially in a currency we are not familiar with (the Honduran lempira), we decide to camp out overnight and tackle the situation in the morning. More border entrepreneurs mingle around our camper like mosquitoes. "No, *gracias*." *Fuck off already*.

I begin the next day in shorts and a T-shirt. There is no

point in suiting up in my ride gear until all the inevitable paperwork is finalized. Thankfully, the forged Precision Drilling letter still holds some weight in these dealings.

We have thought about sneaking across borders under cover of darkness to save time, since not all of them are heavily guarded. But, for several reasons, this will unfortunately not work. Passport stamps are proof for Guinness World Records that we have entered and exited a country. The documentation is also needed when dealing with police and their bribes at random checkpoints along the Pan-American Highway.

The path becomes more and more primitive. In some sections it is nothing more than a creekbed.

Making our way through one town, I navigate through a groundswell of sewage and rainwater. With shit-soaked cycling shoes, I can't help but laugh. Levity in these situations is an acquired skill. And it will be tested.

Honduras is the second-poorest country in Central America. It also has one of the most unequal distributions of income. The people we encounter are skinny and have a look of desperation about them. The intimidation factor feels like Mexico all over again, but perhaps worse.

I now ride with a Leatherman utility knife in my back pocket. Stashed under the driver's seat in the truck, Mark also has a large kitchen knife at the ready.

We cannot afford to be naive about the fact that "Third World" and "turbulent" are some of the words commonly used in Internet travel reports to describe this region. We are now in the human wild.

Passing over backcountry bridges, my attention is drawn to the streams flowing underneath them. It is normal to see communal groups of men and women bathing in the water with their children, all of them naked. Fond camping memories flood back through the aroma of freshly roasted meat and smoke wafting out of the jungle around me.

Stopped at a cantina for a warm meal in the afternoon, Mark and I bond over discussing past relationships, the kind of men we want to be and the type of women we will finally work up the courage to ask out on a date.

Mark is also curious to learn about my upbringing. He wants to better understand how a 22-year-old managed to amass the resources to undertake such a journey, the sometimes misguided importance I place on a positive public image, how I deal with the haters and my fleeting relationship with Adam, my only other support driver.

He is drawn to the fact that I am imperfect in my own little ways. I continue to open up because it feels healthy for the growth of our relationship and for its ultimate success. *Friends share, right?*

I take an active interest in Mark's own misgivings: his past drug use, his ongoing battle with smoking, some risqué sexual encounters and a series of dangerous travel exploits. I also inquire about his family, his love of photography and all the random things he has taught himself how to do, like building furniture and repairing vehicles. He is resourceful in many ways that I could never hope to be.

PAN-AMERICAN HIGHWAY, DAY 81

The loud sound of thunder cracks in the late afternoon sky, signalling more rainfall. I take cover under the dense shade of palm trees beside the road. Mark is parked somewhere out of sight.

Our revamped leapfrog strategy is for him to drive ahead to any intersections where there might be a discrepancy in terms of which way to go. So far, so good. We haven't gotten lost from each other since being in the shitty bowels of southern Mexico.

Another crack of thunder punches through the sky, frighteningly closer than the last. It is a death rattle, though it fades quickly.

Warm steam rises from the wet asphalt.

My skin has never felt so alive. It is stimulated by regular intervals of sun and humidity, of sweating and dryness. Any blisters have hardened over by this point. And my awkward tan lines have only darkened. Hardcore cyclists look upon them with envy.

Mark rarely wears a shirt anymore. He enjoys showing off his bronzed torso, not so subtly pointing to the fact that he looks more chiselled, despite having sat on his ass for almost three months now. Lean genetics are on his side, of course. Endurance muscle memory is on mine.

To prove there is more to a book than its cover, I often reference *our race*. Several weeks back, Mark challenged me to a time trial up a winding coastal mountain in northern California. The result would have made for a great anti-smoking commercial.

The storm has passed and I begin riding again.

A group of eight villagers is standing in a tight circle not far ahead. Oddly, they seem unfazed by my approach.

Peering between them, I catch a glimpse of a man lying in the fetal position. Blood pours from his abdomen, pooling on the red clay of the courtyard. Nothing can be done for the poor fellow.

We watch as his breathing slows, gurgles and then stops altogether. A cold reality hits me. *That second crack wasn't the sound of thunder ... it was a gunshot.*

The first funeral I ever attended was for a friend's father in junior high. I remember the open casket, the lifeless body and the sudden shock of trying to process death. This most recent encounter has a much different aftertaste. Murder ignites a feeling of helplessness in me.

I get back on the bike, frightened.

Catching up to Mark and the truck, I pile in and lock the door. An elderly lady sees me and knocks on the window, trying to sell us some fruit. I shoo her away, worried that she might pull a knife on us. Mark is surprised by my reaction. "What the hell, man?" I fill him in on the murder scene.

An hour passes as I contemplate the next move. Sooner or later, I will have to get back on the bike.

I calm down as I arrive at a gradual understanding that the globe spins on a balance of good and evil. There are no sweeping descents without long, hard climbs. And death makes us appreciate life. Not everyone is inherently evil.

I step back out of the truck and hand the fruit lady a mix of forgotten coins from our change box. The currency has changed five times since leaving Canada. She holds up a bag of bananas. "No, *gracias*" I tell her. The money is meant as a simple peace offering.

PAN-AMERICAN HIGHWAY, DAY 86

I yell into the remote jungle darkness setting in around me: "What the fuck?!" *How does this keep happening?*

I have been riding on my own along this Costa Rican highland road for almost nine hours straight. Worst of all, I only have a few American dollars and no water left.

I last saw Mark at a surprisingly classy McDonald's restaurant in the capital city of San José. Afraid to turn back after a couple of hours alone, I continued on as I have always done in this scenario. *We have to catch up to record pace!* That was 230 kilometres ago.

I'm extremely tired, and my bike is without any lights. The jungle fog only intensifies the dark danger. Fortunately, around a steep switchback, I stumble across a tiny bar on the hillside. *Refuge for my frantic thoughts.*

There is a line of empty stools waiting inside. I flop down at the far end, in a dark corner, so as not to draw attention to my lost plight. Regardless, the overweight bartender walks over and begins speaking to me in Spanish. "No Spanish," I interject. I'm too tired to string together much else.

"No problem," he replies back. "My son es bike racer like tu (My son is a bike racer like you). I know small English." *Thank god.*

I tell him of the epic journey from Alaska, and how I have managed to lose my support companion yet again. Sensing my desperation, he slides over an ice-cold Coke. My legs and arms still have goose bumps from the cold outside. But the sugar is comforting.

An hour passes. The bartender and I continue chatting about bicycle racing while he pounds away a few frosty beers from behind the dim counter. The sport is much more prevalent in this country. So is the American dollar. Ecotourism has had a noticeable impact on the economy.

Another hour passes. The bartender is drunk.

Sweeping the floors, he slaps me on the back: "Okay, we go now. You stay with me tonight. My wife will make us dinner." I accept the warm invitation, relieved. It is well past midnight.

We get in his small red sedan and speed back toward San José. The bartender slurs his words, swerving back and forth on the narrow roads. I white-knuckle the door handle all the while, readying myself for a quick-release bail.

The bartender's wife has stayed up to cook us dinner, just like he said she would. It's a tasty meal of chicken and rice.

They are both incredibly gracious, next offering up a bed in their spare room. *What luck.*

Lying on my back with the sheets pulled up tight, I wonder what horrid thoughts Mark is thinking right now. Somewhere in the jungle darkness, he is still out there, searching.

CHAPTER 13

BORDER PATROL

PAN-AMERICAN HIGHWAY, DAY 87

I'm in a dream.

I see Dana walking along a sandy white beach in Costa Rica with his family. Their attention is fixed on a family of spider monkeys swinging from the jungle canopy. They point up, excited. "Look, there they are!"

I stand in the distance behind them, my bike perched at the side. My father stands next to me. But he looks disappointed. *Why?*

The bartender's son wakes me. I rub my eyes.

The teenager is already suited up in his riding gear, ready to escort me back to the McDonald's restaurant where Mark and I last saw each other. He is half my size and looks like what I imagine a cyclist should: that wiry frame that eludes gravity, perfect for climbing tall mountains. He shakes my hand, excited to help in any way possible. Like his father (who is still fast asleep), he also speaks decent English. "Good morning, amigo!"

He knows that I am keen to get going. Mark likely headed back to the restaurant after a night of frantic searching.

In North America, I could easily have called his cell from a pay phone and saved us from this predicament. Neither of us has phones enabled with an international plan, however. Coverage is also sparse here.

We considered purchasing a pair of two-way radios to

have on us at all times. But this type of communication is connected by a line of sight. It would not work in mountainous regions or beyond a few crowded city blocks.

Our unique perspectives on things make it challenging, at times. And, after getting lost from each other, we don't always share the same method of finding our way back.

For example, yesterday morning I came across a fork in the road. The route we had intended to travel turned into a major highway with a sign that read "*Los peatónes no permitido*" (no pedestrians allowed). I *assumed* Mark would see this sign and take the alternative fork down a quieter road. But no, at speed, such signs are easily missed. He likely continued down the main highway.

Now, hopefully, he's waiting for me.

The bartender's son and I meet up with a small pack of his racing buddies. They lead us at a quick tempo through cramped alleys, narrowly missing parked cars and street vendors. We pass into a suburb of low-lying homes, surrounded by rich green hills. The warm view is straight out of an aromatic coffee commercial.

I have an out-of-body experience. *Wow, I'm really here. I'm riding my bike in Costa Rica. It's beautiful.*

We roll up to the McDonald's. I do a quick scan of the parking lot and neighbouring businesses. The truck is nowhere to be seen. *Okay, don't panic. You'll figure this out.*

The son and I part ways with a handshake. I tell him he is welcome to come visit me in the Great White North. "Gracias, amigo," he enthusiastically shakes my hand. *Amigo.* I like that word. It resonates much better than *gringo.*

Alone again, I head inside and grab a booth seat.

A small army of friendly teens greets me as they go about opening the restaurant. I'm struck by how much they respect their jobs: they smile, wear formal uniforms and work much more diligently than what I am accustomed to. It appears to be an honour to hold a fast food job.

Scanning the room further, I catch a glimpse of a public Internet kiosk. A light bulb turns on.

I boot up my webmail account and search for an old e-mail from Mark's roommate. *Found it!* I type a reply: *Mark and I are lost from each other again. If he happens to contact you, please tell him that I am waiting at the McDonald's in San José and that I am okay.* Satisfied with the details, I press send.

Forty-five minutes later, the truck screeches into the parking lot like a godsend. A bright smile beams across my face.

Mark walks in with tired, puffy eyes. We both hold our breath for a moment, ready to explode with a different version of the last 24 hours. Mark bursts out first, laughing, "Fuck, you are not going to believe…"

I cut him short. "First, let's get breakfast. We have some driving to do."

Mark's expression turns dour. "Yeah … I tried to use your debit card this morning. An ATM machine down the street ate it. It's gone." This would be a bigger concern (Visa does not cover bribes and backwoods barbecues), had we not just overcome a near disaster. *Whatever, we'll figure it out.*

Walking to the truck, I notice that all four hubcaps are missing from the wheels. I shoot Mark a quizzical look, *Huh?* "I'll explain on the way," he tells me.

We scrape together our American change and buy some stale bread to hold us over. The debit machine at McDonald's mocks us all the while. Back along the vibrant green jungle road, the truck splashes through puddles and crumbling dark asphalt. It must have rained throughout the night.

Mark turns a corner and suddenly screeches on the brakes. We are stopped by a mudslide and a steady stream of sludge flowing off a nearby mountain. These sorts of temporary road closures apparently are quite common during the rainy winter months. A Bobcat earthmover is already on the scene.

Scanning the few cars stopped ahead, I notice that most of them are without hubcaps too. It reminds me of my earlier question, "What the hell happened?"

Mark recounts the story of his night alone. As the search hours wore on, he worried that I had been hit by a car and/or had passed out in a ditch. In the midst of his tireless search along the dark highway shoulder, he justifiably ran over several potholes. The jarring contact shook our hubcaps loose.

Seeing the drive from this perspective, I gain a better appreciation for Mark's handling skills. The wide girth of the vehicle does not mix well with the weathered breaks in the road and the added pressure of oncoming traffic. If asked to change spots, I don't know that I would be so brave.

Our path is cleared within the hour.

This is the most time I have spent in the vehicle since having to make the hasty detour to Phoenix, *20-some days ago*. The jungle flies past us in a dizzying series of winding corners. Mark relishes the opportunity to practise his rally car skills. I just try not to vomit.

The expense of extra gas aside, my decision to keep riding into the night may have actually paid off. Mark turns down the blaring Tool track, seemingly more jubilant than usual, and proclaims, "As of today, you're now back on record pace."

"What? No!" I respond.

"Check for yourself."

In the midst of the distracting daily chaos, small chunks of progress had been overlooked. We are often on the road well into the evening, sometimes under cover of darkness, for security reasons and because the weather tends to be calmer. And, often by the prospect of reaching a more enticing stop: a beach, a bar or a cheap motel bed. We've done between 20 and 30 extra kilometres a day since Guatemala, and this has finally made up the difference. Checking our daily mileage against the Italian's, my expression lifts: "Shit, you're right!"

The wind is temporarily back in our sails.

Turning down Mark's tunes again, I tell him we are not through the thick of the storm, however. We have a record of the Italian's mileage, not an exact copy of his route. There is always the chance that somewhere between Alaska and Costa Rica, he and his crew found a few decisive shortcuts.

We finally arrive at *the stop*.

I provide an account of how I happened across the bar in the dead of night, the drunk bartender and the hospitable turn of events. With Mark as my one consistent witness for the record attempt, he is amazed, but somewhat skeptical, as to how we might prove this spectacular series of events if questioned.

I consider how to connect the dots. "Hmm ... well, you saw me start, the bartender saw me finish, the son saw me back, and you can attest to the fact that I didn't have nearly enough money to take a bus or taxi in either direction. Seriously, I need to carry more money!"

"Impressive, dude," Mark says as he writes the son's e-mail address in the witness column of our logbook, then initials the mileage. In addition to the logbook (which should be signed by a notary whenever possible), Guinness World Records requires us to follow up with photos and video of major landmarks along the way.

Looking at the map one last time before hopping back on my bike, I plot an ambitious goal to reach the border of Panama (at Canoas) the following morning. The home stretch through South America is at hand.

PAN-AMERICAN HIGHWAY – PANAMA

Dealing in the U.S. dollar is a small reminder of home (or at least close to it). Aside from better understanding the currency, the American dollar carries a level of integrity that Central American currencies do not. There is far less bribery (zero in Costa Rica). There is also much more infrastructure built up around it. The "greenback" feels like an old-boys club, exclusive.

How did the dollar make it this far south? This question becomes even more curious as we cross over the Bridge of the Americas. Below it are the locks of the Panama Canal, one of the seven engineering wonders of the modern world. Our *Frommer's* travel guide provides a brief history, paraphrased:

Before 1914, ships had to navigate around the tip of South America at Cape Horn. The 80-kilometre Panama Canal cuts travel time between the Pacific and Atlantic oceans in half. The connection with the United States dates back to 1902, when that country purchased the construction and land interests of a failed 1880s French effort to build a canal. The American government had previously contemplated a strategic route through Nicaragua.

Crossing the bridge, we get our first view of modern glass skyscrapers since San Diego, California. The Gulf of Panama harbour is prime real estate for luxury condos, hotels and big business. Bordering slums are still evident, however. They lie in the ugly shadow of American wealth.

I continue on through the city and for another day to where the Pan-American Highway breaks at the forgotten jungle village of Yaviza. Ahead, Central and South America intersect in a 160-kilometre stretch of extreme jungle terrain known as the Darién Gap. We have been warned that our worst nightmares can be found here: drug cartels, kidnapping, hostile Natives, heat, deadly insects and more.

The Darién is one of two "gaps" in the road from Alaska to Argentina. Guinness World Records says that we must fly around it or take a ferry to Colombia. In either case, we must backtrack 281 kilometres to Panama City in order to make travel arrangements. Our loose understanding is that there is a ferry that makes regular trips with cars – that's how the Italian crossed. How do we coordinate this, and with whom? Those are the questions.

I take one last look at Yaviza before hopping into the truck for the three-hour trek north. We have descended into a scene from a National Geographic documentary on an ancient people, complete with dugout canoes and blow darts. Thatched homes on stilts line the muddy banks of the Río Chucunaque. Young kids in worn clothing chase a dog through the alleyway, barefoot.

In my ecotourism program, we once watched a documentary on a group of overweight European tourists exploring a similar region. You see them exit their cruise ship, cameras at the ready, painfully unaware of their eventual impact.

Leaping ahead in time, you see bare-breasted Native women feeling self-conscious about their bodies, wearing shirts (because that's what the pretty white ladies do). Villagers also fight over gifts from the tourists, embracing fear and greed.

A group of kids stop to stare at Mark and me as we pack up for the return trip. They are enamoured of the colour of our skin, our bright clean T-shirts and the massive support vehicle. "We'd better get out of here," I say quietly to Mark, already feeling self-conscious.

The crowded capital of Panama City greets us once again.

Unsure where to park overnight, and not in a position to pay for an expensive hotel, we stop next to one in the heart of downtown. Settling in on the street corner, we discreetly close the blinds and lock the camper door. It would not be a surprise to hear someone knocking on the door in the middle of the night, yelling at us to leave. It has happened before.

The first time this happened to us, we attempted to hide in the far corner of a Target parking lot, in California. In the early morning hours, a mall security guard came banging on the camper door: "You can't overnight here!" It is always an uneasy feeling to pull off for the night in foreign territory, never really knowing who is lurking around outside (and their intentions).

The next morning, we sit down for an expensive buffet breakfast at the adjacent posh hotel. "But we have food in the truck," Mark protests. I explain to him that I want the concierge to see us entering and exiting the hotel, leading him to believe that we are guests (and not squatting out front). He should be able to help with our travel needs and will likely be bilingual, saving us from all that gets lost in translation.

I proceed to make *the ask*.

The concierge looks at me, dumbfounded. "I'm sorry, what ferry, sir?" Apparently, it has been out of operation for some time. The websites I have been relying on for information are outdated.

What first seemed like a relatively straightforward task has suddenly become a big concern. The precious commodity of time is once again in jeopardy. So I plead, pointing to the truck, "Please, you need to help us get to Colombia. I'm in the process of attempting a world record, cycling from Alaska to Argentina."

The concierge politely acknowledges the urgency of the

situation. "Please give me some time to research, sir. You are welcome to go back to your room. I will call you when I find out."

"I'll wait in the lobby, thank you."

Mark and I flop down on a pair of stylish white leather couches. We stare around the expansive lobby, helpless. This is not the kind of situation we can bribe our way out of. There are real logistics involved. There is also a level of Spanish needed beyond "*¿Dónde está el baño?*" (where is the bathroom?). We are in a vulnerable position, on the doorstep of a hostile country that I only know through Arnold Schwarzenegger movies. Colombia, the land of "Freedom and Order," renowned for civil conflict, hostage-taking as a profession and leading global cocaine production.

The concierge speaks fervently in Spanish to someone on the phone. He looks back at me to acknowledge that he is on the job. *Our hotel guests deserve nothing but the best. I'm on it, sir.*

It is another two hours before he acknowledges me again. "You need to ship the truck by vessel" *Maybe the ferry after all,* I wonder. "Please go see this address now." He hands me a slip of paper and tells me how to get there. Motioning with some necessity, "Please, now you go. They close soon."

We race through crowded Panama backstreets in a panicked frenzy, yelling out, "What the hell does that sign say?"

The address only appears by luck down a back alley. "There it is," I point desperately. Mark slams on the brakes.

I run inside while he finds a place to park.

Inside a small, nondescript office, I immediately home in on framed pictures of hulking vessels (the same type of ships we saw navigating the Panama Canal). The reality of the situation begins to sink in: the whimsical dream of a cheap ferry crossing is no more. The truck needs to be shipped on a different freighter. "The fee is US$1,500, cash only," says the owner. The cherry on top is that we cannot travel with the truck. We must fly from Panama City to the destination port at Cartagena, Colombia.

You have no choice. Pay the man.

Next, we are instructed to speed across town to get the truck inspected and receive the required paperwork for exportation. "Please go now," the shipping agent urges. The workday is coming to a close. So again, we hastily push through tight alleyways, sweating nonsensical directions.

Military men with guns and undercarriage mirrors inspect the vehicle at the next location. They hand me a signed form only after receiving assurances that we will not sell the vehicle in Colombia. What the stamped paper says, I'm not entirely certain.

We race another 70 kilometres to the port of Colón on the Caribbean Sea. There I present the documents to the port authority, pray that everything is in order, then watch as a group of scruffy workers drives the truck into a cramped steel shipping container. It is soon lost to view among a few hundred other sea-cans on the deck of a rusted vessel. *Please get there.*

Mark holds on to a duct-taped suitcase, I to my bike, which is now boxed up. Like vagabonds, we board the next bus back to Panama City, still very much in a rush.

We sit apart, next to expressionless locals, sweating in the stuffy hull. A live chicken mills about in a cage stored above us. Below, next to me and in plain view, a young woman breastfeeds her newborn child. I bashfully turn my attention away. Still, I can hear the baby sucking on the heavy milk glands, making me uncomfortable. *Suck, suck, suck,* all the way to Tocumen International Airport.

We purchase two tickets for the next flight to Cartagena.

The next steps happen quickly: passing through security, walking across the hot tarmac to board a propeller pond-hopper that will fly high above the clouded Darién Gap, Mark falling asleep within minutes. I reflect on what has become the costliest challenge yet, and about what mysterious dangers may lie ahead.

The short, ninety-minute flight touches down in the early evening. Stepping out of the plane, Mark and I stick close together, slightly unnerved by an increased military presence in the Colombian airport.

The plan is to push on, despite exhaustion. I believe a quick turnaround may be *the* decisive move in getting ahead of the Guinness World Record. Poorly translated Internet reports have led us to believe that the Italian's ferry crossing took an extra day or two.

After picking up our luggage, we head straight for the car rental counter and arrange for a small sedan. We will press on through the frontier of the Andes Mountains, then backtrack at night in order to pick up the truck, scheduled to arrive in a few days.

The whirlwind day continues. *What day is it, anyway?*

Mark unpacks the suitcase and readies the bike outside. Inside the retro airport washroom, I nervously suit up in my familiar cycling kit, sweat-stained helmet and worn clipless riding shoes. Walking back outside, I notice the street lights turn on. *It's late.*

Turning a corner heading toward our rental car, I see Mark surrounded by military men, some with hands on their hips, others holding guns. A million scenarios play out in my head. Nevertheless, I walk up calmly and attempt to introduce myself as Mark's heterosexual travel companion.

I assume that Mark's Canadian passport, tattoos, smoking and unaccompanied luggage alerted the men to the possibility that he could be an adrenaline-seeking drug smuggler. The addition of a guy in Spandex must add a whole new dimension to the story.

We try to explain that our truck and supplies are being shipped from Panama, making hand gestures of a boat crossing over choppy water, complete with tugboat sound effects. I receive a blank, somewhat quizzical, reaction. The men are not much older than either of us.

Mark takes another approach, holding out a pack of cigarettes. The interrogation squad immediately warms to the nicotine gesture, cracking into laughter as the first few communal puffs are blown. I join in the levity, saying out loud to my companion, "I'm not sure what is so funny, but I think that we are off the hook."

The military men let us go. *Or unleash us?*

We ride on through the first few crowded intersections, apprehensively, our eyes darting around every street corner and dark entrance. My pupils are fully dilated. *Is that person looking at me? Why do they keep staring? And the sliding door on the van looks kidnap-accessible ... yeah, I see you!*

Darkness further exposes our fears.

In view of the clouded high beams and moonlight, I home in on the asphalt goal and try to tune out the fearful unknown that is all around us. Soon, it's just Mark and me on a quiet mountain road. We ride on as long as our wits allow.

The following morning, we awake, our bodies in knots in the passenger and driver's seat respectively, slumped with muscle kinks and puffy red eyes. Licking my gums, I taste stale potato chip plaque. There are a few empty bags in the back seat.

Out the front window, a group of dark-skinned villagers

mills about on the side of a lush green hillside. The warm morning view is invigorating. Still, we're both exhausted.

Nothing about the last couple of days has been fun. Truthfully, not much about the trip has been fun. And then there is *that other issue*, only exacerbated by the shipping debacle.

I turn to my hardened companion. "Hey, Mark..."

"Yeah?" he replies nonchalantly.

"We have run out of money."

CHAPTER 14

THE END OF THE WORLD

At the port in Cartagena, Colombia, three dockworkers back the truck out of the shipping container. Right away, Mark notices a long scrape along a panel on the driver's side. He points it out to the men, frustrated. They throw up their hands: *It was like that when we opened it!*

I shake my head, watching the scene unfold from inside an air-conditioned office of the port master. I'm on the phone.

I dial the lengthy code on the back of my international calling card, the country code next, followed by the area code and phone number, and then wait as the line begins to ring. Over 15,000 kilometres travelled since Alaska and there is still only a one-hour time zone difference from Calgary.

The other end picks up. I hear my mother's voice: "Hello?"

"Hi, Mom, it's your son. Mark and I made it to Colombia ... actually, we have been travelling through the country for a couple of days already. We had to backtrack and pick up the truck."

She senses a problem: "Pick the truck up from where?"

"We ran into some unexpected expenses..."

I tell her about the ferry from the port in Panama that is no more, of instead having to ship the vehicle to Colombia on a freighter and fly across the Darién Gap. The extra $3,000 expense, plus all the other backward dealings have finally become too cumbersome. And, unlike in Mexico, I'm not prepared to crawl back to my sponsors and ask for more help. I'm hoping instead that the Correy Investment Team will come to the rescue.

My parents' financial advisory business has grown steadily in the last couple of years. Never the types to go after a quick buck, they weathered financial storms with a reputation built on sound, long-term investments. They now look forward to selling their client portfolio in return for early retirement.

I could have inherited a multi-million-dollar business. Instead, I sheepishly ask if my parents can lend me $2,000 to finish the journey.

In a stern advisory voice, my mother asks if that is really enough money to finish. *Without any more hiccups, yes. But who am I kidding?* "Okay, more like $3,000," I suggest.

She grows impatient. "What about getting home?!"

"Okay, more like $5,000," I acknowledge.

She agrees to wire the money that afternoon.

I'm thankful for the opportunity this affords me. At the same time, I recognize a failure to take care of myself, to "get off the tit" as my father would say (referring to the warm embrace of a mother's bosom). Of all the adventure stories you read about, I wonder how many expedition leaders needed their parents to bail them out? None that I can recall, or at least none that were reported.

I worry that my parents' support will take away from the rugged nature of the journey, that the Pan-American world record attempt will instead look like a rich kid's summer sabbatical. I want people to know that this journey was not handed to me on a silver platter – I busted my ass to get here. In any case, it would be rude not to thank them. So I do, and half a world apart we hang up with a verbal embrace: "I love you."

For whatever reason, we never say those three words in person.

Since my brother Nathan's passing, none of us have been very good at expressing our feelings. It has been six years now and I can only remember hugging my father once during that time, a few months back at the send-off in Calgary. The farther away I travel, however, the closer we seem to become.

I'm reminded of the time I abruptly moved out of the house for six months after high school. Once my parents and I were back on speaking terms, those were actually some of the most cordial times we experienced, when everyone got along for a change.

Perhaps we sometimes care a little too much for each other. The separation allows us time to breathe, to reflect and learn how to intelligently express those strong emotions.

As I get ready to end the call, I hear my father yell in the background, "Get off the tit!"

LATER THAT SAME DAY

We drive back through the dense green Andes Mountains to where I last finished riding, near the border with Ecuador. Mark is on schmooze detail, responsible for doling out cheap cigarettes at all the military checkpoints.

This brand of military is not the type to ask for a handout outright. They'll just make the camper searches go by a little quicker if Mark shares his addiction.

It is an odd turn of events, thinking back to the early heart-to-heart talks we had in Alaska about how to quit smoking, which continued all the way up to the end of our relative sanity, in California. Part of our sponsorship fund is now directed toward having enough bribe packs on hand.

As always, we want the young guys with guns on our side.

It is apparent that the problems (kidnapping and drugs) we were first concerned about do exist, just not in the open as we expected. The military have confidently pushed the "bad guys" back into the dense mountain jungle.

The Andes, that endless rolling wonder, is much different from any other mountain range we have traversed. The peaks are not so tall, yet rise sharply all the same. A dense canopy of trees above and a blanket of fertile crops on the ground create more shades of green than I can count. It is a compact contrast to the brown textures of modern development.

The action-movie stereotypes are soon forgotten.

Settled in for the night beside a quiet, isolated cantina, I step out of the camper to take a leak before going to bed. Dotting the hillside all around are the faint flickers of fire from inside primitive family huts. From a distance, it looks like welcoming candlelight.

Bird sounds quiet down as the vibrant hum of small insects takes over. Scrolling through Mark's MP3 player, I turn the dial to "Mysterons," by Portishead. The moody trip-hop plays to those relaxed wandering senses that Radiohead normally stimulates. I like it.

As my bladder empties I stare up at the star-filled sky and reflect. Taking into account the dramatic landscape and hospitable locals, I'm confident that this is my favourite part of the journey so far. *Arnold had it wrong.*

PAN-AMERICAN HIGHWAY – ENTERING ECUADOR
Mark parks the truck at the top of the next mountain, and films me labouring up it. I'm happy to see him back in the inspired routine of taking pictures and video. It has been far too long.

Capturing the long climb, I'm more inclined to ride at a

steady tempo (and not stop). Much has changed since those relentless early days at the back, yelling at my father to slow down on the measly Cypress Hills in Saskatchewan. Now I enjoy the vertical challenge.

After 45 minutes of sweating back and forth, I'm presented with a tremendous valley view and refreshing cool breeze. Mark holds out a water bottle as I pass.

Every now and again, a young kid will pull up, seemingly out of nowhere, on a rickety bike. I'm caught off guard, *What? Him again?* Mark later shows me video of one boy hanging on to the back of our truck (reflected in his rearview mirror), using our bumper as a free ride to the top. This escalator service seems to be a common understanding among all passing motorists.

Back down in the fertile valley, we pass by small roadside markets with exotic fruits and flowers for sale. Birds of paradise and gooseberries can be picked from the side of the road.

I'm surprised to see a banana with a Chiquita sticker on it. Normally, this sticker is a corporate symbol, and one that also signifies that the fruit in question has been shipped halfway around the world and is meant to ripen in transit. But no, this particular produce comes from just down the road. It is only a few days old.

Green banana plantations become more prevalent as we pass into the arid regions of northern Ecuador. The stalks and heavy bunches of fruit sprout from dusty desert soil that seems unfit for growth but apparently is just right.

After we wind back up and over the Andes, the humid jungle will greet us once again.

While we are camped at the highest point, a surreal layer of cloud forms beneath us, blocking our view of the Pacific Ocean and most other terrain. Seated on the tailgate with a steaming dinner of beans and rice, Mark and I stare off in soft wonder.

PAN-AMERICAN HIGHWAY – SOUTHERN HEMISPHERE

We pass by the equator without noticing the small tourist pullout at Cayambe, Ecuador. As soon as we are made aware of it by an inquisitive local, though, I ask Mark to drive us back to take some pictures.

He squirms at the thought of another generic tourist shot. "We have to," I remind him, slightly frustrated that this discussion still happens. Guinness requires proof of all major landmarks.

The list of evidence and witnesses is now extensive. At the top of our logbook is a signature from our hostess at the Prudhoe Bay breakfast buffet. That cold Alaska morning seems like a lifetime ago.

Back in Canada, temperatures are starting to dip below freezing, as it is October. Here, it just feels like a cool summer day. The equator is a temperature inversion zone.

The centre of the world...

In the midst of a self-congratulatory moment, Mark yells out from behind the camera, "All done, Ping Pong?" referring to the Asian stereotype of photographing anything and everything. We are like an old married couple, sometimes. Mind you, marriage feels like a fairly straightforward ask at this point.

PAN-AMERICAN HIGHWAY, DAY 100

A few days later, we reach the border of Peru. The entry process is again very bureaucratic and outdated.

Slouched inside a roadside post, weary-looking men in

uniform care very little about our schedule. And we are losing patience. If we really wanted to, we could make a run for the finish at this point. But we stay and play by the rules.

On the other side of the border, a policeman flags us down and rather abruptly hops into the truck. In feverish Spanglish, he tells Mark to turn around, and leads us to another building. As far as we are concerned, though, the paperwork is done. *What is he nitpicking about? Something feels dodgy.*

As soon as the officer gets out of the truck, we make a run for it. "Fuck that!" Mark yells out, on an adrenaline high. Gravel spews up from the tires as we pull away.

No one gives chase.

The day finishes at the small fishing village of Cabo Blanco. Now ahead of the record by a couple of days, we treat ourselves to one of the few motel establishments along the white sandy shore.

In view of a sunset and cool waves crawling up, the proprietor serves a late dinner and tells us a story about the writer Ernest Hemingway and his time spent fishing here in 1956. The famous American author was on location for part of the filming of his Pulitzer Prize-winning and last-published novel, *The Old Man and the Sea.*

The story is about an elderly Cuban fisherman who has gone 84 days without a big catch, amid constant taunting by his peers. Still, he is determined not to give up, and his perseverance soon pays off. The following day, he miraculously hooks a large marlin in the Gulf of Mexico. He fights with the fish for two days before finally gaining the upper hand.

Exhausted, he respectfully calls his foe "brother."

Gazing out over Hemingway's muse seascape, I question

what honour still exists in my own battle. *What value does a world record hold?* All around me, people go about their humble daily lives without a care for such things. My own has diminished greatly.

I stare out at the ocean once more.

Before heading to bed in our open-air bungalow, I express to Mark that "I might not go for the record." Surprisingly unfazed by this, he too seems to realize that the label has lost much of its flair. It is no longer *my marlin*. In fact, I'm feeling more hollow from the impatient confrontations we constantly find ourselves in.

"So, what, you just stop now?" Mark asks.

PAN-AMERICAN HIGHWAY – DETOUR TO CUSCO

Away from the lush highlands, Peru is very similar to the northern desert wastelands of Mexico. Out in the thick of it, there is very little traffic and nothing to hold my attention.

The wind softly whistles along the flat landscape.

In our boredom, we begin to discuss the ambitious idea of taking a detour to the glorious Machu Picchu ruins, one of the "New Seven Wonders of the World." We calculate that it will cost three days of travel time to the interior. On the flipside, this is a once-in-a-lifetime opportunity.

Parked at a gas station slum in San Clemente, an important easterly intersection, I spontaneously slide my bike into the camper and hop into some street clothes. "Let's go for it!" I smile. The cautionary words of a touring cyclist still ring in my ears: *You're going to miss out on the experience.*

We begin our journey east to the ancient Inca city of Cusco.

Only stopping for gas, we pass through forgotten mountain villages with aimless-looking kids and tired seniors walking by. They all share the same red-cheeked complexion. *Sunburn?*

Their clothing is made from the native alpaca wool. The men are dressed in plain, European-influenced formal attire, the women in bright-coloured, handwoven skirts. Most also wear either a cowboy hat or a bowler to block out the intense sun. The mountaintop settlements are all exposed.

After 13 hours of driving, we push on through the cluttered markets of Cusco to the outlying town of Ollantaytambo. Arriving late at night, we park in an unassuming alleyway, not really sure of anything.

We fall asleep to the sound of flute music and a view of the surrounding Andes in moonlit brilliance.

PAN-AMERICAN HIGHWAY – MACHU PICCHU

We wake in the morning to the sound of a bustling town square and Peruvian people talking in an ancient dialect.

Before hopping on a train to the base of Machu Picchu (the road we were following ends at Ollantaytambo), we grab some breakfast. A local vendor is serving up watered-down hot chocolate and fried egg sandwiches. We eat the warm meal next to true local spirit, laughing along to god knows what, maybe ourselves.

After a second round, we grab our cameras and split up to take pictures. The morning sun reflects off cobblestone pathways and homes built of smooth boulders. The architecture is very distinctive and of immense, puzzling construction. Its beauty is unlike any place we have yet experienced.

A group of local kids with dirty hands and nicely parted hair surrounds me while I shoot video. They are curious to see their faces on camera and giggle as I place my sunglasses on one boy's face. He stares at the lens, bug-eyed.

The seclusion is short-lived.

Aboard the rickety valley train, we get our second glimpse of "white people" since the resort towns of Mexico. Both of us are taken aback at how disgusting most of them are. They are overweight and ignorant of the sensitive nature of the cultural ecosystem. So we sit separately and avoid engaging in conversation. The view outside the train is much more captivating.

At the Aguas Calientes departure point, we begin a steep hike up the mountain to the ruins at Machu Picchu. Most tourists choose the air-conditioned buses that snake up an alternative route.

Cresting the sweaty jungle climb, we're greeted with the immediate surprise of a metal turnstile at the park entrance. A maximum of 500 people are allowed to experience the site (not yet visible to us) at any given time. *No problem*, I warmly gesture to the attendant. I am more than happy to embrace their sustainability initiatives.

Just past the ticketing office and around a narrow ledge, the ancient Inca Empire is revealed in all its glory. The rubble city sits atop the edge of a grand mountain stronghold, cradled by the Andes, and constructed from the same bewildering boulders as Ollantaytambo. The view is picturesque.

With one arm around the other's shoulder in a well-timed photo, Mark and I celebrate the moment.

PAN-AMERICAN HIGHWAY – ENTERING ARGENTINA
I'm once again thrust back into the desert sphere, straddling my bike at the San Clemente gas station, bleary-eyed from the 16-hour return trip.

The lone serenity reminds me of cycling across the Canadian prairies. At times, I find peace in nothingness. In other moments, I'm still very aware that it is a slog. Mark drives ahead in ten-kilometre intervals to help break up the vast expanse.

The countdown is on.

Grasslands, wired fencing and farmers on horseback appear farther south. The region begins to acquire a European flavour, especially with the introduction of vineyards near Santiago, Chile.

That scene once again dramatically changes on a switchback climb over the mountains into Mendoza, Argentina. For the first time since Alaska, I shrug back into my winter riding gear. A layer of snow blankets the high-altitude border.

We descend to the windy plains of Argentina. And for a brief moment, we assume that our challenges are behind us.

PAN-AMERICAN HIGHWAY, DAY 126

We stop for groceries in the coastal town of Rivadavia, Argentina. Arriving back at the truck with our arms full, I notice immediately that the doors are unlocked. Our camera gear and laptop have been stolen.

Mark recoils with the keys in his hand. "It's not my fault!! I thought that you locked up!"

Unable to look at him, I turn my attention to the streets. In the distance, a gang of kids runs away with what looks like our black Pelican cases (holding the filmmaking equipment). They disappear before I can catch up to them.

I walk back to the truck, infuriated.

Mark immediately becomes defensive in a way I have never seen before. He considers it both our faults.

I don't agree.

We spend the next several hours filling out a police report

with the help of a kind English teacher who has been called in to translate. Accounting for it all, over $8,000 of equipment has been taken.

In exhausted tears that night, Mark and I sit back in the truck and gaze out over the Atlantic waves rolling in. "What's the point?" he asks. It seems a valid thought, even with less than a week to go.

A moment of leadership is needed from me.

I wipe my cheeks and let out a heavy sigh. "Mark, this is my dream. If I give up on the one thing that means anything, then what is the point of my life? I need you to help me finish this. It is an important accomplishment for *both* of us."

We continue south along the barren windy coast to a ferry crossing at the Strait of Magellan. Rocking back and forth over the frigid waters, I quietly pray: *Please, we're almost there.* Tierra del Fuego National Park awaits us.

Glacial mountains, old growth pine forests and clear blue streams soon envelope us. The scene is reminiscent of the first week of the trip, in Alaska. And, like when we were in the cold north, I'm forced back onto my mountain bike to navigate the gravel roads ahead of us.

PAN-AMERICAN HIGHWAY, DAY 131

The mountain view opens up to a most glorious sight.

The November sun sets across a peaceful settlement with sailboats docked along the Beagle Channel. I have reached the outskirts of Ushuaia, the southernmost city in the world.

The prospect of finishing this journey feels surreal. I look down at my feet pedalling away, then back up at my surroundings. *I'm really here.*

Mark speeds ahead to film me riding in.

Pulling up to a stop sign, tourists cross in front of us without giving a second thought to the story before them.

Ushuaia is a popular destination from which to view penguins in their natural habitat, tour Martial Glacier, hike through the surrounding mountains or charter a boat to Antarctica. None of these activities matter now.

I follow a network of roads down through a few civilized shopping blocks, eventually finding my way to the archipelago shore. Mark is standing there with his camera, ready to give me a tight, supremely relieved bear hug. It feels good.

I sit down next to the pier in silence, feet dangling over the water's edge. Mark eases down next to me.

We gaze out over the pink horizon and watch the seagulls floating on by. A few feet behind us, the last landmark sign reads: "Ushuaia – fin del mundo" (the end of the world).

I'm officially nine days ahead of the record.

"Let's go home," I say, smiling.

PAN-AMERICAN HIGHWAY – RETURNING HOME
After two days of consuming airport carbs, our final flight touches down at the Calgary International Airport.

The expressionless customs agent glances through the worn pages in my Canadian passport. "You have been doing a lot of travelling lately," he states, rhetorically. I tell him of the world record and the 14 countries we visited, now left behind. He then waves me through, tipping his hat as I pass.

My two cardboard bike boxes lie on their sides, hemorrhaging gear from all ends in the oversize-baggage area – a casualty of multiple transfers. I pile the clothing and tools back into the boxes, slightly embarrassed, but nonetheless relieved that everything appears to have made it home.

Our friends are not far behind.

Mark's roommate slides in to shake hands. My sister and my friend Chris are waiting too. As a group of five, we laugh, we hug and then we quietly dissolve into our own familiar conversations.

We walk through the sliding doors and over to the parking lot.

Headed to opposite ends of the lot, Mark and I look back at each other once more. It suddenly dawns on me that this could be the long goodbye. In the "real world," he would otherwise be a stranger, no longer tied to my A-type agenda. I imagine it will feel good to open up, to have some distance.

Chris and I catch up for a few minutes. *Relief* is the first thought that comes to mind.

My sister drives me home, prodding for more details. But I don't say much.

Alone in my basement suite that evening, I stare into the washroom mirror. My hair is four months long, my skin a hardened brown. *Relief*, I think again.

NOVEMBER 18, 2005

A reporter from the *Calgary Herald* phones. He is interested in the dynamic between Mark and me. I try to be diplomatic but I am aware that what slips out may be an oversimplification and possibly get misconstrued.

He then asks what stage the record is at. "My information will soon be submitted to Guinness for review. It will probably take a couple of weeks to have a decision," I tell him.

I drive to Calgary to pick up a copy of the article. Anxiously flipping through the newspaper in the car, I'm surprised when I don't see anything. I flip through again, this time a little more slowly, but nothing. I toss the paper onto the passenger seat. Out of the corner of my eye, I catch a glimpse of the front-page headline: "Calgarian completes 25,000 km epic."

I anxiously call up Mark: "Did you see the article?!"

"Yeah, it makes me out to be an asshole," he says bluntly, referring to a couple of not-so-humorous jabs I made at him running over multiple bikes. "Thanks a lot. Everyone at work is going to think I'm a joke ... Fuck you."

I try to emphasize the good points but am abruptly cut short by the dial tone, and then by worry.

CHAPTER 15

BIGGER THAN SELF

DECEMBER, 2005

During an interview on Citytv Calgary's *Breakfast Television* about my Pan-American world record attempt, host Dave Kelly jokes with me about my demolished bikes, about Mark and me getting lost from each other and how much my butt must hurt from riding over 25,000 kilometres from Prudhoe Bay, Alaska, to Ushuaia, Argentina.

With the height of the *Calgary Herald* front-page tension behind me, I have the foresight to try and steer the interview away from interpersonal challenges and on to the beauty of it all.

I'm realizing how important it is to not let two weeks' worth of setbacks overshadow all the rest. I fall back to saying, "Yes, we had our fair share of challenges ... but I can also appreciate the learning opportunities the journey presented."

No matter what I claim, though, it all comes across as a backhanded compliment to Mark. My ego can't get to a place were I can simply be diplomatic and say, "Mark was awesome! It was the adventure of a lifetime. As for the next challenge, bring it on!" Instead, the story makes me out to be the guy that persevered. No one ever thought to ask, "Did you ever treat Mark poorly?"

Of course I did.

My interviews with local media are picked up in the

national press. Understandably, Mark doesn't want much to do with me. His roommate serves as the go-between, reinforcing the fact that Mark is pissed off, but, surprisingly, also shows sympathy toward me. His final words on the matter are: "I'm not going to tell you what to do next – just do the right thing."

Not being able to speak to Mark in person has put me on edge. I play out a series of damning scenarios in which he provides his own public retort.

A week goes by and not a word is uttered between us.

I consider two possible reasons. In the first, the awkward press attention has shut him away. I had seen this habit of his, of retreating when he felt threatened, a couple of times on the road. In the second scenario, I picture Mark back at work, having moved on, choosing to forget that our journey ever took place.

The complacency involved on his part in the latter scenario bothers me more. I interpret it as a reflection on my leadership, hearkening back to my rocky beginnings as "Hitler" in the Ecotourism program.

Our story is one of complicated personal growth and an equally complicated interpersonal relationship. And the cycling aspect? Merely a stimulus to poke and prod.

I'm asked to speak further about my experiences: at a luncheon for Precision Energy Ltd., a dinner reception for my other generous sponsors, and for enthusiastic local schools that raised donations for the Make-A-Wish Foundation. Naturally, their attention is focused on the record. They want to know how it feels to be the best in the world at something, and, of course, if I will be in the book that Guinness publishes each year.

The celebrity they pursue is unconfirmed, though. Unbeknownst to all, the record logbooks have not been submitted. They remain tucked away in a sealed envelope under my bed.

When my motivation swayed in Ecuador, I promised myself I would not make a decision until I was sure. I'm holding on to the evidence until I can look myself in the mirror and say, *Yes, this is what matters.*

JANUARY, 2006

Dana's mom greets me at the front door, giving me a congratulatory hug as I enter the front hallway. "We're so glad you made it back safe. It sounds like you faced some big challenges," she says kindly. Over her shoulder, I gaze into the living room. The last time I was in their home, Dana was lying on a hospital bed, comatose.

Dana's father walks up and shakes my hand, somewhat guarded. "Welcome back," he says. My visit, in addition to catching up, is also to film an interview for the Pan-American documentary. This is the first time the McKays have felt comfortable enough to proceed.

I point to a couch in the living room. "Before we get started, I want you to know that I carried this with me the entire way." I pull out Dana's plaster thumbprint, still in its Ziploc bag. "It was in my back pocket as I rode along the mosquito-infested gravel roads in Alaska, through the heat in Mexico, all the way to the end of the world at Ushuaia." Both of them smile, their eyes welling up in appreciation.

"So, where would you like to begin?" Dana's father asks softly. With the video camera and microphone pointed in their direction, I ask them to tell me about their son, including the happy memories, the funny ones, and all the trouble he got up to in between.

They point to pictures in a photo album as they reminisce. I see a little guy proudly holding up the first slippery fish he ever caught. On the next page, he is decked out in racing gear, looking smug in front of a motocross dirt bike. Dana is a happy kid.

Toward the end of the album, he is pictured next to a proud junior high teacher, holding up a plaque for "Most Inspirational Student." His face had started to become puffy as a result of the cancer medications. Most of his hair had fallen out, too.

I listen to his parents pour their hearts out. They sit close to one another as they speak, holding hands.

Not once do I stop to change camera angles, adjust the poor lighting or check to see that the sound is recording at a high enough volume. The moment is too powerful.

After 30 minutes, they ask if there is anything else I would like to cover. "I don't think so," I reply. "Thank you so much for sharing those stories with me. I know it must not be easy to relive."

Dana's father looks at me with a forgiving look, choking back the tears. "Nonsense. He's a great kid. We're happy to share."

I begin packing up to leave.

Lacing up my shoes, Dana's mom recalls one final story. Earnestly she begins: "I always told my kids, wherever you go, always take a cellphone and make sure to call when you get to wherever it is you are going. At Dana's funeral, I heard a cellphone ringing. I thought, *How rude, in a place like this.* Then I noticed that the ringing was coming from my purse – it was Dana's cellphone. I had held onto it while he was sick and in the hospital. I realized that it was him calling, telling me he had made it to heaven. He is … he is still with us."

A solitary tear streams down my cheek.

It is apparent that whatever world record aspirations I had before this meeting have now quietly faded into memory. For the sake of our story and my own misguided sense of integrity, I now know what I must do. There is one more scene to film.

APRIL 1, 2006

The first showing of my documentary, called *Longest Road*, is to begin in an hour at the Cineplex theatre in Chinook Centre. Unfortunately, I am nowhere near ready.

Looking at my computer screen, I stare with angst at the editing software's painfully slow "rendering" progress. Even after working away all night, it still only displays 85 per cent complete.

Watching the ticking clock, my fixation turns to panic.

A volunteer from the Make-A-Wish Foundation calls to say that people are starting to arrive at the theatre. The premiere showing is in the morning, scheduled so as not to conflict with the blockbuster schedule. Word has gone out to Dana's family, friends, sponsors, volunteers from the charity and anyone who stopped by my booth at the Outdoor Adventure Show last week.

I frantically acknowledge, "Okay, okay, thank you…"

After I have a quick shower and get dressed, the screen still only reads 85 per cent. *Shit.*

I phone the volunteer back. "The film is not going to be ready in time. I'm going to drive to the theatre and apologize in person. Please stall a bit longer."

My panic slides into shameful embarrassment.

Arriving 25 minutes later, I timidly walk into the dimly lit theatre and begin my apology: "I'm sorry for wasting your time, everyone. This is my first crack at making a documentary. I really tried to get it done in time. If you can make it next Saturday, we are going to try this again, same time." The audience gives me a warm and understanding reception – *it's no problem*. I can relax for a moment.

APRIL 6, 2006

I have been asked to serve as the student representative on a panel discussion that is part the Thomas Wood Distinguished Speaker Series, organized by Mount Royal College. The panel will follow a keynote presentation by adventure photographer Bruce Kirkby. The subject of Kirkby's presentation is "When was your last adventure?"

I'm familiar with Bruce's name but not with his accomplishments. In the days leading up to the event, I check out his website and numerous online articles. Bruce is the author of two bestselling books, *Sand Dance: By Camel Across Arabia's Great Southern Desert* and *The Dolphin's Tooth: A Decade in Search of Adventure*. Besides having trekked across Arabia by camel, he has served as the communications leader for an expedition to the top of Mount Everest, rafted down the Blue Nile, and more. I'm struck with the thought that he is exactly what I want to be: an "Adventurer."

I sit in the crowd during his keynote presentation. Over 600 people have come to hear Bruce speak. I'm captivated by the 38-year-old's stories and stunning pictures projected up on the screen. It makes me curious to delve even deeper into the "real world" questions left untouched. In particular, how does one make a job of this and answer the paternal concerns about job security and paying taxes?

I'm soon called up on stage for the panel.

Having never formally met Bruce, it is an oddly familiar

experience to be involved in a discussion with him. We each share our parallel takes on how to live a life of adventure. And of course, my Pan-American journey is front and centre.

At an after-party for the event sponsor and college dignitaries, I listen to Bruce answer question after question from businessmen in suits, mostly older than him. One gentleman in particular catches my attention. With all sincerity, he asks, "What advice would you give to someone in my position – a guy that has worked at an office job his entire life? How can I break free?" This is how Bruce responded:

> It is much harder at age 40 to drop it all and chase an unusual path. The path itself is no harder, but the price – which often involves eating ichiban soup and living in a basement and holding clothes together with duct tape – though it can be (a bit) romantic for a 20-year-old, takes a far higher toll on a 40-year-old who has other dependants or is even just used to the good life. Accept that change comes slowly; it can seem disappointing what we create in a year, but astounding what we can do in ten. It's never too late! Essentially this type of life boils down to valuing certain things – time, freedom, friends, health etc. – over money. Ignore the bozos who tell you that you can't do it. A bit cliché, but do what you love and you'll end up loving what you do. Start now; there are only so many tomorrows. And never underestimate your ability to delay, and delay and delay.

I accompany Bruce and his equally adventurous wife out to their car after the event. Sensing a confidant and mentor in my midst, I let it slip that things did not go so well with my last support driver. Unlike most with whom I share this experience, Bruce can totally empathize with the situation.

Buried deep inside, there is a story from his past that edges out a smirk. But instead of divulging what happened right then and there, he recommends that we get together for coffee sometime. I seize the opportunity to first invite the couple to the premiere of my film, happening in a few days time. Bruce energetically shakes my hand: "Definitely, we'll be there, brother!"

APRIL 8, 2006

The theatre lights dim. As far back as the final row, I see all eyes looking forward. Bruce and his wife are sitting contentedly up front, my parents and sister behind them. A couple of rows up is Dana's mom, the self-proclaimed "family representative" on these occasions. My friend Chris is seated on one side of me. On the other side are a few friendly volunteers from the Make-A-Wish Foundation. The remaining seats are peppered with blog followers and free giveaways.

The sound of wind comes quietly rushing in.

The screen opens to a shot of me sitting on top of a mountain overlooking the Beagle Channel, flipping Dana's thumbprint through my fingers. At the bottom of the screen, "Day 132" appears. The majestic scene quickly cuts to THE LONGEST ROAD title card in bold Arial all caps.

Enter, the Pan-American Highway.

The quiet audience stares in wonder as I'm pulled into the security booth at Prudhoe Bay; as I enjoy some friendly banter with Mark in the truck while we cross the majestic Golden Gate Bridge; as I read *The Complete Idiot's Guide to Learning Spanish* at the Mexicali border, hug Kelly in Phoenix and dole out bribes in Central America; as I talk with Mark about our conflicts, asking "Is it worth it?"; as I pedal across the lush Andean highlands, play with kids in Ollantaytambo and pose for a picture in front of the first Ushuaia mileage sign.

In the final scene, the audience is transported back to the McKays' living room, where we learn the emotional story of the ringing cellphone at Dana's funeral. Next, the camera cuts to a close-up of the logbooks detailing the world record attempt, in a sealed envelope. And then, the answer to everyone's question: I toss the heavy stack of files into an open fire, destroying any hope of being granted the title of "Fastest to cycle the Pan-American Highway." *There, it's done. Everyone knows now.*

The scene transitions to a black and white image of Dana and me standing next to each other in skates at the Olympic Oval, in Calgary. It is the only shot of the two of us. Paired with my final voice-over, the screen slowly fades to black with this message:

> During the 131 days that Mark and I were on the road, I came to the realization that world records, gold medals and money have no lasting value. Sometimes, the most important thing in life is keeping a promise to a friend.

The lights softly come up.

As I look around the quiet theatre, there is not a dry eye. I too have a hard time holding back. Breaking the silence, my father begins to clap. The rest of the audience follows his lead.

Wiping away my tears, I get up and walk down to the front for the Q&A session. *Everyone knows now...*

I point toward the first hand held high and a young girl asks if I will ever attempt another world record. Surprisingly, I have not considered the question since destroying the logbooks. I give the first response that comes to mind: "Holding a world record is still a goal of mine, just not today. Right now I want to be an advocate for something that's bigger than me."

APRIL 15, 2006

Mark stares intently at me, saying nothing.

Standing in the doorway of his rented home, I hold out a copy of the completed documentary. "Please, it would mean a lot if you took a look at this and told me what you think. If you want me to change anything, please let me know ... I'm trying, here. We have been through too much to end on bad terms."

He takes the DVD and says blankly, "Yeah, whatever."

The door closes in my face.

A week goes by and there is no response. *Really, what should I expect?* He opted not to come to the premiere at the theatre.

The silence once again stirs up paranoia in me. *Could he sue me for defamation of character? If I go ahead and show the DVD again and/or sell it, can he come after me for footage rights? Does he even care? Good or bad, just say something! Fuck.*

Another week goes by and still no response.

Without Mark's blessing, it doesn't feel right to market the DVD on my website (even with all profits going to the Make-A-Wish Foundation). I remove the PayPal link and put the remaining copies in storage.

Instead of feeling down about the mountain of hours that went into filming and editing, however, I choose instead to tip my hat and give one final nod to our stubborn relationship. *Touché, Mark.*

Given a second chance, I would just say, "Thank you."

The next time Bruce Kirkby is in town for a speaking engagement, we schedule a meeting.

Chowing down on a couple of Subway sandwiches at the University of Calgary, I vent some more about my interpersonal issues. Bruce assures me that he has run into the same problems on almost every expedition he has been on. He is not on speaking terms with some of his former team members, often for pointless reasons, he acknowledges. There are ongoing battles over who owns the rights to pictures and video. "You're not alone," he tells me.

Switching gears, I ask how he felt about going to Mount Everest in 1997 as the communications leader for an expedition, working only from base camp. "Do you have any desire to go back and climb it?" I ask. The more I learn about the adventurer game, the more I understand that Everest is a meal ticket for so many. Surviving the climb often segues into book deals and paid speaking gigs. The vain side of me assumes this is an obvious next step.

"Honestly, no. I have absolutely no desire," Bruce admits. "There are so many other places to explore. Everest has become very commercial..."

Bruce has found a balance between adventure, having a career and not selling out. He is the real deal.

I appreciate the opportunity to learn from someone more experienced than me, and to have him help shape my identity. I keep his words in mind during my Directed Field Study (DFS) review at Mount Royal College.

My ecotourism instructor and I sit down for a debrief on the Pan-American journey. He shakes my hand warmly, "Epic. Truly epic." The completion of this trip has afforded me a more personal level of respect, a step beyond regular student–teacher relations. Then again, the Ecotourism program has always been a tightly knit group.

He starts in on the DFS formalities.

There is a booklet with a series of evaluation points ranking from "one" (did not meet expectations) to "five" (met or exceeded the DFS requirements). He asks me to describe a situation in which I applied the ecotourism principles of responsible travel and working to improve the well-being of local peoples.

I enjoy the opportunity to frame my experiences in a learning context, answering, "We often supported the local economy through purchasing from vendors and not from big box stores, and there was an educational component to my blog posts that provided great insight into the areas that we travelled through... Honestly, the only negative impact was bringing along a gas-guzzling truck."

On sustainability I receive a four out of five. The rest of the scores are perfect.

"So, where do you go from here?" my instructor inquires.

I have taken a liking to the title "Adventure Cyclist." As for what this label entails, I now say proudly: "To turn a passion for cycling into my purpose in life." This dream will transcend many mediums, from racing, touring and motivational speaking, to filmmaking, writing and, hopefully, to advocacy someday.

"And to what end?" my instructor asks.

I think of the comic book heroes I read about as a kid (and sometimes still do) and state simply, "To change the world," of course.

CHAPTER 16

TURNING 24

"What's next?" *Ah yes*, the million-dollar question. Every Pan-American conversation begs to know.

Trailing at a close second are queries about world record aspirations that went awry. There is no short answer I can give, however.

Given the opportunity to speak to a group for an hour or more, I'm finding it much easier to frame my decision. It centres on my relationship with Dana.

As I speak to another audience, this time in a grade school gymnasium, then a wide-eyed audience in Calgary, I feel that my message of fighting for something bigger than myself is coming across more clearly. The story elicits laughter, sadness and hope. The unconventional ending also plants a seed for further discussion.

Still, that first question looms: "What's next?"

My bank account is drained. My credit card is maxed out too. I owe my parents several thousands of dollars for bailing Mark and me out in South America. None of my dreams have proven to be sustainable.

I decide that 2006 will be a year to focus on my ecotourism studies and create a business plan for all my future endeavours.

But the adventure sabbatical does not last long.

JUNE, 2006

I receive word that rider Kevin Wallace, from Ontario, has his sights set on the Race Across America (RAAM) solo event in June.

Kevin and I originally met down in Austin, Texas, in 2002, at Lance Armstrong's "Ride for the Roses" event. He and his friend Jeff Rushton were gearing up for a charity ride across Canada, called "Coast-to-Coast Against Cancer." Two years later, they raced RAAM as a two-person team. The duo set a blistering record of six days, fourteen hours, seven minutes.

On June 20, Kevin and 19 other solo riders, aided by their support crews, set off from the pier in Oceanside, California, near San Diego. The finish, in Atlantic City, New Jersey, is 4733 kilometres and 14 states away. (Various eastern seaboard cities have hosted the RAAM finish over the years, most recently Annapolis, Maryland.)

A note on the challenge severity from Kevin's website, www.teamrace.com:

> In 1993 *Outside Magazine*, the biggest and most popular magazine on outdoor sports, commissioned a panel of experts to rank the world's toughest events. Using such criteria as the "Mule Factor" – the distances involved; the "Forum" – how tough the course is; the "Anguish Index" – how hard the competitors "have to work to convince themselves that what they're doing is only mildly insane and self-destructive;" and the "O Factor" – a combination of the cost to do the event and the dropout rate. Given these criteria,

as judged by a number of multi-sport athletes and observers, the ranking came out as follows:

1. Race Across America: 676.2 points
2. Vendée Globe Around-the-World Sailing Race: 675.0 points
3. Iditarod Sled Dog Race: 417.5 points
4. U.S. Army's Best Ranger Competition: 402.5 points
5. Raid Gauloises Wilderness Competition: 399.0 points
6. La Traversée Internationale (25-mile swim): 301.4 points
7. Badwater 146-Mile Cross Country Run: 113.4 points
8. Hawaii Ironman Triathlon: 67.2 points

The Race Across America website further boasts that "This Ain't No Tour," referring to the Tour de France, the most widely recognized cycling event in the world. The official website (www.raceacrossamerica.org) explains why:

> RAAM is a race! But unlike the three great European Grand Tours (Tour de France, Vuelta Ciclista a España and Giro d'Italia), RAAM is not a stage race. RAAM is one continuous stage, similar to a time trial. Once the clock starts it does not stop until the finish line. RAAM is about 30 per cent longer than the Tour de France. Moreover, racers must complete the distance in roughly half the time allowed for the Tour.
>
> More importantly, RAAM is not limited to professional cyclists. RAAM is open to professional and amateur athletes alike. While solo racers must

qualify to compete, anyone may organize a team and race.

Racers must traverse 3000 miles across 12 states and climb over 170,000 vertical feet. Team racers have a maximum of nine days and most finish in about seven and a half days. Teams will ride 350 to 500 miles a day, racing non-stop. Solo racers have a maximum of 12 days to complete the race, with the fastest finishing in just over eight days. Solo racers will ride 250 to 350 miles a day, balancing speed and the need for sleep.

I follow the online race coverage with great interest. Riders battle extreme heat in the southwest, sustained Colorado climbs, Oz-like blowing winds and boredom across the central states, the rolling Appalachian mountains and crippling, mind-numbing fatigue, of course.

Perennial favorite Jure Robič, from Slovenia, drops out in Colorado due to a viral infection. While he is still in hospital, Kevin and his well-financed crew finish in a respectable fifth place with a time of ten days, three hours, fifty-seven minutes.

The celebratory moment bridges a gap.

I'm reminded of the evening my father and I happened across coverage of the race, in our motel room on our first tour across Canada in 1996. The blurred line between abstract ideas, big dreams and reality is all of a sudden no more.

I'm drawn in further. In fact, I feel a kinship with the monumental challenge. *I must do it.*

My first and last opportunity to qualify for RAAM 2007 is at the "Bike Sebring 12/24 Hours" event in Sebring, Florida, held in February, just four months before the California start of RAAM. The day of the Sebring qualifier also happens to be the day I turn 24.

The flat Florida terrain and warmer temperatures make Sebring the "easiest" qualifier, so my research tells me.

The race is a time-trial format: just you against the clock. Racers set out from the Sebring International Raceway for a 142.4-kilometre out and back loop in the orange grove countryside. They then circle a shorter, 17.6-kilometre loop continuously until the halfway point in the race.

As soon as the race clock strikes the 12th hour, riders are diverted onto a still shorter, 4.8-kilometre loop around the raceway. This final leg is closed to traffic and lit with glow sticks through the night.

For those athletes hell-bent on qualifying for RAAM, the UltraMarathon Cycling Association (the governing body for international ultra races) stipulates that you must ride *at least* 680 kilometres in that 24-hour period.

If you choose to race RAAM on a team (two-, four- and eight-person options), no qualification is necessary. This is because team riders compete in a relay format, so individually they may only be on the bike for as little as three hours a day (in the case of the eight-person option). In comparison, solo riders rarely get away with sleeping for more than three hours a day. The 12-day cut-off is ever-present.

My interest does not waver.

The farthest I have ever ridden in one day is 300 kilometres, however. It happened when Mark and I got lost from each other in Costa Rica and I stayed the night with the bartender. *So, half of Sebring.*

I proceed with the ignorance of a runner who finishes a half marathon in good spirits, then signs up for a full marathon on the assumption that he or she must merely budget twice the time. *And besides, I'll be, like, the youngest out there.* Forty is the average age for most ultra cyclists.

I'll have more energy and ride faster.

My excitement overtakes my reason.

During the first week of the winter semester at Mount Royal College, I pull out my worn credit card (since buffered with fortuitous scholarship money), sign up for the race, purchase my flight tickets to Orlando, rent a car and a hotel room and purchase the necessary Ultra Cycling membership.

Meanwhile, my parents have begun their transition to retirement from their business and have purchased a piece of property on a lake in British Columbia. They're still young by retirement standards, but they have done well for themselves. "And it's time," they smile. I rarely see them in formal work attire anymore. Jeans, casual polo shirts and a greater sense of peace have come into their lives.

The five-day work week becomes a three-day work week. And then, one day, they officially announce their retirement.

Our Calgary home goes up for sale soon after.

For all the difficult memories, I'm still sad to see the house in transition. But perhaps the challenge is more about seeing my parents spend more time at a second home in British Columbia, my sister going off to college a few hours north and for my last year to be spent alone in a new dorm room.

Adulthood hovers on the horizon.

I get settled into my tiny dorm residence, complete with a single bed, computer desk, small closet to store my canned goods and clothes, shared washroom and a communal kitchen.

I'm situated right across from the college gym.

I can see the indoor running track from my bedroom window – a subtle reminder to train. And when free time presents itself, to train some more.

With only a few months left to build toward the RAAM qualifying race in Florida, I put together a plan of regular three-hour workouts, six times a week. My time at the National Sport School has given me discipline.

I dive right in.

Oatmeal in the morning, class until the afternoon, back to my room to eat a pile of macaroni and tuna, rest for an hour while that settles, then off to the gym for a workout involving one to two hours of cardio, then weights, then back to the room to study, then bed. Meanwhile, my roommates watch from the sidelines as they get high on potent marijuana and regularly skip class.

After a couple of weary transition weeks, my workout routine becomes enjoyable, even addictive. The euphoria carries over into my studies too.

I become obsessed with getting the best grades possible. In my microeconomics correspondence course, for example, I stay up all night retaking the weekly test until I get 100 per cent. And though these tests are only worth a small percentage of our overall grade, I'm actually taken aback that more people do not try to ace every test. *Why wouldn't you aspire toward a perfect score?*

My motivations have clearly changed since high school. I'm no longer concerned with holding up a degree for employers to take notice of. Instead, I consider each class project as a small complement to my Adventure Cycling career, and ultimate reflection of my passion.

In a Web 2.0 class, I improve my website. In a public speaking class, I hone my storytelling technique. In a marketing class, I trim the fat off my business plan. And in Wilderness Survival Skills, I learn how to do more with less.

Friends in the traditional sense slip further out of my life. Chris is one of the few to hold on, though I can see his interest waning. There is also a new girl in the dorm scene that makes an honest effort to build a relationship with me. But I am a self-proclaimed "bad friend."

When I am challenged on the subject, I grow frustrated for having to justify the path that I have chosen. *You need to understand,* my selfish nature is what led to my last breakup.

I'm on a mission.

SEBRING QUALIFIER – FEBRUARY 18, 2007

It begins to rain at 2:00 a.m. The Sebring International Raceway is a lonely, quiet place. Anyone that isn't trying to qualify for RAAM calls it quits.

For the next four and a half hours, it's just me and a handful of guys circling in the dark.

Stopping for a short break, I take the opportunity to stretch and urinate. A few racers pass behind on the track. But I think nothing of it. A thick yellow stream exits below, lit only by starlight.

This is war, a battle of attrition.

Feeling woozy, my tired body rocks forward and back, caught in a drunk-like stupor. Neon yellow sputters down my leg. The lack of control aside, the urine stings on release. *What holy hell is this?* I question, now wide-eyed with new concern.

My ragtag crew of local volunteers (found through the race forum) inquires as to the mysterious ailment. One of the race organizers says it is my body getting rid of excess electrolytes found in the Gatorade I have been drinking on every lap. The Gatorade is complemented by Ensure "nutritional shakes," my primary calorie source.

More than 24 hours in, I continue to pick up new bottles of each mixture out of necessity rather than excitement. Liquid nutrition is the way to go, so I have learned. Fluids are more easily digested than solid food and create less bulk in your stomach. But the lack of variety is taunting my early-morning motivation.

Gazing over at what other crews have to offer their riders, I'm envious of the warm chicken noodle soup and chocolate brownies. A strong rider speeds by me and yells out to his crew, "Gummies on the next lap!"

At 6:30 a.m., the race clock finally stops. Every fibre of my being is drained of energy.

For the few of us that are left, there is no marching band or excited cheers from admiring fans. I thank the two volunteers who helped me, and then ride directly over to the rental car. Back on the track, the race organizers hold a small awards ceremony. But I'm not interested.

Half asleep, I turn the key in the ignition. Pulling out of the raceway parking lot, I notice the sun beginning to rise out the passenger-side window. It is a beautiful Sunday morning in Florida. The warmth nurtures my downtrodden spirits.

Arriving back at the motel, I find myself without a room, since I could not afford the night in between, when I was racing. Speaking with the front desk clerk, I plead, "If there is any way that you can get me into a room now, I would greatly appreciate it." He says that he will do what he can, and that if I want to rest in the car, he will come let me know when the room is ready. Standard check-in time isn't for another five hours.

I hobble back out to the rental and tilt back in the driver's seat. My eyelids immediately grow heavy as I succumb to exhaustion. Unfortunately, the fear that the clerk may rattle on the window at any moment keeps me from giving in to sleep. Instead, I lie there with my mouth open, head tilted to one side, drifting in and out.

Then, black.

I'm caught off guard by a knock on the window. *Did I doze off?* The desk clerk holds up a room key. Looking at my watch, I see that two hours have passed. It feels like I had lain back only moments ago.

I slowly pry the car door open, swing one leg out, then the other. Hunched for a moment on my knees, I take in the sounds of Canada geese swimming in a marsh next door.

I stand up and embrace the fresh air.

My bike rolls along as I steady it with one hand while I carry my suitcase in the other. The black plastic wheels of the suitcase bump and grind along the uneven asphalt. In comparison, my bike glides along with relative ease.

Making my way up the stairs to the top floor, squeezing between a cleaning crew with vacuums and pull carts, I find my room and immediately collapse face down on the bed. The force of gravity has never been so strong.

My eyes begin to close, that sweet surrender. But just before a full blackout, the bedside phone rings. I pick up. "Hello?"

It's my mother. "Happy birthday, son," she says warmly. I pause for a moment, feeling a conflicted sense of pride and disappointment. She asks how the race went.

"I cycled 600 kilometres. I missed qualifying by 50 miles." I don't bother sharing that I placed first in the 20 to 24 age group. The mileage record for that category was also within reach. I unknowingly missed it by a few miles.

It was a humbling moment.

I celebrate my 24th birthday with the understanding that RAAM 2007 is not in the cards. Conversely, I'm proud to have reached a new mileage milestone. Six hundred kilometres is a hell of a long way to ride in one day.

FEBRUARY 20, 2007

I pack up my belongings, grab a couple of meagre-looking continental pastries and begin the drive back north to Orlando.

Having slept through most of my birthday, as well as the following day (a Monday), my energy level has pretty much returned to normal. The race pains linger in other ways, though, mainly through numbness in my hands and feet, tenderness along my undercarriage, a few saddle sores, and dehydrated eyes.

I pull onto the highway.

A few weeks before the RAAM qualifier, I contacted two Rotary Clubs in Orlando to see if they would be interested in having me come out to speak. In addition to the qualifier, I saw my trip as an opportunity to step beyond the speaking safety net I had grown accustomed to in Calgary, where most of my engagements have been through contacts I already know, such as sponsors and school principals. Over a year had passed since returning home from Argentina. It was time to test my story with an audience not already familiar with my previous accomplishments.

The first Rotary Club meeting is at a gorgeous golf course on the southwest edge of the city. Walking into the clubhouse, I feel a little underdressed. A server wearing a pressed uniform walks briskly past. I ask, "Excuse me, where does the Rotary Club meet?" He points me toward an elegant patio, complete with a buffet spread and a lectern on a podium with chairs gathered around it.

Rotary Clubs, so I have learned, are a great way to gain speaking experience. They are a community service organization whose membership consists of local business people that meet once a week. Traditionally, a new speaker is invited to present for 30 minutes at each gathering. It is a way for Rotary Club members to keep abreast of community news and worthwhile initiatives.

Members begin to arrive for lunch. "Are you our speaker today?" one of the gentlemen asks. He has a firm handshake and a confident moustache.

I respond modestly, "Yes."

"Good! You are a cyclist of some sort, we hear." *Of some sort, yes.*

The chapter president gives a brief introduction and then waves me over to the microphone. "Is it alright if I don't stand behind the lectern?" I ask. In my opinion, the lectern-and-podium setup represents a certain formality (or staleness) in presentations. The same can be said of PowerPoint slides: memories of lifeless student lectures will forever haunt my thoughts.

I'm inspired to test new anecdotes.

Instead of starting in on the obvious Pan-American world record attempt and running through a laundry list of the countries and challenges, I begin with a memory of my father and me cycling across Canada. "The cycling chapter of my life began at age 13," I tell them. "My father called it 'Manhood Training.'"

I go with what feels natural. I tell them of cycling as a way to cross-train for hockey, of being bullied in that sport and of all the adventures since. "And what brings you down to Florida?" one of the men asks.

Framing the qualification around my earlier stories, my motives all of a sudden become clear. It is not the adrenaline rush that draws me, nor the "toughest" label. The Race Across America represents a full-circle journey. Yet, one critical piece is missing.

The relationship with my father has remained mostly civil. Our last confrontation happened during my first year of college, the year I dropped out and touted the idea of becoming a professional bike racer. Annoyed, my father told me bluntly to "get real."

Past emotions quickly boiled over. I stormed out of the room, yelling, "I'm not going to live a conventional, boring life!" *If only he could see the world through my eyes.*

LATER THAT AFTERNOON

I check into a plain stucco motel in Orlando, right next to the big theme parks, though I am oddly uninterested in showy attractions. My thoughts are consumed with creating a different experience.

I pick up the phone in my room and dial long distance back to Calgary. My mother answers. "Mom, can you put Dad on the line?" I ask. Having grown accustomed to playing the mediator between us, she is a little surprised that I'm requesting a direct connection. She passes the phone over.

"How's the weather?" he starts in.

"Alright."

"Your mother told me you didn't qualify. I guess RAAM is out of the picture and you can get back to..."

I cut him off short and ask straight out, "Will you be my crew chief?"

"For what?" he asks, puzzled.

"For RAAM in 2008. Dad, we first learned about the race

while cycling across Canada together. It would be a fitting full-circle journey if I kept working toward this goal. And even though we have had our differences, I can't think of a better person to get me and my crew to the finish in Annapolis."

The line goes silent for a moment.

His tone changes to one of all-business, mixed with a hint of excitement. "Okay, I'm in. Now let's look for a *real* qualifier. No more riding around in circles."

I'm 13 years old again.

CHAPTER 17

VALEDICTORIAN

FEBRUARY 25, 2007
Sitting at the short desk in my dorm room, I press the record button on a fixed digital video camera. After clearing
my throat, I start in on a public account of the Bike Sebring
12/24 Hours qualifier and all it was meant to be. "RAAM is
not going to happen this year," I finally admit.

Much has been learned, however. I have a better understanding of pacing, of nutrition and of all the intricate details
that are often overlooked during shorter races. For example,
using risers to elevate my aero bars (aero bars are an aerodynamic forward extension of traditional handlebars, commonly used among triathletes). This subtle shift encourages
me to tuck down in a slightly more upright, comfortable position. Additional positive outcomes from using these extended handlebars include less neck strain, less weight on
my sit bones and hands (reducing numbness and friction)
and less wind resistance (compared to being upright the entire time).

"I have my sights set on another qualifier this summer.
It's called the Race Across Oregon," I continue. The two-day
race makes sense because of its relative proximity to Calgary.
On the flip side, RAO is also considered the most difficult
preliminary event for the Race Across America, covering 856
kilometres and 40,000 feet of exposed climbs through the
Cascade Mountains. In comparison, the ascent up Mount

Everest is 11,560 feet (from basecamp to summit on the South Ridge route).

My father agrees to be the crew chief again, along with Curtis, a recent ecotourism graduate. Curtis is full of energy and always ready to dispense a quick dose of wit. Together, we are the "Three Amigos."

MARCH, 2008

I sign up for an account on a new "social media" platform called Facebook. The interconnected sharing website (including YouTube) plays to the storyteller in me.

Feeling the Hollywood bug bite, I reacquaint myself with Lisa Cichelly, a contact in the film and television industry. She and I had originally met when I was seeking advice on producing my *Longest Road* documentary. Back then, I had imagined a much more elaborate setup, including multiple support vehicles and crew, filming 24/7. *Embarrassing.*

My ask is now twofold.

I'm curious to see if she is interested in optioning my evolving RAAM story, "following father and son on a full-circle journey." She is. I also ask if there are any entry-level positions I can jump into, in between studying and training.

I'm hired on as a part-time production assistant for a reality television show involving misbehaving dogs and their equally misguided owners. Utilizing my limited filmmaking experience, the job entails going to applicants' homes to shoot submission videos and then editing those (resulting in a rough version of the show itself, essentially). The producers then decide which ones make it through. I also help as a production assistant on set, managing craft services (food for the crew) and transcribing interviews.

It's not all glitz and glamour, however.

Right from the get-go, it is apparent that the host of the show has a very strong ego. That pompous confidence is effective on camera but makes him difficult to deal with away from the limelight, at least in my case. He leaves me more than one voice mail saying that my videos are "fucking shit."

I laugh on the receiving end, fuming out loud, "I can't believe this asshole!"

"That's just how the industry is," Lisa subtly defends. *Fine, but I'm not going to put up with it.*

Knowing that I am not an easy fire (because of my option agreement with the company), the host and I instead try to keep our distance.

I'm firing on all cylinders now.

My grades are doing well, and over $8,000 in scholarships have rolled in. I also receive a grant from the Canadian Film and Television Production Association to continue working with Lisa, now as a producer in training, learning how to find funding for projects and assemble all the moving parts.

The cherry on top arrives on Mount Royal College letterhead. It is a note from the school president, informing me that I have been nominated as a candidate for valedictorian by students and staff in my Ecotourism program. Adrenaline hits in the spring sunshine.

Running back to my dorm room, I blast "Speed of Sound" by Coldplay. I'm overjoyed.

APRIL, 2008

The interview process begins with five other candidates sitting in a room together. Each of us gives a brief synopsis of our time at the college, followed by a one-on-one interview in a private room. I'm asked by the selection committee, "Given the opportunity, what would you speak about?"

I look at the panel and smile. "I'm not going to pretend to know what each student, as part of the graduating class, has gone through. Instead of speaking to the journey, I'll home in on that intimidating next step – leaving college, headed out into the unknown."

The head interviewer then asks what my message will be. I pause for a moment to consider. *What is the one thing that I can speak about with conviction?* And I realize that the answer is to be found in my rich cycling history. "I'll speak of a need to turn our passion into purpose," I say proudly.

A week later, I get *the* call.

On June 1, I will address an honoured crowd of a couple thousand students, their friends, parents, siblings, neighbours and a host of celebrated dignitaries as the 2007 Mount Royal College valedictorian.

Full of pent-up energy, I lace up my running shoes.

Two hours later, I find myself standing on the east side of Calgary, huffing with pride, watching the sun set across a golden wheat field. Closing my eyes, I hear the music again.

JUNE 1, 2007

My second home looks much different than what I am accustomed to. The main gym is dressed in formal banners, with row upon row of students in royal-blue graduation gowns, smiling.

My heart pounds. Sitting on the wide black stage with school and provincial dignitaries, I'm anxious for my turn to speak. But first a sea of students must cross the stage to collect their parchment and honorary handshake. The line of thousands dwindles to hundreds, then to just a few.

The air in the auditorium grows quiet as the speaker introduces me as this year's valedictorian.

I stand up and walk a few incredible feet to the podium.

There is no questioning the formality of the occasion. Gripping either side of the sturdy wooden lectern, I look ahead and pick out my ecotourism peers. Not once in the past four years have I seen them dressed so formally. A few smile as I catch their gaze.

Take a deep breath, smile back.

I begin by asking who among the crowd uses Facebook. Hands shoot up and there is a communal chuckle. The site has seen an incredible surge in popularity over the last year, having grown from a private forum for Ivy League university students to a public addiction. I'm playing to our need to share.

I dare not look over at my father for fear of telepathic prosecution. Ever the traditionalist, he places a much higher value on face-to-face connections versus the virtual type. He is sitting next to my sister, mother and aunt on bleachers on the far left side of the room.

I delve deeper by suggesting there is a need to give our respective Facebook statuses a facelift, to give our path meaning. *Shit*, I'm not sure it makes any sense now that I say it out loud. I grip the lectern a little more tightly, in embarrassment. *Forget it, they're all still smiling.*

"I am a firm believer that any challenge can be overcome, should the passion to do so be there," I proclaim. "But passion alone will only get us so far, and this is why many of us arrived here at the college. We had a need to turn our passion into a purpose. Whether you were here for four years, two years or just for today, I would like to believe that we have all found some purpose in our time at Mount Royal."

I talk about cycling to the end of the world.

Arriving home, my speech now nearing its end, I explain that my purpose is the pursuit of a dream. "And not a dream that can be defined in black and white terms, but rather, a feeling inside that speaks to me with a quiet confidence and says, *One day you will change the world.* And so will you."

On that closing, the crowd begins to clap in unison. The school president comes over and shakes my hand.

The 2007 graduating class is instructed to flip their tassels to the right side. "You are now college graduates," the president says joyously. Students stand up in excitement. A few throw their caps up swirling into the air.

My family gathers outside in the warm summer sun for group pictures. Everyone is bubbly and proud. My father takes me aside and says he wasn't a fan of my speech. He gives me that look again, that questioning smirk, telling me to *get real.*

I'm shaken free of his judgment by his sister, my aunt. She tells me how proud she is, and that she is glad to have made the trip east to be a part of this special occasion.

She and my uncle live on the west coast, kid-free, working from home as advertising consultants. They helped develop one of the original BlackBerry smartphone campaigns, I'm told. My mother takes a picture of the two of us with our arms around each other's backs. She is the cool aunt, non-judgmental.

JUNE 26, 2007

My father calls me into the sunroom of our still-unsold Calgary home. I'm living back in my basement "cave" for the summer, preparing for the Race Across Oregon. My mother nods apologetically as I leave the kitchen. *Yeah, it's one of those serious chats.*

We sit down across from each other. Naturally, I have a defiant grin on my face, assuming he is going to lay into one of those "this-is-what-it-is-going-to-be-like-when-the-real-world-hits" speeches. *I'm not 13 years old anymore, Dad.* He instead asks about my recent training.

Yesterday, I rode for a couple of hours into the night around our community. The goal was to become more familiar with racing in the dark. I cycled a four-kilometre loop, stopping occasionally at a stockpile of water bottles at the end of our driveway. At around 1:00 a.m., I decided to call it quits, mainly out of boredom. Having raced the Bike Sebring 12/24 Hours earlier this year, I figure I have a good enough grasp on night riding.

"You're riding around in loops again," my father says. "If you ask me, this kind of training will not prepare you for Oregon."

Knowing I have my finger on the pulse of ultra racing, he asks what other riders are doing for training. "Well, most try to get in a couple hours before work, then a couple after," I respond.

He shakes his head. "No, you have more flexibility. What does that Jure Robič guy do?" My father wants to better understand the mindset of a RAAM legend.

I read through a brief bio of the Slovenian army soldier on www.wikipedia.org:

> Robič has won the Race Across America (RAAM) 3 times: in 2004, 2005, and 2007.
>
> On 19 September 2004, Robič broke the world 24-hour road record by cycling 834.77 km (518.70 mi.). In 2005 he won le Tour Direct (7d 19h 40m), a 4023 km (2,500 mi.) race on a course derived from classic Tour de France routes. Jure won the DOS-Ras Race Across Slovenia four times, the Tour Direct twice and the Tortour in 2010.

Robič is renowned for pushing himself to extreme mental breakdown during endurance races. He has been laboratory tested, and his abilities to produce power and to transport oxygen were found to be parallel those of other top ultra-endurance athletes worldwide. During the 2004 Race Across America, it was reported that he had only eight hours of sleep during his eight-day, 2,958.5-mile (4,761.2 km) ride across the United States.

From 1988 to 1994 Jure was part of the Slovenian Cycling National Team and he was also a National road champion. In his career he won more than 100 races and has been on the podium at least 150 times. He was also a winner of Maraton Franja, Juriš na Vršič.

In addition to sporting achievements Jure Robič was the recipient of the Sportsman of the Year awards for special achievements, Slovenian year for special achievements and awards for fair play and tolerance in sport.

In short, he rides more than everyone else.

My father probes some more: "All barriers aside, what would be the optimal way to train for this particular race?"

I tell him I would drive the Oregon course in advance. Doing so would allow me to better anticipate the challenges, and strategize ahead of time. I would also go on a couple of long tours beforehand to get my body used to the rigours of riding for hours on end, day after day. I don't have the same discipline at home.

"So, why not do that?" he asks outright.

"Truthfully, because I didn't think you would support that

idea." Five years ago we got in a fight over this very situation: me dreaming on the bike versus finding a more substantial career path. It has always been a raw nerve.

I'm caught off guard by what my father, turned crew chief, says next. "I want you to do well, not just finish," he instructs. If it takes driving down to Portland beforehand, then do it. And if you want to get in the miles, why not ride to the cottage (on Shuswap Lake, in British Columbia) and back a couple of times, over 600 kilometres each way. You'll get plenty of hill training climbing up and over the Rockies."

Submitting to this rare moment of agreement, I ask his opinion on when to begin. "Why not leave for Portland right now?" my father responds, straight-faced. *Who is this man?*

In shock, I nod and begin moving toward the garage. "Well, okay, then ... I'll grab my keys." Rounding the kitchen corner, I do a double take to make sure that he isn't pulling my leg. *No? Huh.*

I hug my mother as I exit through the back door. Armed with a set of MapQuest directions and a stack of CDs, I climb into the Tahoe, turn the key in the ignition and pull away. America's most bike-friendly city is a 15-hour drive to the southwest, one way, without stopping. Driving the course will take another nine hours.

I'll do it all without sleeping.

Darkness (and the first yawn) rolls in as I speed through the mountain town of Fernie, British Columbia, and soon into the United States. My sleep-deprived focus is drawn to blurry headlights and thickening veins of interstate traffic. Fighting to keep my attention is part of the training. I lose if I pull over.

Through a midnight blur, the sun rises across oily fast-food wrappers on the dash. I step out of the truck, crunching them into my hand, and stretch into the smoggy city air. Rolling my shoulders and neck, I proceed to the entrance of the Race Across Oregon host hotel.

Surveying the humid lobby, complete with chlorinated indoor pool, I try to imagine what it will look like in less than a month's time when race crews are buzzing around. I ask where the action officially begins. "Oh, *that* group, they usually start out in the back parking lot," a senior manager directs me, with some bias.

Satisfied I have covered off all the relevant points, I hop back into the truck and begin following a series of printed route cues. They direct me out of the city, speeding over twisty mountain roads toward scorching eastern plains. The route doubles back and finishes at the Timberline Lodge, atop Mount Hood. The lodge is famous for those exterior shots in the movie *The Shining*.

It takes me ten hours to get there, including two stops for gas.

In sight of the infamous lodge, I stumble out of the truck and stretch once again, this time into fresh mountain air at dusk. The engine hood is hot to the touch.

Staring wide-eyed across the rolling forested lowlands, I call my father to humbly acknowledge out loud, "You are not going to believe that a person can ride this distance in such a short period of time and over so many arduous climbs. But we have to."

RACE ACROSS OREGON – JULY 20, 2007
Race director George Thomas tells the crowd of riders and their support crews what to expect over the next two days.

Scanning the hotel lobby, I see over a dozen pods of people in matching T-shirts, looking on confidently. My father and Curtis both smile, oblivious to the intimidation factor.

At the end of the mandatory briefing, my father asks George if he can demonstrate the suggested water bottle handoff – there was a particular method that was referred to in his talk. With riders speeding by, it's important to consider the physics (coming up fast to a crewperson who is stationary) so as not to break an arm or drop a bottle. I appreciate my father's willingness to learn from the best, but I also cringe at the rookie nature of the question. The people in the matching T-shirts have likely dialed in this procedure already.

We are the last to leave the lobby, and we head to bed soon after. Curtis and I share a room; my father is in another. We collectively set our bedside alarms for 3:30 a.m. and double up with a wakeup call.

Getting under the crisp white sheets, I take one last look at my hardware. Bow Cycle has generously sponsored two Kona road bikes. One of them, my climbing steed (for how it is geared), is a curious shade of pink. The guys at the shop tried to pass it off as another colour. "No, that's pink," I laugh. *But real men wear pink.*

My eyes close.

RACE ACROSS OREGON – JULY 21, 2007

Anxious alarms begin screaming four hours later. I nearly fall out of bed trying to smack them into submission.

I make my way into the bathroom and pour boiling water (from the cheap in-room coffee pot) into a plastic container filled with plain oatmeal. Curtis films me chowing down on the slop. It tastes like wallpaper paste and very well could be.

My father knocks on the door, "Are you guys ready?"

Curtis and I carry the two bikes, each of them cleaned, lubed and fixed with numbered race plates. My father handles our cooler. Together, we make our way out to the quiet hotel lobby. Into the crisp, early-morning air, only my rear wheels make a sound, softly ticking around.

Other crews huddle around their riders in the darkness. They stand beside idling vans filled with food, varieties of tools and mounted spare bikes – none much better off than the next. Altogether, there are 11 "solos" and 30 team participants. Only one other rider is close to me in age.

At 5:30 a.m. we head off together as a pack in what George Thomas has termed a "neutral start." He leads us along a bike path to the quieter outskirts of town. Meanwhile, our support crews drive along an alternate route.

Having scouted this section in advance, I'm well aware of where the first attack will likely happen. We make a right-hand turn – also the end of the "neutral start" – that morphs into a short but painful climb along a residential street. Five of us shoot off the front immediately, our lungs primed to burst.

We race along quiet roads to an opening at Highway 26, where our support crews are waiting. Picking out my comrades, I shoot them a determined grin. They clap and cheer as we fly by. Neither of them has seen a bike race before.

The first-placed crews anxiously jump back in their vehicles and pull onto the highway behind us. The next stretch entails a 59-kilometre climb up to Mount Hood. The route actually passes by the turnoff for Timberline Lodge before looping back at the end of 856 kilometres. But that hopeful thought is a world away.

Curtis and my father speed ahead to the first bottle exchange near the top of the climb. (Early in the race, there are designated stops to avoid causing congestion.) Gatorade and

Ensure are once again my go-to nutrition. A more suitable alternative has yet to make itself known to me.

Up ahead, I see my father starting to run on the highway shoulder, trying to match my speed as best he can with a bottle outstretched behind like a baton pass. I reach to grab it but miss. *Shit.*

Farther down the road, Curtis begins to run, also with a bottle in hand. I stop pedalling to focus more on the grab. *Success.*

Spraying sugary electrolyte drink into my mouth, I smile at the thought that they came up with the idea to double up without any instruction from George. That fact alone reassures me that they are resourceful as a pair and can handle the host of new tasks that are fast approaching, such as managing any gear breakdowns and navigating the route once the pack thins out. I can settle in and focus on riding.

Driving up beside me, my father acknowledges that I am in third or fourth place, and riding strong up the climbs on "Pepto" (the pink climbing bike). He doesn't mock the colour anymore. "You're doing well!" he instead calls out. And I realize that I'm energized by the encouragement, just like the thumbs-up hockey days.

At the mountain summit, I pull over to quickly pee. As I anxiously watch from the corner of my eye, a few riders seize the opportunity to pass me. Shaking with adrenaline, I piss on myself by accident.

Back on the bike, I begin a long descent down Mount Hood to the town of Dufur, where green farmlands quickly dry into an arid basin at the intersection of Highway 197. The temperature grows hot very quickly. And, it seems, the honeymoon phase is over.

The midday sun hits me hard. My body is in revolt from drinking all the Gatorade (sipping some every 15 minutes).

With each swallow, I can feel the sugar granules tearing into my gums, like a sour candy licked too many times. "Maybe just water for bit," I say to Curtis through the open window of the truck.

He and my father have gotten into the habit of driving beside me when it is safe to do so. They offer words of encouragement, handing off bottles to me, as well as energy bars and bananas. And they tell dirty jokes. On this last point, Curtis holds the titles of king, president and CEO. The pair also provide regular updates on my pace and progress, as reported by intermittent checkpoint call-ins.

In order to qualify for RAAM, I must finish within 15 per cent of the winner's time. Once that person is out of sight, it becomes a guessing game as to how close we are to them. Racers are not tracked by GPS, and cellphone coverage is almost non-existent. George Thomas and the race volunteers repeat one strategy to combat the unknown: "Stay on the bike."

Catching just a glimpse of a follow vehicle rounding a blind valley corner is all the motivation I need. The competition becomes even more apparent as the sun begins to set. As I gaze up a lengthy switchback climb, four-way flashers abound. Classic rock also faintly echoes down toward me from externally mounted speakers. *I'm coming for you,* my gaze calls out.

My eyelids grow heavier with each passing hour. Curtis and my father are exhausted too. "Why don't we pull over and close our eyes for 15 minutes?" I suggest through the truck's open window.

We congregate at the next pullout, collapsing into the leather seats of my parents' new Jeep Grand Cherokee. My head flops back into the comfort of the passenger seat, still upright. The deepest of sleeps is not far behind.

Ten minutes pass.

A tap on the driver's side window startles me. It is a race official. "You need to get him back on the bike," the older gentleman encourages. I see that my father has stayed awake the entire time. He acknowledges the volunteer and thanks him for keeping our best interests in mind. Like the old farmer in Saskatchewan, and his son who eventually did come and work in the big city, I'm again reminded of my father's respect for people.

Not wanting to disappoint him, I turn on my iPod and push off in range of the Jeep's high beams. After 20 sluggish minutes, I finally settle back into a rhythm. *Don't think about the saddle sores, keep your eyes open. Don't think about the saddle sores, keep your eyes open. Don't think.*

The hilly Oregon shadows taunt from the sidelines.

We pass the 24-hour mark and start in on the dawn of a new day. At this point in the Sebring qualifier, I was packing my bike and heading back to the motel. Out here, however, there is still another 380 kilometres to go. Rounding a bend at the far end of the course, I take note of the snowcapped mountain finish on the western horizon. *It's only getting closer.*

The basin temperature remains excruciatingly hot.

We happen across a lone competitor struggling up a climb, just past the Warm Springs River. He is lost from his crew (they missed a turn after stopping to buy ice) and humbly asks if we can spare some water. Not thinking twice about it, Curtis and my father stay behind to help while I continue up the road.

I'm sweating buckets and cramping by the time the next bottle is exchanged. Receiving the handoff from my father, I have no choice but to stomach more warm Gatorade and

Ensure. My bowels churn something foul, though, and I burp up stomach acid. I am hunched over my bike in search of sympathy, but my father offers a dose of tough love instead: "This is what you wanted." There is no pity party to be had.

By late afternoon, I finally reach the long, 55-kilometre climb back up to Mount Hood. Peering up the winding mountain road with trepidatious prayers, I understand that my RAAM qualification hangs in an uncertain balance. So, *Whatever you have left.*

The dry basin is lost behind a wall of coniferous trees growing thicker. I hold a steady tempo for 20 minutes, long enough for the ailing rider behind to fall away. Once out of view, I put in a couple of powered insurance efforts. "Out of sight, out of mind," my ecotourism instructors taught. I'm hoping to break his will, and in effect kill his need to pursue.

Now, where are the others?

It has been over half a day since the three race leaders slowly slipped away. They may have already finished – without cell coverage, it is impossible to know for sure. My father and Curtis appear concerned. *Tick, tock.*

My body cries out to stop, or at least to slow a little. Instead, Curtis runs up beside me and calmly asks me to pick up my pace. "How close is it?" I yell back. He falls back without saying anything else. He doesn't know.

Fuck! Not again.

So much has been invested in this qualifier. Money aside, I think back to the countless training hours at Mount Royal College, the failed attempt in Florida, scouting out the Oregon route in advance, and of course the three 1200-kilometre round-trip Shuswap training rides that followed.

Darkness sets in on the unrelenting mountain.

Through fatigue and near delirium, that infamous Timberline Lodge turnoff finally arrives. Ten kilometres and a soul-sucking 6–10 per cent grade are all that remain.

"Please," I say out loud. *Let it be.*

Halfway up the climb, the uncommon sight of a white officiating sedan drives past. Blaring on the horn and waving a cowbell out the window, the husband and wife team yell out, "You can do it!"

With what little of my raspy voice remains, I cry out helplessly, "Am I on track to qualify??"

"You sure are!" they excitedly reply back. And in a heartbeat, I feel a tremendous weight lifted.

I stop to drink from one of my bottles. Hunched over the front end of the bike, my breathing grows heavy. I sink even deeper, my legs spread out wide for support. Behind me, the sound of the Jeep's four-way flashers cradles my eyes closed.

In a daze, I begin to tip over. Curtis and my father rush to my side, each holding onto an arm. "You're so close. Just another couple of miles," my father says softly.

I mumble incoherently, "Are you surrr iss mils?"

Come on, they pull me up.

Finding my balance, I push off one last time.

Around a mountain corner, a finish banner and a dimly lit crowd of cheering volunteers come into view. I coast across the lodge parking lot with prideful tears, immediately falling limp at the sight of the race clock, finally stopped, showing 41 hours and 31 minutes.

"Incredible, just incredible," my father says aloud.

Eleven months and counting until "the Toughest Race in the World."

CHAPTER 18

STAY ON THE BIKE

SEPTEMBER, 2007

A potential title sponsor for my bid for the Race Across America sits directly across from my new agent and me. The Calgary business executive spends most of the time during our expensive downtown lunch face down in his BlackBerry, occasionally nodding. This shorthand is the norm now and is not considered rude.

Similar meetings have been fruitful for a pair of Olympic athletes my agent also manages. Admittedly, however, this is his agency's first foray into the "Adventurer" realm.

My lunch companions pick at their heavy pasta meals, while I prod at my abdomen under the table, slowly chewing on a crisp garden salad. My hockey player frame has continued to drop weight since the Race Across Oregon: those two days of epic climbing in the heat have squeezed me dry. And though I'm slim by most standards, I'm intrigued by the more vascular ideal. I have entered into the endurance psyche of shaving weight and maintaining a lean figure.

My agent gives me a soft poke. *Focus.*

Sensing my turn to shine, I begin in on the father–son connection behind RAAM. I speak enthusiastically about cycling across Canada as a teenager and of learning a respect for the open road through "Manhood Training." The man nods blankly again, his finger scrolling through a new e-mail.

I bite my lip. *Remember, you need this.*

My agent jumps in to make *the ask*. "We're looking for a title sponsor that will go all in ... $30,000." Before the meeting, my agent explained to me that the $5,000 buffer (my budget is only $25,000) will help to support lead-up training costs. He encourages me to see this as a career, not a one-off race. I respect that.

Much to my surprise, the executive tentatively agrees to the proposition. We shake hands.

Outside the restaurant, my agent and I enthusiastically slap each other on the back. The encouraging prospect is a huge weight off my shoulders, a celebration worth sharing.

I call up my father and describe the luncheon. His tone is decidedly more reserved. "Just be cautious. I dealt with these types of guys for over 20 years in the financial industry. Many of them talk a big game but don't last long. Don't count your chips until the cheque is cashed, okay?"

My optimistic RAAM preparations continue moving forward.

Thinking back to only one year ago, it scares me to acknowledge how different my race support would have been had I qualified at the Bike Sebring 12/24 Hours race. Visions of a weary three-person crew in a crammed minivan, and outrageous debt, come to mind.

It is generally understood that a bare-bones budget for RAAM falls in the $15,000 range. The main costs are an RV rental (which functions as a roaming headquarters), a follow vehicle, flights, gas and food for the rider and support crew. Of course, this assumes you already have everything you need for your bike(s), such as a vehicle rack, spare parts, clothing and expensive tools.

Sufficient financial backing is a key difference between simply surviving for 12 days (or less), and setting yourself up for success. It allows for a better crew rotation, quality food on board, efficient sleep breaks and a backup equipment reserve, among other perks. No bonus points are awarded for a minimalist approach.

OCTOBER, 2007

My friend Bruce Kirkby has been busy working with CBC Television as host of their new reality show called *No Opportunity Wasted*. Each episode showcases three contestants who take on unique challenges to help overcome a particular fear and ultimately realize a lifelong dream. The show is a Canadian adaptation of a United States-originated concept produced by Phil Keoghan of *The Amazing Race* fame.

Aside from a welcome dose of positive Canadian reality television, I'm excited about the doors this will open for Bruce. But of course, he remains humble.

At our next face-to-face meeting, rather than gloat, he instead tells me about a young guy in an upcoming episode: "Another cyclist, like you." His name is Jay. The 32-year-old downhill mountain biker was paralyzed four years ago from the waist down after a horrendous crash at Panorama Mountain Resort. Wheelchair-bound, Jay still lives for the thrill. The show recently helped him to experience the beauty of assisted ocean surfing.

Bruce also mentions that Jay is trying to raise money for a wheelchair that uses functional electrical stimulation (FES). The $18,000 piece of equipment will further his rehab and better position him for stem cell treatment. "You two should hook up!" Bruce encourages.

Of course, I'm intrigued to learn more. But I have also grown increasingly disillusioned with organized charity.

The uphill battle began with finding a charitable endorsement for "Ride for Life" in 2002. You would think the bureaucratic leash would loosen its noose after raising over $30,000 – not to mention public awareness – for various causes since then, but no. My ideas are still met with criticism and stonewalling. Nevertheless, I cannot deny that my heart still yearns to be a part of something bigger than myself. *Perhaps there is another way?*

I schedule a meeting with Jay at his apartment in Calgary.

Like the first time I met Dana and his cancer, I'm thrust back into a crash course in humility as Jay rolls out of the lobby elevator with his emaciated legs, the left one dangling. His scarred hand extends out to mine, "It's great to meet you, man! Bruce filled me in on your adventures."

Jay's girlfriend is quick to welcome us inside their apartment. She tours me around the small IKEA living room, highlighting daily tasks she helps with, including physiotherapy. Jay is classified a quadriplegic, but he still has some movement in his arms. He also has some sensation in his legs, which I find fascinating. "It feels like when you fall asleep on your arm," he educates. The therapy helps to stimulate those confused nerves.

After a quiet moment at the dinner table, the couple surprises me with the goal to see Jay walk again. When I ask how I can help, I'm further educated on the FES wheelchair. It would put Jay's weight partially back on his legs, while holding him upright and providing electro muscle stimulation. I had never seen anything like it. And of course, it is very expensive.

My Race Across America bid can be used as a lightning rod to raise funds for the new wheelchair. Bruce and the soon-to-be-aired *No Opportunity Wasted* episode will also add credibility. And perhaps I can again find inspiration in the grand ambitions of a fellow cyclist.

"Count me in," I tell them.

NOVEMBER, 2007

Since graduating from college, I have been living in a cramped basement rental in Calgary. The owner of the home is an elderly Greek lady with a thick accent. She charges me less rent in return for cutting grass and weeding around the property. Fresh baking and lemonade are a nice bonus.

My otherwise solo routine involves walking to work at the film and television production company around 6:00 a.m., receiving my tutelage there from 7:00 a.m. to 4:00 p.m., running home, eating a hearty dinner of pasta and tuna (a cheap craving I developed during my dorm-living days), then hitting the gym at Mount Royal College for two hours. There is very little time for a social life.

My best friend Chris and I meet only sporadically.

Much has changed since the days when he and I lived together in downtown Calgary, working the same restaurant job at Jack Astor's. Chris is now a University of Calgary graduate, moving up the ranks in the geomatics profession. He also has his own apartment and a girlfriend too. He is busy in his own right.

Nevertheless, I ask him if he would like to be a part of my eight-person support crew for RAAM. The ignorant side of me assumes he has the same flexibility as me and the same desire to help. This turns out not to be the case, as he explains in a poignant e-mail: "The only time we do anything anymore is when it revolves around one of your projects," he unleashes.

On reading that final line, I'm struck with a new kind of heartbreak. Chris has been a brother to me since junior high. We have shared aspirations, drunken laughs and copious campfire dreams. Yet, somewhere along the line, I forgot to repay his courtesy. *How could I have let it get to this point?*

I immediately reply back: "You're absolutely right ... I'm sorry!" But I have exhausted our friendship, my last one remaining.

Chris does not respond.

LATE FEBRUARY, 2008

I take stock of all my gear through the Tahoe rear-view mirror. There is my bike and a sleeping bag, plus four plastic shelving containers full of clothing, tools, spare parts and nothing else. The trunk is loaded with everything I need to begin focused, warm-weather training.

Turning forward in the driver's seat, I feel my eyes grow heavy with the fading sunset. *Next stop, California.*

Signalling a right at the state line, I pull over at a rest area and flop down in the back. With my legs propped up on the back seat, I listen to the soothing sound of a semi-trailer truck idling nearby. Reminiscing, I think back to that last important conversation with my father: "All barriers aside, what is the best way to train for RAAM?" he had asked.

Building on the success of our Oregon game plan, I'd responded: "I should head down to Arizona and spend a month training in the heat. Before that, it would make sense to pre-ride the first leg of the course, from Oceanside, California, to Flagstaff, Arizona. We should try to minimize any surprises during those first two days of racing," I strategized.

Of course, these plans are put into motion under the pretense that a title sponsor agreement is nearly inked. "The timing is a little tight, don't you think?" I say to my agent, growing concerned about the cavalier luncheon we had with the BlackBerry-obsessed Calgary businessman, and the questionable validity of an executive handshake. RAAM begins in just under three months.

My agent once again assures me and tells me not to worry. "The markets are in a bit of a rough patch right now. He'll get back to us soon enough. We've done a couple of deals together," he encourages. So, *continue as planned.*

Before passing through San Francisco, I take a side trip to the prestigious university campus at Berkeley. The thought of pursuing a master's degree has crossed my mind. I could, potentially, develop an expertise in environmental planning. My cycling knowledge would be a great asset in the global shift toward bike-friendly city planning. *Perhaps.*

I continue around the "City by the Bay," my old friend.

Driving another seven hours straight through the night, I finally pull up at a beachfront parking lot in the laid-back surroundings of Oceanside. My eyes close as early-morning surfers begin to walk by. *I'm really here. This is it.*

MARCH 4, 2008
Waking in the stuffy back-seat heat, I step out of the truck and walk down to the end of the infamous wooden pier (of RAAM starting line lore). Within a few strides, I feel a rush of blood return to my legs. My other senses are imprinted with a glow of sea breeze and deep-fried boardwalk fare wafting by.

There's no better time than now.

I tape a series of printed race directional cues to the handlebars of my orange Kona road bike (the all-purpose steed).

Not long after, I push off along a vacant bike path paralleled by dry soccer fields and residential streets, heading east out of town. This is the "parade start," not the official start. I continue on to an abandoned bridge where the race actually begins.

Stopped at a ceremonial crack in the pavement, I pause to commit to memory the sounds of highway traffic and the sight of clear blue sky, the dry hillside on the horizon and scattered broken glass. *Now, imagine that the race has begun.*

Continuing on, the route begins climbing away from the coast.

Labouring up the first sustained switchback, questions begin swirling in my mind about how fast the leaders will ride this early section, and where exactly our support vehicles can stop. (Stops are limited until after the first 72 kilometres, headed up Palomar Mountain.) Also, *how many water bottles should I carry? Which bike should I use? And should I shave my head for better airflow?*

Satisfied that I have seen all I can in one day, I start back down toward the coast in view of a warm California sunset.

With two hours of backtracking still ahead, I'm keenly aware of three factors starting to work against me: the early setting sun, shining right in my eyes, the darkness that follows and a lack of paved shoulder to buffer me from rural traffic. My father always warned me against riding at this time of day.

Dumb, Ryan. You know better.

Nearing the outskirts of Oceanside, the road flattens and the speed limit drops to 50 mph. The low-lying sun is nearly blinding now, and made even more troubling by panicked traffic coming up from behind. It takes just one poignant honk for me to recognize the full severity of the situation.

I grip onto the cork handlebar wrap a little more tightly.

And then it hits.

Instantaneous black.

I feel warm asphalt along the right side of my body.

Opening my eyes, the horizon spins out of control. It feels like someone cracked me over the head with a baseball bat, and then another swipe to my spine, paralyzing me from the neck down. Maybe someone did. *Am I lying down?*

Looking back, I nearly witness the end of things as two cars screech around my motionless body, just barely missing my fragile melon head. I instantly recognize the dire need to move, but I can't

One car stops. Then a couple more.

I faintly comprehend that people are running toward me. Someone grabs my arm and pulls me to the side of the road. I still can't get up on my own. *Was I just hit by a car?*

As the spinning horizon slowly rights itself, a fire truck and two police cruisers pull up. Someone in uniform begins asking me questions, but I can't focus.

I faintly notice the debris of a car mirror on the road, my bike still lying in the middle of it. Blood drips from my right elbow, as well as from my kneecaps, my brow and from my lacerated knuckles. The fiery sensation of pain and stiffness soon follows.

I was hit. It happened so quickly.

Someone asks if I need an ambulance. *Probably.* But for fear of an exorbitant hospital fee (I'm unsure of what travel insurance covers), and worry that I am already making enough of a scene, I instead choose to focus on the second victim. "Is my bike okay?" I ask, slightly panicked.

The first witness on the scene chimes in, still looking concerned: "Aside from some cosmetic damage, yes, I think so … Are you sure you don't want an ambulance, though?" *Nah.*

An elderly couple stands timidly to the side, listening.

Someone had had to flag them down and they were the last to arrive on the scene. They hadn't yet noticed the missing passenger-side mirror on their car.

In a quiet moment between questions, they step in closer to offer an apology, their hands softly trembling with guilt. Looking up to see a well of concern in their pale, wrinkled faces, I again shrug off any need for more attention. It was clearly an accident. *And yes, I'll share some of the blame.*

A policeman helps me to my feet. "Had it been an illegal," (a Mexican immigrant) "they probably would have backed up and finished the job. You're extremely lucky," he says, rather ominously.

After learning I am Canadian and only passing through, one of the witnesses offers to drive me back to Oceanside to find a hotel for the night. "First, would you mind taking a picture?" I ask. *This is definitely going on Facebook.* And perhaps I should also document the scene for legal reasons, though I'm not entirely sure what those reasons could be. *Do I need this for insurance? And will insurance even cover any of the damage to my bike? What about going to the hospital?*

I hobble over to the tiny sedan belonging to the lady who offered to drive me to a hotel. *Careful not to get blood on her seats.*

Looking back at the scene as we pull away, it all starts to make sense. I realize that the broken mirror must have hooked my left arm and quickly flipped me over the car. I must have also rolled across the pavement a short distance. The large scrape on my hip, which looks like raw meat through my torn shorts, is proof of that.

PHOENIX TRAINING – LATE MARCH, 2008

Hunched over my aero bars with feet firmly planted on the ground, I take a moment to appreciate the Arizona desert landscape. There is no traffic on this calm, isolated stretch of highway.

Closing my eyes and listening to the soft wind, I gently rub a nagging elbow wound. A scab has formed where I must have first hit the pavement in the accident back at Oceanside. The pain has lasted longer than I thought it would. *Probably a hairline fracture.*

I could have pushed for more money.

Two weeks after I arrived in Phoenix, an insurance company called me up out of the blue to offer an injury settlement. I had no plans to follow up – the elderly couple didn't mean to hit me. And, of course, I take responsibility for the fact that I was riding at dusk. But since the insurance company is so eager to settle, I decide to help them out where I can.

I provide a list of all the bike components I will need to replace, and also make sure to clearly state that "this is my job, not just a paid vacation." My agent would be proud.

A cheque for US$3,500 promptly arrives in the mail. The influx of cash provides a welcome answer to how I will cover my expenses in the short term. The potential title sponsorship remains in an uncommunicative holding pattern.

The plan is to train in Arizona for a month and a half. Kelly's mom has arranged for me to stay in the pool house of a local open-arms Christian family. I'm thankful again for her willingness to help me at every turn.

After being dropped off at the home of my new adopted family, I only see Debbie and Kelly a few more times. We get together for lunch on one occasion, where I'm introduced to the new boyfriend: a tall, athletic Greek guy working toward becoming a police officer. I'm happy for Kelly.

Sensing that I am more alone, the patriarch at my new home invites me to share in family dinners. The transition into their fold feels very natural.

I leave them in the cool mornings, headed for another 160 kilometres on the bike, followed by one to two hours at the gym and a chocolate milk grocery stop on the way home. This becomes a regular routine.

Eat, ride, press, stretch, sleep, repeat.

I work away on my laptop computer in what downtime remains. There are still many RAAM logistics to coordinate, including vehicle rentals, hotel rooms at the start line, how to transport all of our gear to Oceanside, sponsor promos, fundraising for Jay's FES wheelchair and finding a less sugary alternative to my flawed race nutrition.

On a whim, I click through to one of the race sponsor links. It's for a company called Hammer Nutrition. The Montana-based business is offering 50 per cent off their extensive fuelling line to all solo racers. It's a tough deal to pass up, considering how much I expect to consume over 12 days. The race endorsement also carries some weight.

I go for broke and order $2,000 worth. What remains of the insurance settlement evaporates with a "Checkout" click.

Keep the faith.

A few days before packing up to head home, I get a call from my agent with that long-awaited sponsorship update. "Okay, there is some good news: the markets have been through a rough patch, as we know. He can still give you $5,000."

Fuck off!

On principle, I flat out decline. "He strung us along! I committed to this race long ago under the false hope of $30,000. This is just a drop in the bucket. I can't do it," I reply in frustration.

My agent tries to convince me that any amount of support is positive and that I should never turn down money. I wholeheartedly disagree. *This is exactly how my father thought it would play out. Fuck.*

I call him.

He responds to the news in an authoritative tone. "Your mother and I will cover your race expenses. You can use our motorhome and Jeep for support vehicles. And if you ask your sister nicely, she may also let you use her Jetta. We are going to help, but I want you to know something: this time, you are going to pay us back. Do you understand?"

I agree with disheartened emotion. *The work of my agent and the title sponsorship was supposed to be a sure thing. It was going to validate everything.*

My father tells me to pull it together. "Forget them. We need to focus on the real objective now."

CHAPTER 19

JURE GIVES ME THE LOOK

MAY 14, 2008

An incredible desert valley landscape comes into view. I stop to catch my breath and gaze on for miles in every direction. Only a small stretch of pavement separates the road from the frontier below. Overhead, a lone eagle circles in the blinding sun...

I waved goodbye to my adopted Arizona family yesterday evening. Pushing through the night along Interstate 15, I fought the need to sleep in order to reach *this* northern isolation by first light. It's now 2:30 a.m.

Parked in the pale moonlight on a high ridge, I gaze out over the familiar red rock desert valley near the north rim of the Grand Canyon. In the distance is the quiet outpost and Colorado River crossing of Lee's Ferry. The air is absolutely still.

It has been six years since I first camped out here on my inaugural solo tour to surprise Kelly in Phoenix, and six years since I decided to turn a passion for cycling into my purpose in life. *This place has meaning.*

Reflecting on this, with my feet kicked up on the dashboard, my eyes grow heavy with one last comforting thought: after two focused months down south, I'm confident I have done all I can to prepare for RAAM. Mind you, a level of uncertainty will always exist as to what is the best training regime for "the toughest sporting event in the world."

One strategy is to ride as many kilometres as possible in a training day. Conversely, there are those who never ride more than 160 kilometres each training day – a proven strategy used by Jonathan Boyer, a former Tour de France rider who raced and won RAAM in 1985, then again in 2006. Quality over quantity has been my approach also.

The next morning, I continue up through barren northern Arizona, on to Utah and northward to my parents' home in British Columbia. Counting the kilometres as they tick by, I hum along to a selection of worn Coldplay CDs while chowing down on a calorie-dense care package of fruit, nuts, crackers, juice, beef jerky and a small assortment of candy: one last gift from Debbie.

I have a big, lean smile on my face.

Crossing over a nameless mountain border town into Canada, I nearly lose myself on a GPS detour along an abandoned logging road. It's my first time using this prospective RAAM technology. I'm testing it out on my laptop, propped up in the passenger seat beside me. Watching my tires spin out at the crest of what now looks like an old ATV hunting trail (complete with encroaching trees and worn, muddy tracks), I learn a quick lesson in trusting my better instincts over new technology.

Drawn to the random adventure, though, I naively and swiftly push on through the muck.

As I slip into one of my father's oversized business suits, he helps me adjust the tie, also borrowed from him. Reflected in the mirror, he gives me a look that is warm but stern. *You cut it a little close. Now remember, this is her day.*

Standing behind rows of family and friends seated outside the quaint Quaaout Lodge, I begin filming my sister and brother-in-law-to-be as they exchange wedding vows up front. Vibrant green grass, tall coniferous trees and a calm Little Shuswap Lake serve as the picturesque backdrop.

I have only chatted with Leland, her fiancé, once or twice before. He met my sister at the Augustana campus of the University of Alberta, in Camrose, Alberta, during a time when my sister and I were separated by studies and I was busy racing from Alaska to Argentina, training for RAAM or just "too busy" to make plans. Naturally, I feel a little awkward knowing that this relative stranger is soon going to be part of our family.

Leland has just taken on a physical education teaching position in smalltown central Alberta. He is tall, skinny and active in all the sports where lanky guys have an advantage. Mind you, he's extremely lucky to still be able to share his love of sport.

Last year, my sister broke the news that Leland (known to me at the time only as "the boyfriend") had been in a bad accident. His ATV rolled over while he was driving up a steep embankment, falling backwards and crushing his head on impact. Thankfully, a few joyriding family members were on hand to rush him to the nearest hospital.

We would later learn he would need to have his skull reconstructed and plastic surgery to help make sense of his face again.

Trying to make light of the situation, I jokingly referred

to him at one point as the "Six Million Dollar Man," from that 1970s TV show. "We can rebuild him, faster, stronger..."

My sister instantly broke down in tears when I said this. It was at that moment that I realized she was in love.

As I watch the two of them up at the altar now, Leland is the one in tears. With painful scars on his face, he reads aloud: "For better or for worse."

He seems like a good man.

MAY 30, 2008

I'm in a tuck position, full aero, speeding along at 40 km/h on a quiet lakeside road.

My parents coast beside me on their two-person moped, smiling ear to ear. The last time my father was this close to me on a bike, I was 15 years old and we were headlong into a 2400-kilometre ride from Fort Lauderdale, Florida, to Grimsby, Ontario – our third big tour together, following one from Charlottetown, Prince Edward Island, to Grimsby, and "Manhood Training" across Canada before that.

I'm testing out a new Kona time-trial bike, recently sponsored by Bow Cycle in Calgary, using "deep dish" wheels, with greater surface depth than traditional rims (for aerodynamics) and a more aggressive approach. The hunched "time-trial position" is much different than what I am accustomed to.

After just 45 minutes, I take note of an uncomfortable strain in my shoulders and neck. The elusive "Shermer's Neck" injury is a concern. The problem was first reported in the 1983 RAAM, when racer Michael Shermer was forced to drop out after nearly 3200 kilometres because of a "quick meltdown" that occurred when his neck muscles suddenly weakened and were no longer able to support his head. Neck braces have since become a necessary tool to have on hand during the race, should the hellish ailment arise.

This position is too aggressive. But the streamlined ensemble looks intimidating, so I'll keep it. If I learned anything from my recently retired cycling hero Lance Armstrong, it's that in the business of sport, a strong performance is complemented by an equally threatening image.

The media spotlight that RAAM briefly shines is not lost on me, either, especially since I will be the youngest competitor, at 25 years of age. The average age is 41. Online chatter has begun hyping the underdog, the unknown young variable: "The kid who has cycled great distances."

Delving deeper into the mixed bag of ultra-marathon online forums (fuelled further by a few too many miles spent riding alone), I learn that an endurance mental edge generally hardens with age. Granted, a loss of top-end speed is expected as slow-twitch muscle fibres take over. The latter can be used to my advantage, however.

But does speed really matter?

One of the race veterans has actually projected his finish time, estimated to the minute. Hearing the guy boast out loud with such certainty, I have to wonder how his mental edge (and that of his crew) differs from mine. He sees all the variables in play.

Pulling away from a branching paranoia, I turn back to look at my mother's beaming smile on the moped. It has become apparent that RAAM is more than a full-circle journey for my father and me. It is an essential break from routine and an infusion of life for us all.

It is a family affair.

In addition to my parents, there are my aunt Jillian (my mother's sister); her boyfriend, Bob; Leland; Curtis of course; and feisty Megan, a recent sports therapy graduate from Mount Royal College. I will depend on Megan and my sister (a nurse in training) to help keep on top of mounting muscle aches. There are also serious health threats to consider. *Knock on wood.*

The crew assembles at my parents' cottage that evening.

With everyone all smiles and laughing like new friends, it is difficult for me not to jump right into leading our focused team-training weekend. But it's not my place. Instead I say to my father, the crew chief, aside, "They need to understand how difficult this is going to be."

Unpaid hours, summer heat, questionable fast-food choices, sleep deprivation and mounting personality tics are never a good combination. Successful crews must set aside all these issues for the sake of their rider.

As for maintaining those strained relationships after the race, so far I'm batting 0 for 2 with Adam and Mark. This track record has me particularly concerned for my aunt and her boyfriend, both in their sixties.

Over a homemade team dinner in view of the quiet Shuswap Lake, I pick up on a mounting tension between Aunt Jillian and Bob, beginning with subtle sarcastic pokes, often laughed off. It is disheartening to think that the challenges ahead may push their relationship to the breaking point. *They are both good people.*

Alone later that evening, my father catches me tearing up after witnessing a more concerning argument. "Is it really worth it if we are going to break them up?" I ask, in need of a moment to vent. The pre-race demands are weighing heavy on my mind.

My father reassures me: "Whatever happens at the end of the race, you need to know it was in motion well before we began. And that is not our focus. Your crew is not going to let you down."

We dive headfirst into team meetings. On the agenda, we're set to tackle simulated rollouts (both during the day and at night), seminars on preparing my Hammer Nutrition food, going through the race rules in depth, discussing individual responsibilities and upcoming deadlines and strategizing on how best to organize the support vehicles for the drive south.

Three days later I stand at the edge of my parents' driveway and wave goodbye to the newly prepped crew. The plan is for me to fly down separately – a strategy that will greatly reduce travel time and help keep my legs feeling fresh. It also affords me the opportunity to wholeheartedly embrace these last few moments of calm.

One week to go.

JUNE 6, 2008

Reunited in sunny Oceanside, we patiently wait inside a community hall with over 100 anxious racers and their crews for the opening race introductions. Seated ahead of us is a row of hardened European faces. King among them is the steel gaze of RAAM legend Jure Robič.

I poke my dad in the leg and point inconspicuously: *That's him.*

Not once does Jure turn his shaved head to look at the other riders. Still, I want him to notice me, to justify my existence, to say, "Yes, you have earned a spot at the table." But he's in the zone, focused only on his own performance. *He's out for flesh.*

Meanwhile, giggling can be heard from farther down our row. My mother and aunt joke about something, completely oblivious to the tension in the room. *Please, God,* I hope no one is taking bets right now.

One last sleepless night.

RACE ACROSS AMERICA, DAY 1

Our humble group of nine part ways after compassionate hugs and "good luck" wishes all around. The RV and Jetta team members head straight for the second time station in Death Valley, several hours away. Somewhere in between, my father and Curtis will be stationed in the Jeep.

Back at the pier, I stand confidently among a sea of Lycra.

We are individually called to the start line in front of a small crowd of local riders and fans. On hearing my name announced, someone yells out, "You got this, Ryan!" I turn to see a rider I had befriended during the Race Across Oregon, now dressed in plain clothes. His support means the world to me.

The attractive female announcer then calls out: "Three, two, one…!" followed by a ceremonial gunshot into the early afternoon sky.

We ride as a group along the familiar bike path, relatively silent in our own thoughts. There are 27 solo racers this year, including two women. Historically, half of us will drop out due to physical or mental breakdown.

We pass the spot where I was hit by the car, then on to the abandoned bridge I scouted previously. The race officials stagger us in one-minute intervals from that point on.

One by one, riders sprint away with all eyes watching.

The line shortens and I can feel my pulse quicken. I'm excited, but I also feel like a lemming marching off into some uncertain horror. And then an official starts counting down for me, racer #124, pointing to me: "Three, two, one…!" *Blast-off.*

I charge to the end of the bridge.

My pace is not sustainable for the long haul, but I'm also aware that the leaders (mainly Jure) will try to ride most of us off their wheel. Not until a considerable gap opens up will they settle into a more realistic tempo. And that could be at least a day from now, maybe two.

Enter, the mental game. Do you channel your energy into catching the rider ahead? Or, do you focus on staying ahead of the one coming up behind you?

As I pass the next-youngest rider, 31-year-old Timothy Case, he looks up from his aero bars and calls out in a tone that hints at an early defeat, "See you at the finish line!" *Good, one down.*

I speed up a little to make sure he doesn't have second thoughts.

I pass the rural parking area where support crews are allowed to make first contact with their riders. Thankfully, my follow vehicle has arrived in time. "All good?" Curtis yells out, running up beside me. I offer a purposeful thumbs-up.

He and my father hop back in the Jeep and speed ahead to the next dusty pullout, over five kilometres away.

It is important for me to start thinking about, and making sure I specifically call out for, what I will need at these short stops. Already the temperature is creeping into sweltering 100-degree Fahrenheit territory. *A glass of cold water would be nice.*

But first, a series of exposed rolling climbs awaits me.

Austrian Gerhard Gulewicz passes me on a tight switchback corner. Like a jittery lone wolf, he gives me a quick glance and then hurries on without speaking a word. He appears concerned about a larger predator trailing somewhere behind us.

I push a little harder to stay on the contender's wheel.

We reach the base of Palomar Mountain, the king on this section of the coastal range. Keeping an eye on Gerhard, I'm all of a sudden surprised when Jure Robič rides up beside me, in stealth mode. My fanboy gratitude acknowledges him aloud, "It is an honour to ride with you." But he does not respond. Instead, his tinted gaze scans me from head to toe, then pulls away without remorse.

I'm not ready to go down that easy.

Reaching the first summit time station, at Lake Henshaw, I learn I'm in fourth place. I'm also parched. I have only gone through one water bottle in 87 kilometres. It was filled with HEED, my Hammer Nutrition electrolyte drink. I toss the empty bottle into the ditch, then catch another from my father as he runs up beside me.

Race veteran David Haase soon passes me with the same steady determination as the three before him. I'm now in fifth place.

Argh, I feel a cramp in my right calf muscle. The left quickly follows suit. *Push through it.*

I follow David down the "glass elevator," a drop of 914 metres over a distance of 14 kilometres into the small desert settlement of Borrego Springs. So begins our trek through Death Valley, easily one of the toughest sections of the race. Temperatures soar in the wasteland, and very few (if any) cyclists have time to acclimatize. Racers that live in cooler climates are at a particular disadvantage.

It's like my training in Arizona never happened.

Sweat percolates from underneath the brim of my helmet, dripping down and collecting in a stressed cascade of wrinkles. I wipe away the first salty wave with my glove, then, settle back into aero position, full grimace. *Fuck* I'm dehydrated. Worst of all, I know exactly what happens next.

My quadricep muscles join the lower half of my legs in

debilitating, painful cramps. I have the good sense to keep pedalling so that they will not lock up altogether. *But how long until they do?*

Looking ahead, I see the highway straighten out and open farther into the gates of hell. Lucifer throws me a high-five as the RAAM media truck passes by. *Great, perfect timing.*

Feeling as though my body is about to go through something awful, I shy away from the attention.

As expected, the freight train hits with great intensity. All at once, my biceps, triceps, neck muscles and fingers fully contract in excruciating lockdown, preventing me from squeezing on the brakes with any reasonable force. The only option is to roll to a stop and hope someone catches me.

Sensing that I am in distress, the Jeep races on ahead to the nearest pullout. Curtis and my father jump out with a pair of fresh water bottles in hand, not yet aware of my incapacitation. I try to yell out but my cheek muscles also seize up.

I begin a frightened wobble.

Just in time, the two of them grab me under my shoulders and pull me away. "Sit down here," my father says, setting me down in a lawn chair next to the Jeep. "Now tilt your head back, we'll pour some cool water on you." My core temperature has skyrocketed.

Next, I'm directed to throw back a handful of Hammer Endurolyte capsules (a condensed electrolyte). "Chew them up in your mouth," my father says, looking concerned. I do as he says. I could swallow them whole, but that would slow the rate of digestion. I need them to work fast. Almost instantly, an overwhelming blast of sodium and other bitter minerals slams into my nauseated senses.

I take a swig of water and groan. My head hangs limp like a rag doll over the back of the chair. "We're going to start feeding you these every hour," my father holds strong. I let out a faint "Okay," nearly depleted, at the mercy of their support.

The RV and Jetta pull off into the sandbox.

My entire crew scrambles to help where they can. Two of them massage my legs, two others work on my shoulders, one applies a bag of ice to my forehead and everyone else offers encouraging words from behind. But I cannot fully embrace their generosity.

Distracted by a creeping sense of dread, I take stock of three engines left in idle, and the prospect that this may only be purgatory. I may well have yet to discover the true depths of Race Across America hell.

CHAPTER 20

I QUIT

The sun begins to rise across the dry desert landscape. Pedalling slowly toward those comforting orange and yellow hues in the east, I feel my eyelids heavy and unwilling to keep up with the task at hand. *I need to sleep, even just for an hour.*

Late last night (early this morning?) we crossed from California into Arizona. I missed seeing the familiar state sign, my attention caught in the busy-ness of an Interstate detour and the flashing lights of riders ahead. We have since migrated back to a quiet frontier road and away from that opening shot of Oceanside adrenaline.

With a stretch of asphalt to spare, Curtis and my father pull up beside me in the Jeep.

They are quieter than usual and they share the same tired expression. The pair has yet to swap out of that experienced "follow position," and I'm concerned. "We'll stay with you until we find our rhythm," my father assures me, referring to the three-vehicle rotation and our rookie crew. *Still, we should stop. But where?*

We have travelled over 456 kilometres in 17 hours and 13 minutes. Curtis yells out that the aptly named "Hope" RV resort and mercantile is not far. "The rest of the crew will be waiting there," he further encourages. "You'll get to sleep soon!"

Thank god. I am utterly and literally drained.

A layer of salt coats my skin. The sweat that has seeped from my pores accounts for five pounds in lost water weight (3 per cent of my body mass). This fact is concerning, as dehydration symptoms become noticeable after just a 2 per cent loss.

Delving deeper into physiology, the body of an adult male is composed of approximately 60 per cent water. The "fluid of life" is necessary for every bodily function, including digestion and nerve function. Consequently, a loss of water thickens the blood and places a greater demand on the heart. Electrolyte loss can also lead to kidney damage and worse. Death is the final straw.

These extremes are tested regularly during RAAM. It is not uncommon to see a rider hooked up to an intravenous drip of saline (sodium chloride) while sleeping. Unfortunately, the level of expertise required to administer an IV is beyond that of my crew. In place of "the drip," my Endurolyte capsule and water bottle regime continues.

How much farther?

The weight of my torso collapses deeper into the aero bars, causing my bike to weave back and forth. "Get to the RV!" my father yells across Curtis, looking concerned. "And then you can sleep." *But what would Jure do?* History shows he would soldier on. Gerhard Gulewicz and David Haase would likely do the same.

I let out a conflicted breath.

Seeing the crew clapping for me up ahead, I slowly veer off onto the dusty shoulder, wearily dismount and step into our comfortable RV. In doing so, I accept the outcome of my first decisive race decision: stopping for an extended break will likely take me out of contention. *Fuck. Okay.*

After downing a bottle of Recoverite (a Hammer Nutrition recovery drink) and eating a little bit of solid food,

I quickly strip down and step into the cramped RV shower. Naked, I see that painful saddle sores have started to form around my crotch and inner thighs. My exposed skin also radiates, red.

As I relax for a moment, the lukewarm stream provides a stinging sense of relief. *You have an hour break.*

After brushing my teeth, I flop down on a bed in the back and feel my eyes close like heavy shutters. Outside, I can hear the hum of our generator powering the air conditioning, of crewmembers shuffling around (no matter how quiet they try to be) and the occasional clapping of other crews parked in the same lot. Adrenaline remains in constant flow, reminding me that I'm being passed at this very moment. *But they'll have to rest too.*

Balancing recovery with gaining ground has always been a point of interest for race followers. In 2006, RAAM officials actually tested out a mandatory 40-hour rest break, to be divided among the 54 time stations at each rider's discretion. That is not the case anymore; the masochists balked at the idea. They considered it a penalty rather than a privilege.

My mother gently shakes my arm, "It's time to get up."

Our strategy moving forward allows for one hour of rest during the hottest part of the day, and then another two to three just before sunrise. Longer rest periods will make it nearly impossible to finish on time. Saving the bulk of my sleep for the early morning plays into my usual rest patterns. There is also a mental boost, and familiarity, in rising with the sun. Sunrise signals a new day and the fact that we made it one step closer.

An hour of rest makes a world of difference. Falling into REM (rapid eye movement) sleep is ideal. Normally accounting for about 20 per cent of our sleep time, this is the part of the sleep cycle that maintains healthy circadian rhythms, marked by changes in melatonin secretion, cortisol levels in our plasma and a stable core temperature. And it goes without saying that quality sleep on RAAM is crucial, as quantity is in short supply.

But let's not kid ourselves. No matter how much I rest, I'll never feel fully rested. Still, having the opportunity to shower, eat, brush my teeth and change into a fresh set of riding clothes does lift my spirits.

Speaking of clothing, Bow Cycle has generously sponsored a new kit for each riding day. This will help ensure that the material covering my heinie is always taut, thus reducing saddle sores caused by bunched friction points. Excessive, perhaps, but the ultra-devil is in just such details.

Zipping up a clean new jersey, I gaze into the bathroom mirror and take stock of my slender frame. Looking up into a pair of tired, red eyes, I muster a simple rally for Round Two. *Here we go.*

My crew is in good spirits as I exit the RV and straddle the orange steed. Back in the driver's seat of the Jeep, my father turns the key in the ignition – *Come on.* Pulling my mother aside, I ask her to keep an eye on "the chief." "He's no good to us if he runs himself into the ground," I say. She gives me a half smile, acknowledging the risk.

Thankfully, Curtis has gone down for a rest.

It is Leland's turn in the "Navigator" position. His role is to give plenty of advance warning about approaching turns via cues provided in a thick "Race Bible." He also prepares all my snacks and water bottle mixes. The more we can coordinate on the move, the better. Even though a two-minute stop sounds minor enough, multiply two minutes by one stop every hour by 12 days, and you have 576 minutes spent off the bike, which equates to 9.6 hours of wasted time.

To the disciplined rider, those 9.6 hours could instead be utilized for a quarter-race-worth of three-hour sleep breaks. But of course, it is much easier to talk about saving this time than it is to put it into practice. A tired mind grasps instant gratification, not rules and procedure.

"Go ahead," my father waves. There is no traffic coming up behind us.

The route takes us farther into the desert and its blinding midday heat, through the ponderosa pines of Prescott National Forest, around the switchback artisan hillside town of Jerome, past the popular red rock getaway of Sedona and, finally, up a 46-kilometre forested climb to the northern Arizona mountain town of Flagstaff. We reach the chilly 2100-metre elevation just after sunset.

Undiscovered country lies ahead. Thankfully, I'm surrounded by a few familiar faces. Kelly's mom and a training buddy have driven north from Phoenix to see me ride through. They stand outside the RV for over two hours while I have my third sleep break.

RACE ACROSS AMERICA, DAY 3

Waking groggily, I share a quick hug with Debbie before I push off into the relative unknown, headed for Utah. Darkness soon surrounds us on the open country descent, save for the Jeep's headlights and an unobstructed patchwork of stars above.

I'm now in 13th place.

Racers pass each other when they sleep; my anxious mind has accepted this fact. Still, it piques my curiosity to know that Jure blazed through this region a whole ten hours ago.

That's a huge lead, considering that the majority of those ahead of me are all within a two-and-a-half-hour grasp; one less sleep break, essentially.

I remind myself that a lot can happen in 4823 kilometres. All it takes is one crash, one bout of dehydration or one nagging pain that gets worse, and in an instant, a strong rider is assimilated into the 50 per cent attrition rate. Mind you, I would never wish ill toward anyone.

Every qualified rider is a gladiator.

Perhaps the strongest among us, 62-year-old race veteran David Jones, passes me at the entrance to the fabled western landscape of Monument Valley, Utah. "Why would you ever want to do this more than once?" I ask as he slowly rides up beside me.

Feeling great pain, even he is unsure in the moment. "Ask me again at the finish," David responds. Riders are allowed to ride together for 15 minutes every hour. It is in these brief exchanges that racers bond. Not surprisingly, you begin to feel more like brothers in arms rather than friendly foes.

Still, experience continues to beat down youth.

I continue on alone through the valley of mesa monoliths interspersed with sun-bleached trailer homes. Remnants of the Navajo Nation.

Looking back along Highway 163, déjà vu strikes as I recognize a scene from my favourite Oscar-winning film, *Forrest Gump*. I'm on the same stretch of vacant highway where Tom Hanks's title character decides to finally stop running, and turns around and leaves his band of scruffy followers to go home after crossing the United States multiple times, because, "I just felt like runnin.'"

Even though Forrest is a fictional character, the landscape reminds me of the film's grand emotion and the draw to living an extraordinary life. Like listening to Coldplay, it strikes a particularly inspired chord in me. "This is the place!" I yell out to my crew, beaming.

As darkness begins to descend on day three, so does the cooler mountain air of Colorado.

Curtis yells from the shoulder as I pass through the touristy town of Cortez, "The one-armed man is after you!" a reference to the movie *The Fugitive*. Following closely on my heels is 52-year-old Beny Furrer, from Switzerland, who is in fact a one-armed killer of another variety.

I look back to see Beny gripping onto to his custom-made, solo shifter–brake, switching to a harder gear, his quad muscles pumping. *Fuck*, he is determined to catch me. In response, I'm determined not to be humiliated, although I applaud his push past adversity. *But hell, he's quick.*

Anxious to get ahead, I throw down a powered effort up a long climb, pulling away, while taking advantage of my ability to stand and use both arms for leverage (thrusting my weight into the pedals). *Good luck to you, Beny.*

With twilight fading behind the mountains, cars passing in the opposite direction begin shining their blinding high beams, no doubt confused by the combination of a cyclist in silhouette and flashing hazard lights trailing close behind.

Enter, another night.

Staring into the path of the Jeep's headlights for seven hours straight is not unlike solitary confinement. I think about how good it will feel to finish this race, but the thought rides away from me because the end is still so bloody far.

In place of optimism I think about keeping my eyes open, and of the two riders who have died swerving into traffic. *It's never-ending.*

As I pull up to a long-awaited RV stop, my aunt Jill greets me with a heartfelt hug as I plead for a longer sleep break. Her boyfriend offers a quiet thumbs-up from the driver's seat.

I unbuckle my stiff cycling shoes and my mom hands me a bowl of warm chicken noodle soup. Megan checks my vitals while I slurp, my eyes half-closed.

With additional helping hands, my sister massages my legs, quickly inducing me into a coma-like sleep on our dining table, now folded down into a bed. My father and Curtis are in the back, also sleeping.

"Where's Leland?" I slur. As I ready myself for the next push, I learn that Leland has ventured off in search of gas and energy drinks. But I can't think about that now.

As I descend 3300 metres through the creeping shadow of Wolf Creek Pass, in Colorado, the temperature falls quickly, and much lower than I had anticipated for any section of the race.

Nearing the bottom, in complete darkness, I'm quickly forced to layer up in a variety of spare clothing, including two pairs of wool socks, leather driving gloves and my sister's purple winter jacket (and matching headband) – an otherwise "cute" ensemble.

Between shivers, the fashion faux pas escapes me.

RACE ACROSS AMERICA, DAY 4

Ahead is the city of Taos, New Mexico. The popular ski destination is the first of three time cut-offs during the race. And even though I'm well within a safe range, my mental alertness and already suspect math skills are failing me. *What if we have a breakdown of some sort? How close are we really?*

Getting me back on track in the dead of night, Leland pounds the theme from *Top Gun* out our one loudspeaker, now duct-taped to the door of the Jeep. The iconic 80s theme wouldn't be my first go-to song, but it gets both him and Megan jamming in the Jeep. I'm also pretty sure that it intimidates the other riders, looking back.

On the *highway to the danger zone*, I pass one sleepy caravan, then two, and one more before the high wears off.

Even with the extra push, shock hits us as we reach the time station in question and are told that we cannot continue. "Not to worry, you just need to wait for a bit," an official clarifies. He then goes on to tell us that a rider ahead was beaten up by a couple of drunken assholes in a pickup truck. They are now holding everyone back until the police have cleared the way.

A perfect time to lie down.

When I'm awakened from an undisturbed three-hour coma, it's still pitch black outside. *More cold and nothingness. Argh!*

In an effort to stimulate my senses, I swap out my usual iPod playlist for an audio book (race rules state that one earbud can be used while riding). The narrator comes on, "You are listening to *The Art of War*, by Sun Tzu." He goes on to read the surprisingly simple text, outlining ancient battle-field strategy for generals, which I thought might have a real-time application. But the soft drone of it all begins to put me back to sleep. And, unfortunately, my overplayed beats have also lost their lustre.

I turn off the device and tune back in to the crickets and muted hum of the Jeep, rolling, as always, in the darkness behind me.

Tasked with keeping me attentive, "the dirty twosome," as Leland and Curtis have become known, drive up beside me and engage in delirious banter. "You know that Leland is banging your sister, right?" Curtis yells across from the driver's side. He and Leland begin chuckling, their brains fuelled on Red Bull and Rockstar energy drinks and a host of grab-'n'-go snacks. I begin laughing too, despite the dig. It's the closest I have come to a guys' get-together in a long while.

RACE ACROSS AMERICA, DAY 6

My sister helps pull my cycling jersey over my tight shoulders. Feeling feeble, like an old man, I'm now almost entirely dependent on my crew to help me change my clothes. It is day six of the race.

Last night, we passed the halfway point, in Pratt, Kansas. Zipping up my top, I think about the brightly coloured neon sign I saw on somebody's front lawn, that landmark piss-off, reading "Congratulations – You're almost there!" *What the fuck!? No we're not.*

I have started to swear a lot, often in my head but sometimes out loud. No one tells me to mind my words. The crew appreciates that my body is going through something fierce, and that swearing opens up a mental spill release, if only just for a moment.

Fuuuuck, my tender sit bones cry out in agony as I attempt to sit down again on the hard leather bicycle seat. Not able to sustain the pain, I stand back up to pedal.

After 15 minutes of this, I slowly try again to set down my weight. *Come on.* Letting out a squeamish breath, I force myself back into an unavoidable level of discomfort. *You have to.*

My nose whistles with the next agonizing inhale.

Since reaching the flatlands of Kansas, the ever-present dry winds have been the cause of terrible nosebleeds, and consequently having to pack my nasal passages with Vaseline. The crew is understandably concerned to see more bloodstains soaked into my jersey.

Every body part now hurts or has lost feeling. Of particular concern is constant pressure on my penile region, which makes it difficult for me to anticipate when I need to urinate.

Feeling a small dribble in my shorts, I scramble to the side of the road for yet another impromptu stop. The Jeep quickly reacts, pulling up behind me to block my business from passing east–west traffic. My crew directs me to a sheltered pocket, between the open passenger and back doors.

A vacant country road extends south from the gravel shoulder.

In the open afternoon air, I pull out my poor, battered fellow and try to hold steady. Staring past the amalgamation of saddle sores, it is refreshing to see primitive earth, rather than asphalt, on the ground. This allows for a momentary reprieve from everything asphalt carries with it: the sight of oncoming rumble strips, traffic cones, glass, devilish mileage signs and worse.

I stretch my neck, twisting and cracking to each side.

Just as the mellow yellow begins to flow, a family in a minivan comes into full view ahead of me on the country road. Without hesitation, Leland jumps in front of me to block the obscenity. He does not flinch as urine splashes off the ground and onto his running shoes. Instead, he looks at me, wide-eyed but with levity, and proclaims, "You'll remember this for the rest of your life."

And now, finally, I can call you brother.

Continuing on, Timothy Case (whom I last saw outside of Oceanside, California) passes me on a particularly monotonous stretch of rolling prairie hills and a debilitating headwind. *And he thought he wouldn't see me again* – saying, "See you at the finish line," as I blazed past in the opening minutes of the race.

We chat for a few moments like old friends caught in the

same war. Still, feeling a sense of defeat, I let him ride off, no doubt on a high from what is becoming an increasingly uncommon occurrence: that is, passing another racer. The solo contingent has long since separated into an ebb and flow. We rarely see each other anymore.

Realizing I am falling farther down the ranks, I pull off the road and begin to sob.

My father jumps out of the Jeep, now piddling behind me. "What's wrong?" he asks.

Looking away, I tell him: "I don't think that I can do it." The hare has been caught. This is no longer a race.

He pats me on the back. "Just get to the next time station, okay?"

I feel like a weakling.

Austrian Franz Preihs passes me, despite having a broken collarbone. (He accidentally ran into a construction sign on the shoulder, just yesterday.) He looks over at me, sees me having another bloody nose moment and still finds the time to ask if I am okay. It is a weird kind of respect, like two fighters who hug after a boxing match.

I wave him off. Any physical advantage I had at the start has all but withered away.

On a long climb, swaying from side to side, I happen across Caroline van den Bulk – the only other Canadian racer, and one of only two women. She started a day ahead of the solo men. She is also the first rider I have passed in some time.

Her crew cheers me on from the top of the climb. "Go, Canada!" they yell with red and white maple leaf flags waving high. But I'm exhausted, and after only a few more yards I stop to take a short break in the Jeep.

Megan encourages me to ride the high. "You just passed the first person that started ahead of you." But I don't care. My will to race is gone. I think of Caroline, who has tried her hand at RAAM once before and failed, and come to realize the futility of continuing to punish my body just for the sake of finishing.

My mood swings dramatically. *What's the point…?*

One moment my spirits are up, enthused perhaps by a new, less painful riding position or spurred on by the cheers of a nearby time station and potential break. My mood changes at the drop of a hat, though, as I protest to stop, stretch, pee and/or collapse over my bars and sulk further.

RACE ACROSS AMERICA, DAY 7

Just past the Missouri capital of Jefferson City, I'm passed by Jim Rees, a 45-year-old motivational speaker from London, England. Back in Oceanside he was one of the only riders I had a chance to chat with for any length of time. He made a point of encouraging me with the personal mottos "We are all built for greatness" and "Accentuate the positive." But the Jim I see now is a changed man. He doesn't say a word or look over at me. His dark eyes remain fixed ahead, likely caught in the bowels of a lurid hallucination.

RACE ACROSS AMERICA, DAY 8

Our bodies have crossed into a new dimension, some worse than others. We have travelled nearly 3274 kilometres.

Pushing farther into the cornfield abyss, I fall asleep on my bike in the first early hours of the day.

Hunched over like dead weight, I swerve into the dark ditch beside the road without warning. The grass slows me down a little as I run into the fence alongside the road and collapse off of the bike at, of all places, the ominous gates of a rural cemetery.

My crew panics at the desperation of the situation, and also at the irony of where I have stopped.

Immediately, someone drapes a warm blanket over me. "Just a little bit farther," someone else says. The RV is waiting at the banks of the Mississippi River, the two-thirds point of the race. Still, my eyes are too heavy to open.

They help me back onto my feet. "Open your eyes, Ryan!"

The Jeep follows more closely behind me now, remaining on high alert for any redneck traffic coming up behind us.

After 20 tense minutes, I reach the RV. But instead of going right inside to sleep, I stand apart from my crew, my thoughts stuck in the doldrums of misery.

A light misting of rain falls around us.

From the corner of my eye, I see my crew quietly milling about in the ambience of a flickering gas station light. It is apparent that they are unsure how to right the situation. No matter, my mind is already made up.

My father is the first to approach me. He doesn't ask how I am. He already knows. *Now listen.*

With complete confidence, and without question, I turn to him and freely admit, "Dad, I'm not tough enough … I quit."

CHAPTER 21

MISSING PERSON

RACE ACROSS AMERICA, DAY 8 CONTINUED

Rain continues to sprinkle down in the darkness. *I'm done with cycling.*

In the hour before "I quit," my mind had set a course north to barren Fort McMurray to start making some of *that* Alberta oil money. It is the only way I can pay my parents back (in the next decade, that is) for this abysmal dissolution of passion and begin moving the hell on. Or rather, lose myself.

In the roughneck mix, there would be no cycling news and no one to take me to task over this failure that the so-called Adventure Cyclist was ultimately broken on the bike and forced to drop out of one of the sport's most hallowed challenges. Still, the decision to quit RAAM is not without great personal heartache.

My father remains silent as I lay it on the line. "I mean it, I'm done. And I'm okay with it, I have already thought it through ... I'm going to get a real job and pay taxes, just like you always pester me about."

I walk over to the RV, prop my bike up alongside it and head straight for the bed in the back. Unlike previous sleep breaks, this time I hope to close my eyes for the remainder of the night and wake up rested, and ultimately a changed man, no longer a foolish dreamer.

My mind shuts off completely.

It is still dark when someone nudges my arm. Rolling over to look down the aisle, I see something curious: my father is walking around in a white T-shirt and spare pair of my Spandex riding shorts. *What the hell?* He fills a water bottle at the kitchen sink, then steps outside.

I hear the retractable RV steps unfold. *Fuck, come on!*

I plead with my mother, who is quietly milling about inside. "I'm done. I can't ride any farther. Please!" She motions to the door and says that my father is anxious to go on one last ride with me. "With what (bike)?" I shoot back. Outside, the self-titled authority on "Manhood Training" circles on my pink climbing machine. It's 4:00 a.m.

"You're not going to make your old man finish this alone, are you?!" my father yells out. *Goddamn it.*

Fumbling down the steps, I angrily protest, "I'm fucking done, seriously."

Sensing forward progress, my sister and Curtis hop in the Jetta. Leland mischievously slides into the Jeep. Their engines begin humming once again, ever so anxious. *Fuck!*

"Ride with me to the next time station," my father coddles me.

"Fine, but after that I'm done," I state bluntly. My father gives a thumbs-up to the vehicles, then begins slowly pedalling. Like a distraught little lamb, I keep pace at his right side.

Curtis and my sister, Trisha, speed on ahead. The Jetta "backup car" is now responsible for scouting out turns ahead of us and marking them in advance. Quite often, whoever is riding in that vehicle will jump out and point enthusiastically in the direction I need to go, maybe even doing a little dance, just for a laugh. It helps to better anticipate turns and adjust my speed. It is one less thing to think about, especially through busier areas.

Leland falls in behind my father and me with the Jeep, his headlights now leading the way for the two of us.

Climbing a short hill, my father comments on the featherlight frame between his legs: "Jesus, no wonder you can climb so well." He has never ridden such an expensive bike. The pink Kona "King Zing" retails for $5,999 in Canada. My main bike, the orange "Zing Supreme," sells for $2,999. And the green time-trial bike, which I have barely touched, is north of both those figures.

Collecting dust in my parents' garage is an old steel road bike with downtube shifters. The last time my father rode it was when we cycled from Fort Lauderdale, Florida, to Grimsby, Ontario, in 1998. In the ten years since, the cycling industry has evolved in many ways. Bikes are lighter, especially those with carbon fibre frames. "How do you shift gears on this thing?" my father asks, as he grinds up a steeper grade.

"The shifters are connected to the brake levers," I point, realizing now how foreign it all must be to him.

In the midst of further education, the gas station lights of misery fade out of view. We soon ride over the grand Mississippi River onto the humid Illinois flood plain and my father's scheme to keep me on the bike.

Trying my best to keep up, I'm afraid to ask *What's next?*

"Let's just have some fun," he grins at the sign of a new dawn.

Feeling the world open up in a warm glow, my emotions calm and I begin to think critically about riding with my father. It occurs to me that this may be an extreme violation of the race rules. "We called race HQ, they are allowing it for now," my mother says. Yet, there is a difference between being allowed for the long term or only the short term.

I shy away from the thought that we are being given special attention, as well as that I may have to openly admit to having a mental breakdown. As far as I know, no one else has their father along to guide them. This is not Baby Me Across America.

What a cluster fuck.

RACE ACROSS AMERICA, DAY 9

Stopped for a short break, I straddle my bike, numb to the world, looking on as my father refills his water bottles at the Jeep. He takes a bite out of one of my Honey Stinger energy bars, pauses to assess its curious texture, and continues on, happy as can be. Meanwhile, the crew evaluates the scene with a curious energy from afar, none quite sure what to make of the chief's new on-bike rotation.

We stand in the shadow of Main Street, USA: that traditional small-town scene of old brick buildings, barbershops and mothballed clothing stores. The only activity we can see is a group of older men in a country diner, hunched at the counter. They sit with their hands folded around cups of hot coffee and "home-cooked" meals. There are no signs of their kids, grandkids or any youth in general. They are the last guards of the small-town farming industry.

An elderly lady waves to us as she shuffles around a corner. My father smiles and tips his (my) helmet. *Why the hell is everyone so cheery?* I give a small wave back.

"Okay, are you ready to go?" my father asks.

"Whatever." I'm frustrated to continue on in this highly manipulative manner. *Just have some fun,* he says. *Just like the old days,* he babbles on.

The irony of the father–son story becoming richer for this experience is not lost on me. Still, I wanted to be viewed as the underdog powerhouse, not the bleeding-heart narrative we have become.

My relatively untrained father rides on without me, easily able to sustain what would otherwise be a painfully slow pace by traditional racing standards. My average speed is 16 km/h.

Just like when we ventured across Canada when I was 13, fighting those prairie headwinds, I yell ahead and try to make it clear that it is a challenge to keep up. He falls back.

Face to face, he can see my agony more clearly. I anxiously shift my weight from one saddle sore to another. The bags under my eyes have their own baggage. And having continued to shed weight each day (it is impossible to keep up with the caloric demands), my clothing now hangs from a gaunt, awkwardly tanned torso.

On a cellular level, I feel strung out, like a junkie without a care. In fact, the thought of getting side-swiped by a passing vehicle doesn't seem so horrible to me. *If only I could commit*, I consider, wavering back and forth across the white line.

Concerned by my apathy, the chief suddenly changes his tune: "We're getting you off that Hammer shit and onto some real food," he fires at me. He was never sold on the liquid nutrition strategy, despite over 20 years of science and racer testimonial backing it up. *But are we using it correctly?* All he knows is that my mood perks up whenever a pizza box is passed around.

The crew begins passing me food out the window every 15 minutes. It might be a banana, or a new take on an old favourite, like a Hammer Bar dipped in chocolate pudding. When I have time to stop and eat, it's peanut butter sandwiches, pasta, soup, cottage cheese and a large bottle of Hammer Recoverite to top off the meal.

Concerned about increasing constipation, I'm forced to stop more often. Sitting in the tiny RV bathroom stall, the dump of all dumps is soon at hand. And these dumps don't flush without a fight. "Just leave it," my mother says. "It needs to soak."

Such moments of levity are a godsend.

On an upswing, I ask my father to ride behind me instead of ahead. Even though I appreciate his company, I'm concerned that having him continually out front, and to have other teams see this, in broad daylight, is going to put race officials in an awkward position.

After three days and two long nights together, I finally tell him, "I'm fine to carry on alone." He appears let down by the prospect of not finishing together, yet he understands the reason why. It was a special thing he did, no doubt. But we must honour the integrity of the solo division.

Now, the team riders, who started two days after the solo riders, approach like a bullet train in packs of two, four and eight. They wear elongated, aerodynamic helmets and tight skin suits. All of them are on time-trial bikes, hunched in a tuck position, with legs spinning furiously. Still, despite their record-breaking intentions, many make an effort to slow down and pat me on the back. "I don't know how you guys do it," one guy says in a Texan accent, referring to the solo riders.

"Fuckin' rock star!" screams another.

The respect of fellow RAAM racers means the world to me. Their words are an important reminder that attempting the solo challenge is no small feat. In fact, only five Canadians have ever finished the race. And in the entire history of RAAM, I'm nearly the youngest to get this far. (An 18-year-old freak of nature from Alaska holds the record for the youngest competitor to reach this point in the race.)

Getting back to the task at hand, fellow Canadian Caroline van den Bulk and I continue to leapfrog each other amid shared cheers from our support crews. The supportive back and forth endures all the way to the foot of the rolling Appalachian range.

Unfortunately for team van den Bulk, climbing remains my strength. Knowing this, my father pulls me aside during a short break, when we are parked next to her crew. "If you want to finish in Annapolis before the cut-off time of 12 days, you've got to get going," he says discreetly.

A sad reality sets in as I look back to see Caroline struggling to squat in the grassy ditch. Her crew holds up towels on either side of her to create a small privacy tent. They do not have the luxury of an RV. The woman is tough as nails, and could care less about what passersby think. *You do what you have to.*

Sensing that this is our final meeting, the mood around her camp immediately turns less jovial. Having started a day ahead of me, she is cutting it close for time. This is the same position she was in last year, unfortunately. It is sickening to know that after pedalling 4000 kilometres, Caroline will now have to sleep less and somehow pick up her average speed.

Conversely, I have experienced my first ray of hope.

Munching on a handful of colourful gummy bears at a rest stop outside of Smithsburg, Maryland, Leland walks up to me and hands me the Race Bible. "What's up?" I ask.

"Take a look at the bottom of the page," he tells me. My eyes pace down a series of mileage cues. At the bottom right-hand side, a tally reads "361 miles to go." We both nod our heads in mutual understanding and smile. *Another day and a half.* I have 581 kilometres left to go.

To no one's surprise, Jure Robič has already crossed the finish line in first place. *Wow*, I think, on hearing the news.

Good for him. "I too shall finish this fucker," I proclaim out loud.

The energy of the crew changes from a meandering question mark to finishing strong. Climbing up one steep Appalachian pitch after another, they blast "Viva la Vida," the title song off of Coldplay's triumphant new album, out of the loudspeaker. *Nothing can stop us!*

In the midst of our high, a redneck in a truck swerves up ahead of us and honks for us to get out of the way. On instinct, my middle finger shoots straight up, like a defiant pirate flag.

The driver immediately screeches on the brakes and falls back beside me. Rolling down his window, the bearded stranger then proceeds to yell: "You want to fight, asshole?" and some other bullshit.

But I'm no longer an injured animal, limping along. "I dare you to stop and get out!" I yell back, coasting alongside his truck with a fierce gaze. *I fucking dare you.*

The driver assesses the rage monster before him, and peels away in defeat. "I'm back!" I yell out, in defiance.

RACE ACROSS AMERICA, DAY 11

Just 210 kilometres left to go.

In the middle of the night, we pass through the Gettysburg National Military Park, in Pennsylvania. My father and I rode through here previously on our tour up from Florida. At the time, he tried to educate me about the important battles that took place here, and how these vacant grassy fields were actually the epicentre of the American Civil War. The scene is hauntingly quiet now.

The following morning, we hit the home stretch through Maryland.

On the outskirts of Annapolis, Leland and Megan (in the follow vehicle) pull ahead to a gas station coming up on my right. They see me about to stop and motion down the road, "Keep going! We'll catch up." I nod and continue on. Time is still a precious commodity.

I pass through one set of traffic lights, then another. The gas station is soon out of sight, replaced by a congested wall of city traffic, mini-malls and an intuitive sense of concern on my part.

Fifteen minutes pass, and still no sign of the Jeep. My pace slows as I look back over my shoulder. *Where are they?*

It's 10:00 a.m. I have less than two hours to finish before the cut-off. I haven't used a cyclo computer since the start of the race, so as not to focus on slowly ticking kilometres. Now, I have no idea how much farther I need to ride.

The highway has begun a slight descent toward the Atlantic coast. Though no water is in sight, I'm sure that this is the right direction. Faint remnants of white chalk arrows are visible on the asphalt, usually an indication of a race route. Whether these are for RAAM, that is the question.

Shit, do I turn back and try to find them? No, I don't have time. I decide to follow the arrows. They soon lead me off the main highway, onto a quieter country road.

A vehicle I do not recognize has been trailing me intently for the last few kilometres. A dishevelled man wearing a retro cycling cap pulls up beside me in his equally dishevelled truck, and inquires, "Are you doing RAAM?"

"Yes, but I'm embarrassed to say that I have gotten lost from my crew. Also, I'm not sure if I'm going the right way ... I'm worried that I'll miss the time cut-off." The man is a local. "Not to worry!" he laughs.

He pulls in behind me, the same as the Jeep would, and

shouts out turns as they come up. *But what about my crew?* I begin to worry. They are likely frantic and hunting for me in an entirely different area, on the assumption I would have continued straight on the highway.

The man and I stop at a convenience store with a pay phone. He gives me a couple of quarters to call my crew.

Holding up the receiver, I pause, "Shoot, I don't know any of their numbers." Each vehicle has a disposable phone with a local number. No one ever thought I would need to have that information on hand.

After an hour, I come to terms with the fact that *this is how it is going to be*. Without my usual support team, however, I'm now without food and water. "Here, take some of this loaf of bread," the man gestures to a grocery bag. I stuff two pieces of the bleached white in my mouth, and stuff another two into my jersey pocket. He then hands me a gallon of water for my empty bottles.

My new friend and I pass by the second-last time station without knowing it. Usually, those volunteers would radio ahead to the finish and give them your ETA.

Pulling back up to a busy highway, we make a right turn when it is safe, a quick left, then a right into a mall parking lot. Directly ahead of us is a red van with race decals and two race officials sitting on the bumper, chatting nonchalantly. *Holy shit*, it suddenly hits me: this is the official finish! Riders are escorted from here to the ceremonial finish, where you cross under the infamous RAAM banner.

I ride right up to the two men.

They look at me and do a double take. One of them steps back in utter surprise, and shouts out, "Shit, you're Ryan! The police are out looking for you, along with your crew." He immediately calls off the cavalry, passing me a Gatorade in between an elated explanation.

"Are you ready?" he asks. I nod.

The van pulls ahead, followed closely by another race vehicle on my rear. They begin ceremoniously honking their horns as we make our way down to the cobbles surrounding the Annapolis pier. Tourists on narrow streets stop and stare. Some begin to clap as they realize what is going on.

Ahead I see the white Race Across America banner atop a finish gate, the ocean close behind. The majority of my crew (not everyone was able to make it in time) stands and claps to one side. My parents both have tears in their eyes. My new friend is there too.

I receive the "Youngest Finisher" award, with a time of 11 days, 21 hours and 44 minutes, at a ceremonial dinner for riders who finished that day. Afterward, my crew and I head back down to the pier to cheer Caroline on as she crosses the finish, albeit unofficially.

She misses the time cut-off by only a few hours. Still, she has completed something pretty amazing.

We share a hug.

RETURNING HOME

Curtis, Megan and I take turns driving back across the country in the Jeep. We learn quickly that I'm only able to hold the wheel for 15 minutes at a stretch before I start to doze off. My feet have also swollen to almost double their size and are in pain when not propped up on the cramped dash. My recovery has begun.

After dropping Megan off in Calgary, Curtis and I continue

on to my parents' home in British Columbia, where Curtis kept his own vehicle and where I will continue recovering.

As Curtis readies for a quick turnaround, since he is headed back to his day job in Calgary, I give him a hug and say with all sincerity, "Thanks, man!"

I'm now all alone.

LATE JUNE, 2008

I wake up in a cold sweat, with the bedsheets tangled around my feet. I have been unconsciously pedalling under the covers, like a lost fool.

Still in a daze, my attention turns to the blinking LED power light on a computer monitor in the corner of the bedroom. I pull myself to the edge of the bed, my fingers tightly gripping the covers in the darkness.

My mind can't let go. It feels like I'm supposed to be somewhere.

The next morning, I walk out to the end of my parents' dock and look out over the calm Shuswap Lake. Thinking back over the events of the past few weeks, I feel proud of all that my crew were able to accomplish. *They were brilliant.* Still, I can't help but feel like I failed.

PART III

THIS MOUNTAIN OF MINE

CHAPTER 22

GET A REAL JOB, PAY TAXES

JULY, 2008

I have been recovering at my parents' lake home in British Columbia for over a month now. They expect nothing of me.

Enjoying the comfortably cool indoors, I take spontaneous naps, regularly massage my swollen feet and embrace being pampered by my mother. In an effort to get some fat back on my skinny frame, she has prepared a bevy of home-cooked meals and sugary baked goods. Still, I have a sick appreciation for the wiry image (I am 11 pounds lighter) that stares back at me in the mirror. "You're too skinny," my mom comments, not looking impressed.

Other than my weight, the last remaining physical evidence of the Race Across America is a set of awkward tan lines and dry, cracked skin along my nether region. My broken confidence remains the most painful wound, however. It quietly mocks me, speaking from afar: *Your family babied you across America. They are the only reason you completed the race.*

I think back to the finish in Annapolis, of standing alone atop the ceremony stage, having a medal draped around my neck and of adoring praise from a small crowd of local race volunteers. It didn't feel right. The saving grace was when the MC invited my crew onto the stage for a group picture, then passed me the microphone and allowed me to express my gratitude. *This is all due to them.*

The thought of having almost dropped out scares me. *Thank god* for my father's intervention. "You would have been eaten alive by those guys," he laughs, referring to the roughnecks and my suggested "easy" alternative of working on a northern oil rig. "You need some more calluses on your hands, first," he further jabs.

Nevertheless, he does disagree with my assessment of the events that transpired, as well as my unfortunate disconnect. "Only one person pedalled that bike across the country," he reminds me. Yet, on the day of my "wedding," I walked up to the altar, looked my passion in the eyes and told it that I was no longer in love. How can that feeling be dismissed so quickly?

My mother interrupts one of my lost, longing stares out the living room window. "Would you like to go for a ride down to the corner store?" she asks with a heartwarming smile and tears in her eyes. She wants to see me smile again.

I crack a small grin. *Of course I will.* I can't say no to my mother.

We walk outside into the morning sunshine.

A pair of small bluebirds chirp and sing to each other from a nearby tree. Ahead, a fluffy squirrel scampers by with a nut for safekeeping.

Opening the garage, I take a deep breath. *There it is.* I haven't touched my bike since the end of the race.

My mother proceeds to roll her casual bike (outfitted with a wealth of hand-me-downs, including touring packs, a racing helmet and stylish sunglasses) out into the open air.

I stand pensive for a moment, noticing that my orange frame has accumulated a light layer of dust. It sparkles and fades in the light that softly flows in.

Feeling a range of memories flood back (of grand vistas, aero bar elbow creases and nighttime shouting matches), I instinctively move my hand across the polished surface, hearing the beast purr again. *Quite the adventure we had, hey?*

Throwing my right leg up and over, I cautiously sit down on the worn leather. The excruciating pain is immediate. Sores along my inner thighs crack (even after applying moisturizer) as they conform to the saddle curvature, forcing a muted yelp. "Errr, fuck."

Pushing off alongside my mother, we crest a steep gravel driveway, then begin coasting down the lake road, running parallel to it. The morning sun greets us again, shining through an alley of tall conifers and warming as we pass. *Another perfect day.*

But I'm too exhausted to care.

Pushing down on the pedals, my legs lack the ability to contract with any pleasurable force. The synergy that I had with the machine is all but gone.

Trying to jump-start my enthusiasm, my mom stands awkwardly (she is relatively new to distance riding) and does her best to sprint ahead. She looks back after the first jump, taunting me. "What the fuck?" I grumble.

For the first time in weeks, she takes noticeable offence. "Stop swearing, it's very rude. You never used to do it," she scolds.

I apologize. It's time I got my head screwed on right.

AUGUST, 2008

Having begun to accept RAAM in my heart, I drive back east to Alberta with the notion that obsessive cycling and I are ready to part, amicably. The father–son element, which represents the contentious heart of that dream, has finally come full circle.

Staring out at the wondrous Trans-Canada mountain landscape, I smile, feeling slightly emotional, yet happy at the same time. *I'm ready to move on. There are other passions to explore.*

On the horizon is the small farming community of Bentley, Alberta. Leland and my sister have said I can stay with them at their rented condo until I find work in Calgary. "Just for a couple weeks," I assured.

At 25 years old, it is difficult not to feel a little ashamed. Many of my high school friends have established their professional foothold, have married and are well on their way to a white picket dream. Me, on the other hand, I don't have a cent to my name, and now I'm moving in with my younger sister.

Seeking a "real job" and becoming financially secure has its draw. I'm intrigued by the thought of having a domain to call my own, to have equity and physical proof of what my hard work can achieve. The last 12 years have been spent building something far more vague: a story. And unfortunately, it's difficult to monetize words, especially those describing atypical athletic pursuits. "Give me another year," I would always tell my parents. "I'm close to something."

But, no. *If I haven't figured it out by now, it's probably not going to happen.*

My parents and I are finally in agreement.

Moving forward, it will be nice to receive a regular paycheque. Maybe I can also start dating again. The not-so--subtle jabs from friends and family are growing tiresome. For my birthday last year, my sister bought me *The 40-Year-Old Virgin* on DVD. The year before that it was a blow-up doll with blonde hair and perky plastic lips. And, "No, I'm not gay!" I insist defensively. "I'm just busy."

I wanted to change the world.

The Rockies descend into the foothills, trailing into familiar badlands and soon the Calgary city limits. I turn north on the QEII Highway, back into a prairie abyss. Central Alberta beckons.

My understanding of Bentley is that there is a farmers market on Saturdays. The Bentley Generals Hockey Club is the social focal point of the town. And seemingly endless gravel roads sprawl off in parallel compass lines. Life appears very simple on the surface.

Leland greets me at the door of their humble condo, hugging me in a brotherly embrace. "Hey, man," he says in a cutesy voice. My sister rolls her eyes in the background. Leland and I have obviously grown comfortable around each other.

"Hey," I reply back with a thankful smile. And for good measure, I quickly remind them that my stay will only be a week or two, until I find work in Calgary. It's not a problem, they assure me.

I immediately set up in the spare bedroom and begin searching through online job postings.

Through the evening, the next day and the night after, I begin to surmise that my qualifications are mostly irrelevant on paper. It is apparent that my invented occupation as "Adventure Cyclist" may not carry much weight. So, I default to "Semi-Pro Cyclist" and other tangibles like "Valedictorian" and "Athlete Ambassador" for *insert charity name here*. I top it off with my logo at the top of the page, positioned with distinction.

Still, I am unsure how to apply myself in a more traditional sense, beyond the low-pay realm of guiding and outdoor education, that is. So I submit my résumé to all job postings with companies that offer reasonable enough pay and appear to have not only an appreciation for motivation but also low education barriers to entry. *The right people will pick up on this.*

A week passes without any response.

In the second week, I hear back from a handful of not-for-profit groups seeking an ambassador "to help attract potential donors through speaking engagements." They each seem like a perfect fit in their own way, and not such a far stretch from what I had been using my story to help achieve since Ride for Life in 2002.

I begin going for interviews.

After the first enthusiastic round of buttoned-up shirt-and-tie meetings, my intuition tells me to actually pull back and re-evaluate what public speaking means to me. The employers all require me to follow a script. And the story that helped land me the interview is, in fact, not of interest to their narrative. They only care that I have public speaking experience. I decline.

I get asked back to downtown Calgary to interview for something far more substantial. "$100,000 to start," says the man in the suit. *Huh.*

He phones that evening and asks me back for a second interview.

We meet for dinner, this time at a swanky restaurant with hipster track lighting, rich mahogany interiors and wine flowing. I pick up on the fact that he orders an expensive steak. I order something far less pricey, despite not having to pay. "Get a steak," he encourages. *Okay, he's got my attention.*

"I respect the distances you have cycled," he tells me next. And even though training will be required, many of my "street skills" will carry over. "High performance athletes make good business people. They understand goal setting and are more dedicated to a goal," he explains further. Having a former NHL hockey player and an Olympic athlete on his company's payroll have proven this point.

"Think it over this weekend and get back to me. We would be thrilled to have you on our team," he says. We shake hands.

Walking back to my truck on a quiet downtown street in the late evening, I'm caught in the wanderlust of a prosperous new opportunity. *This will change everything.*

In that orange streetlamp haze, I accidentally walk two blocks too far. *Wow, come on, Ryan.*

As I turn around at a dark corner, a scraggly homeless man extends his hand from the gutter. "Spare some change?" he speaks through a matted white beard.

Fishing through my pockets, I tell him, "I'm sorry, I have none to spare." *I really don't.* High-interest credit cards are my sole currency, and a facade at that.

Doubling back to the parking shelter on the opposite side of the street, I pass a 24-hour fitness facility located a couple floors up in a high-rise building. Along the exterior window, I watch a row of young professionals work out. They run in unison on identical treadmills overlooking the dark city street. I imagine what it would be like to be one among them...

After hitting the gym for an hour, we'd clean up in trendy, chic outfits, then text to meet at a nearby rooftop lounge. Over appetizers and cocktails, one of the roundtable hipsters might ask about my path leading up to this point, and recoil, "You did what? No way!"

Cutting out early, I walk a few blocks home to my simply modern, one-bedroom bachelor pad. Early tomorrow morning, the plan is to head west to Banff with my hiking group. And then, on Sunday, I'll take my four-legged companion out for a walk, finishing up in the afternoon at a coffee shop, sketching memories for a book on my adventures.

That doesn't sound too bad. Not bad at all.

Back in real time, I unlock the creaky truck door and slide into the driver's seat. The parking structure is empty, save for a lone security guard patrolling in a golf cart.

I turn the key in the ignition, ever so lightly, just enough to power on the radio. The CBC nightly news crackles to life. "Canadian track cyclist Zach Bell finished seventh in the Men's Points race today." The date is August 15, 2008. Zach is representing Canada at the Beijing Summer Olympics.

It is a serendipitous moment.

Zach and I began racing together on the road in 2002 for the Synergy racing club in Calgary (we also trained together at the Olympic Oval during this time). Sharing many personality traits, we ended up as roomies on many of those first-year road trips across Alberta. I always enjoyed his company: never cocky or arrogant, always humble.

Before the start of a big race, I would often sit at the edge of my motel bed and watch Zach tinker with his bike setup. He always put in more time than the rest of us.

During our very first road race together, he got away from the peloton (the main group of riders) and almost lapped us. I came in third, thinking I was in second. He was that far ahead.

The quiet guy with the big legs quickly transitioned from college wrestler, hailing from the Yukon wild, to road racer, to track cyclist, and now to a key rider on the national team, all in the span of a couple of years.

I wonder...

On Monday morning, I call the man in the suit. "Thank you

for considering me. You have presented a tremendous opportunity, and one that is not easily dismissed. It's just ... something has come up."

CHAPTER 23

DISTANCE DEFIER

AUGUST 18, 2008

My Skype line dials out. Picking up on the other end is my former teammate and track-enthused roomie Zach Bell. He is fresh from competing at the smoggy Beijing Summer Olympics.

Not having spoken much in the last couple of years, we exchange pleasantries, chatting about those early years and all the interesting building blocks since. Zach has been racing with some of Canada's best on the Symmetrics squad, Canada's first real hope at a professional road cycling team. Unfortunately, they recently lost their title sponsorship and had to disband.

I proceed to ask him about the state of cycling at the national team level and what it takes to *make it*. "The Olympic team," I clarify.

A floodgate of patriotic enthusiasm opened last week. Seated in my truck after that steak dinner and follow-up job interview in Calgary, I listened with great interest to all the Olympic news from afar.

As a result of that patriotic 180-degree about-face on cycling, I grew feverishly inspired by the grand Olympic ideal, and by the sport of ultracycling, which remains an obscure, underground racing scene. Perhaps it was time for the sport to step out of the Olympic shadow. *There's absolutely no reason why I should not at least ask "What if?"* I'm on my way to a full recovery from RAAM, I'm fit and I have the where-withal to ask even tougher questions.

"You know what, if anyone were to ever take on such a goal, you would think it would be someone with your story and similar determination," Zach cautiously agrees. He then lays out the playing field, including the main athletes in contention and which disciplines have the best odds. Currently, Olympic cycling consists of BMX racing, cross-country mountain biking, road cycling and track racing.

I have no interest in BMX.

When we weigh the pros and cons of road cycling, Zach explains, "You have to be faster than Svein Tuft," the 2006–2007 Union Cycliste Internationale America Tour Champion. "If you're not, there's no point." The way Zach says this, I infer that Zach believes Svein could beat *him*.

Intimidation aside, I don't see the building blocks in place for the road scene, such as an established development and training program. So that option is out.

Zach proceeds to tell me about track racing. "The qualification is simple: just you, the track and a clock. There's no complicated racing schedule, only a time standard." Essentially, I could find out very quickly if I stood a chance.

The Canadian track scene is also gaining support because of Zach's success. Yet it only has a small pool of dedicated athletes to draw from, and surprisingly, almost all of them are from my training stint at the National Cycling Centre in 2001. He encourages me to embrace this as the best option for moving forward. Plus, I can always use him as a resource.

We never discuss the cross-country mountain biking scene. Those obscure ranks are already filled with a handful of veteran World Cup podium contenders such as British Columbia native Geoff Kabush. *And why would I bother to reinvent the wheel?* Track cycling is clearly my best bet. I get it.

I go to bed encouraged.

The next morning, I ask Trisha and Leland if I can extend my stay indefinitely.

Fortunately, the opportunity to split the monthly rent and coexist as *Three's Company* is greeted with open arms.

I'm more concerned with what my parents are going to say. The final RAAM invoice, still hot from the printer, is imprinted with a hard $20,000.

I brace for impact as my father calls, expecting an update on job prospects. "Don't get mad," I cushion the blow. "It's going to be a little while before I can pay you back. I'm going to try and make the Olympic team for London 2012."

There is a pause on his end.

"It sounds like a good idea," he surprises me. "How does one go about making the road cycling team?"

A little taken aback by the support, I take a second to gather myself. "No, Dad, sorry, I'm going to try to get on the track team. My chances are much better than road. Road cyclists are a dime a dozen, and many of them are strong."

Another pause.

"Is track the one where you ride around and around like the Indy 500?"

I cough. "Well, sort of, yes."

"Have you considered the fact that you didn't like track cycling the first go-round? More importantly, no one cares about it. Can you name three professional track cyclists? I think you need to consider the long-term viability of this," the dormant investment advisor speaks.

He has a point.

Cross-country mountain biking is a more tangible alternative that plays to my adventurous side. It is also the most foreign to me, having never owned one of those bloated-looking metal bikes or ridden off-road any great distance.

My perception of the community is of bearded, weed-smoking dudes who love to scream downhill, drink Red Bull and fly off dirt jumps – which is more of an ignorant stereotype of downhill riding, a subcategory of cross-country mountain biking, as I find out. Cross-country is about backwoods endurance, sprinkled with just enough "technical" riding to shame the fearful.

The unknown intrigues me. *And perhaps, selecting a completely new discipline would be an adventure in itself.*

That afternoon, I type "cross-country mountain bike" into YouTube and begin scrolling through a long list of racing videos. They feature burly riders careening down "singletrack" trails, ascending up and over hidden mountain passes, splashing in the mud and sweating just the same as any road rider.

I'm intrigued by the potential of exploring trails that were once an afterthought in my mountain periphery (during my road racing days). Those days had their ups and downs too. Sure I loved gliding along on black asphalt, but I also had to deal with headwinds, impatient drivers and nefarious cracks in the road, for starters.

A road seems so limiting now. A dirt path, on the other hand, has many incarnations.

Best Body Fitness is a training facility located in the summer vacation town of Sylvan Lake, just a short drive south from my newly adopted home of Bentley.

Owner Scott McDermott is an Ironman veteran.

Having lost his curly long locks to the '80s, Scott has evolved the rocker tune, accepted being bald and swam/biked/ran into his late thirties with great entrepreneurial zest. He is 190 pounds of solid energy, often leaping down two flights of stairs from his office to greet members working out on the floor below.

We share a similar plight.

Surrounded by heavy-lifting "gronks" (all-arms, energy-drink-loving roughnecks), we are like two peas in a neatly shaven endurance pod. Mind you, the community of Sylvan Lake is making an effort to break beyond stereotypes by hosting an annual half Ironman, or half iron distance race, when not under the Ironman banner. Otherwise, sport boats and beer drinking populate the lake.

Scott and I had met previously, before the Race Across America, during a two-week winter training stint in the area. After making an effort to engage with the "new guy" in the gym, Scott took an interest in my story and made me the following offer: "If you ever need a job, just say the word." I politely declined, since Calgary was where I expected to end up after the race.

AUGUST 24, 2008

Scott is away racing Ironman Canada in Penticton, British Columbia, when I decide to finally take him up on the offer.

The assistant manager, unaware of our connection, is slightly dumbfounded when Scott instructs over voice mail to hire me on the spot. "No interview is needed." I'm flattered but also hesitant to jump right into a slightly-better-than-minimum-wage job with both feet. The $100,000 turndown still taunts me. *Are you sure?*

I just need to go for it.

Working the front desk at the gym will afford me the flexibility to train toward my new Olympic goal. It will also surround me with like-minded athletes.

Continuing to live with my sister and Leland in Bentley will cut down on the cost of renting my own place. The quiet central Alberta location will also keep me focused, like Rocky Balboa preparing for his fight with Drago in remote Siberia, in *Rocky IV*.

And these are the trade-offs, I tell myself.

AUGUST 25, 2008

I swallow my pride and begin my job-training with the front-desk manager. She is a couple years younger than me, having just graduated from high school.

Kelsey instructs me on how to fill out membership application forms, how to run the gym management software, how to open the facility, how to close, what to clean and more.

Following my first shift, I throw on a pair of technical shorts and go for a jog on one of the treadmills in the cardio section. I notice curious eyes darting my way, since, naturally, my stance is poised and stiff. *It will feel like home soon enough*, I'm sure.

SEPTEMBER, 2008

Leland stands over my shoulder as I write a pitch to *Mountain Bike* magazine. "Can a seasoned endurance athlete transition from the road to mountain bike, and in the span of four years speed up the ranks from amateur to member of the London Olympic team?" That is the story.

It's a ballsy idea from which many editors have already

balked, dismissing the dream as ignorant. But *Mountain Bike* decides to give me a try, agreeing to post monthly updates on my progress. It will be my first time working with an editor and having my writing published.

On a suggestion from Scott, I pose the same question to the local Sylvan Lake newspaper. I'm well aware that this goal will require community support: financial backing for regular travel and expensive bikes does not materialize from part-time work. My column will focus on the question How do "we" build an Olympic dream?

Back in the big city, the Olympic goal regains the interest of my agent, with whom I am still on strained terms. He and I have recently had a long coffee shop heart-to-heart, though, about managing client expectations. He apologizes again for the RAAM sponsorship fallout and for possibly overhyping the opportunity. I apologize for putting all my eggs in one basket and for turning down the sponsorship offer at a reduced value.

I'm willing to give the relationship a second chance.

Within a week, my first paid speaking gig materializes. Then another. Both fell to me because higher-profile athletes were originally booked but ended up having a scheduling conflict.

I learn that my story now has relevance in the market for traditional "Reach-for-your-goals-with-(insert Olympic hopeful's name here)" speaking topics. A story that originates in what is, to many, the still foreign world of Adventure Cycling adds some original spice.

No one questions whether the Olympic goal I have set for myself is attainable.

NOVEMBER, 2008

Avenue magazine decides to profile me in a feature about outstanding Calgarians. It comes as a shock when I learn I will be on the magazine's front cover. The *Calgary Herald* does the same by choosing me as one of "20 Compelling Calgarians."

I'm humbled. Never has anything I have done received so much attention. And all this happens before the first off-road pedal stroke.

DECEMBER, 2008

I drive back to my parents' home on the Shuswap for Christmas. The morning of, I lay out two presents before them. One is an envelope with a cheque for $1,000: "The first of many in repaying you for RAAM," I smile. The second is a wrapped copy of the *Avenue* magazine cover. It comes as a validating surprise to my mother and father.

JANUARY, 2009

I begin to make inroads with a rep at Specialized Bicycles. He is already familiar with my story, having seen me speak at Bow Cycle about my Argentina tour, and is happy to help with loaning a full-suspension mountain bike for the following season. Unfortunately, he can't get me anything for a fast-approaching training trip to California (elite and pro cyclists head there in the colder months). I don't balk at the idea of giving myself the same advantage.

I need to turn pro in less than two years.

Understanding my needs, a new personal sponsor, whom I met on a flight last year, has arranged for me to stay in San Diego for all of March and part of April.

Scott is supportive of the time off: "Do what you gotta do, buddy. Enjoy!"

I arrive in San Diego with my orange Kona road bike packed in a rented plastic case along with a few changes of clothes.

As I exit the airport, the late afternoon California sunshine immediately takes me back to the start line at RAAM. *It will be nice to enjoy the coast this go-round.*

There is a 160-kilometre loop out to familiar Oceanside and back that quickly becomes my favourite.

The Pacific Coast Highway is an important part of my cycling story. It feels like a second home, having cycled up it on Ride for Life, then back down it en route to Argentina. Helping with my transition to warmer weather, surfing beauties walk by and wave as I grab an authentic Mexican burrito on the cheap.

Sometimes my route deviates inland, but for the most part I stick to the coast.

The ocean view is far more enticing than riding toward the dry coastal hills, where temperatures steadily rise and the California dream of wealth and privilege transitions into wall-to-wall traffic and a ballooning Hispanic lower class.

I'm training for my first mountain-bike race, the Sea Otter Classic, a respected early-season festival of cycling events for both on-road and off, in the arid coastal hills of Monterey, California. I'm signed up in the Category 3 cross-country (XC) event.

This is a diverse bottom rung. Many of the riders I'm

paired with have either never raced before, do not have enough points to upgrade or just don't care to push themselves any further. There are two categories, based on ability, above us. Category 1 is considered pro by most standards.

Come race day on April 17, I'm still without a mountain bike. In a last-minute frenzy, my Specialized Bicycles acquaintance connects me with their global marketing manager, who happens to be on site. Nic Simms meets me at the race expo, quickly shakes my hand, then leads me back to their elaborate team tent to grab a demo bike.

Higher on his priority list, however, are Rebecca Rusch (a multiple 24-hour mountain-bike racing champion) and Christoph Sauser (Olympian and World Champion cross-country rider), both of whom are sitting in the shade just outside. They are cooling down after a "hot lap," a race-pace practice run around the track. With cool towels and water bottles in hand, both are signing posters for a lineup of fans. I have no idea who they are.

Nic leads me past the star riders and into a utility coach parked alongside. Inside the polished metal workstation is a row of shiny new mountain bikes, parts and tools galore. "Take this," Nic says, with haste. It is next year's "29er" (referring to its 29-inch wheel), a revolution in big-wheel stability, supposedly. He shows me how the shocks work, gives me a crash course on braking (disc brakes are new to me), shows me how to shift with my thumbs (another departure from the road bike) and discusses how the bike handles. He then hands me a CO_2 cartridge. "What's this for?" I ask.

He tells me that it is to pump up my tires. "It's faster than a hand pump and less of a hazard if it falls out of your pocket." *Huh.*

I have to jet to the start line now.

With 20 minutes to go, hundreds of riders have begun to

seed themselves in respective age waves. I'm in the 25 to 29 mix.

"Hopefully, I come back with a medal," I proclaim with great pride. Nic smirks, not really sure what to make of my blind Canadian ambition. *Sure thing*, he tips his head.

Coasting through the expo crowd, my body quivers slightly and I feel a surge of adrenaline. *This is bonkers*, I still have no idea how the bike handles.

I find my starting wave and immediately shuffle through to the front. It is not so much a case of being overly confident as it is about creating opportunity. With such a large crowd, I know enough to anticipate that a bottleneck will form in the tight single track. Over 300 riders stand behind me.

The wave ahead of me shoots off. My grip tightens.

The announcer counts us down: "Three, two, one, GO!"

I immediately fire ahead with a few close followers behind me. The first mile is on the Laguna Seca racetrack, familiar paved territory. I'm determined to get the lead going into the first single-track offshoot. And I do.

I have never been at the front of a race. The feeling is both empowering and scary, and without a moment to consider which influences the other.

I'm setting the pace through uncharted waters. Knowing how the bike reacts on dirt and sand at speed remains a question mark. *Fly like a bat out of hell on the straightaways. Remain cautious with the rest.*

My fingers hover over the brakes as things start to get dicey.

We descend through a small sapling forest, around a series of tight downhill bends. My foot clips the high side of an off-camber corner (an angled track, not cut into the slope, that does not complement the force of gravity) as I duck to miss a branch, sending my heart racing.

I ascend alone out of the forest, pushing nervously past waves of riders ahead of me, huffing. "On your left!" I yell out repeatedly.

I arrive back in view of the Laguna racetrack, turn on the afterburner and fight with every last breath. Crossing under the finish arch, I throw up my arms and celebrate. *I can't believe it, I won!*

The next rider crosses the finish line over six minutes behind me.

Upon hearing of my win, the Alberta Bicycle Association upgrades me to Category 2.

From here on in, local race points are what I'm after. The better I place, the more points I'll receive. And the more points I have in the bank, the more likely I am to be upgraded.

I sign up for every race in Alberta, and even one on the west coast that requires four days of driving, $500 in gas, a $40 ferry trip and over $300 in hotel costs. I'm playing the odds, travelling to races that offer the most points, not necessarily those with the best competition. The sooner I can be upgraded to Category 1, the more time I'll have to mature at the elite level.

By the end of the 2009 season, I have earned a spot as one of the top Category 2 racers in Alberta. That said, the final ascent to Category 1 has slowed.

Podium spots are traded back and forth between a deep talent pool, particularly on courses that are littered with technical terrain, like mud, single-track and other opportunities to tear my flesh open. Fortunately, I feel my skill evolving with each weekend scar. Never have I ended up with so many cuts and bruises from crashing into trees, sliding down steep slopes and doing other dumb things so quickly.

In between bloodied battles, I refocus on my work at the gym. I apply Polysporin antibiotic ointment, stretch, use a foam roller to massage my legs and stay away from too much strenuous activity.

Behind the scenes, my agent and I have been working diligently on building further relations with Planet Foods in Calgary. They are one of the top distributors of natural and organic foods in Canada.

During RAAM, I supplemented my whole-food intake with a generous supply of their energy bars and electrolyte gummy chews in addition to Hammer Nutrition products. Building on that support, Planet Foods has also agreed to sponsor my entry, and that of a teammate, in the legendary TransRockies, a seven-day mountain-bike race through the heart of the Rocky Mountains. It is a perfect final test for Year One of this new adventure.

Upping the ante, I'm determined to partner with a rider who's stronger than me. This person will help pace me through the foreign terrain, showing me how to navigate the best lines. They will push me beyond my comfort zone and ultimately to the next level for the following season.

Bow Cycle connects me with one of their part-time employees. Brian Bain is shorter than me and has a clubfoot, but apparently he is also a strong contender in Category 1. He accepts the challenge and agrees to be patient with me. "It doesn't really matter if I'm faster than you. We have to cross through the time checks *together*," he points out.

Our unique bond is tested to the max on the final day of the race, heading into Fernie, British Columbia.

Fighting neck and neck for third place with a team from Pennsylvania, I find it difficult to keep up with Brian on the climbs, since he weighs much less than me. "I'll swallow my pride. Go ahead, push me," I suggest. He gets a hand on my back and thrusts me forward. We gain a small lead.

Sensing that the end is near, my chain creates one last challenge and snaps with an ill-timed thrust. Instead of wasting time trying to fix it (mashing the next two new links together), I take a gamble and continue on foot, running down the last mountain descent, while Brian coasts slowly ahead. Both of our anxiety levels are at max capacity.

We finally reach pavement.

The finish is in sight. "Grab onto my seat!" Brian yells back. He'll tow me in the rest of the way.

My partner huffs and puffs, fighting to get this locomotive back up to speed. All I can do is sit back and offer cheers of encouragement.

We cross the finish line in third place.

Brian immediately collapses to the ground, looking back as the fourth-place team comes roaring down Main Street, only a few blocks behind us. "Congrats, man!" I slap him on the back. A podium finish at TransRockies is a sizable accomplishment in the mountain-bike realm.

AUGUST, 2010

I return to TransRockies to challenge their new three-day solo option (TR3). This category has recently been allotted a rare number of Union Cycliste Internationale (UCI) world ranking points. Garner enough of these points and you can race internationally. Races in Canada with this number of UCI points are normally tough to come by.

Most of the local elite racers will stay away, though, because of the steep entry fee and because UCI points have no value to them. A limited number of pro riders who do not have to pay their own way, however, will be drawn to the points. Riders such as Adam Craig (a multiple Olympian), Carl Decker (World Downhill Champion) and a handful of riders from the Canadian national team may want to race. But overall, the combined talent pool will still be smaller than usual.

Again, I'm playing the odds.

My goal is to acquire just one point. If I do, I can apply to race for the national team at the UCI Mountain Bike Marathon World Championships in Italy next year. I see this as an important opportunity to make myself known.

The race begins at an early hour, just as the sun begins to peek over the misty mountains surrounding Fernie.

At the sound of a horn, a pack of 20 elite riders shoots off the front almost immediately. Over 300 team riders and TR3 solos are left in their caffeinated wake.

Thirty minutes later a group of ten lean riders power ahead from the initial lead group, and I'm among them. Pushing the pace even faster, we soon spread into our own anabolic rhythm of grunts and personal pain.

Ahead is a lengthy mountain climb.

Reaching the first skyward pitch, sweating profusely, I see Adam Craig and the national team riders cresting on a switchback high above. It is a humbling moment of awe, respect and realization of how much higher my bar needs to be set.

By the end of day three, I finish ninth overall. I'm awarded 20 UCI points.

Driving back to Bentley with the windows down and the stereo blaring, I rejoice in having surpassed my one-point goal. Although, in the back of my mind, I'm concerned that the maturing talent pool will soon catch up with my grand ambition. *These are the guys I need to beat.*

To cap off another great racing season, in which I also placed third at the Category 2 national mountain-bike championship in Canmore, Alberta, I plan a special event at Best Body Fitness as a way to bring the active-minded of Sylvan Lake together and also maintain community support (I have several small donors) heading into the winter.

The lost opportunity to hold a world record for cycling the Pan-American Highway in 2005 has stuck with me. And though it was not what mattered in the end, it is still very much a personal goal of mine to be "the best" at something.

Speaking of which, spinning is on my mind. For the last couple of months, I have been getting more involved in leading spin classes at Best Body Fitness, often two to three sessions a week, in addition to managing the front desk. Through a Google search, I find an eight-day, eight-hour record for consecutive time spent "static cycling" on a stationary bike. The challenge was originally conceived by a retired DEA (Drug Enforcement Agency) agent from the United States.

As for the rules, they are relatively straightforward: you must ride at least 19.2 kilometres in an hour, during which time you must pedal *continuously*. For every hour you complete, you can take five minutes off the bike. You can choose to bank that time, for sleeping, mainly, or use it then and there for washroom breaks and/or stretching. Incomplete hours result in a one-hour penalty. If you receive this penalty and you haven't banked enough time, then BONG, your record attempt is over.

Compared to RAAM, this should be a walk in the park. I'll be sheltered from the elements, I'll have the ability to moderate my gears at will (and why would I add tension to the wheel?), plus have many of the same support crew from RAAM, and more.

AUGUST 13, 2010

I take on a 24-hour solo training ride in the centre of town under an open-walled event tent as part of our "Shake the Lake" outdoor music and action-sports festival. I also hope to promote the other ride, for the world record, now planned for October.

Leland and my sister are there for the entire effort. They hand me food and water and help me to pass the time with jokes, YouTube videos and memories of racing RAAM.

In the middle of the night, it is just the three of us in the dark parking lot, though an eclectic security guard is never far away. Drunken teens walk by and cheer me on.

Coming up to the sunny 1:00 p.m. planned stop time the following afternoon, a small crowd cheers me on as my bike odometer ticks over one last kilometre, closing at 870 kilometres. I stand out of the saddle and give a little wave.

Despite my wobbly legs and keen desire to fully dismount, I rejoice for a moment. My body and mind have reaffirmed that *yes, you can do this.*

Projectile vomit spews out of my mouth. *Ugh, what the fuck?*

Slowly walking over to my bed, still nauseated, I step in another pile of red slime. That one is an hour old.

I lie down. *Ugh, here it comes again.*

My energy is so depleted that I just roll over and puke onto the pillows. It is a helpless and untimely scene. Two days to go until the record attempt spin and I am the sickest I have ever been.

My sister knocks on the front door, perhaps sensing my need for help. She and Leland recently moved into their own place. She walks in to find me in just my underwear, covered in puke. She takes on the thankless task of helping me clean up. "I see that you had licorice," she points to one pile of vomit. *I likes my candy.*

We postpone the record attempt an additional two days. "And you need to get the doctor's approval to proceed," Scott says. He claims that my condition is a liability for the gym, and that he is concerned as a friend also. He then hands me a long grocery list of easily digested calorie-dense foods to buy, such as avocados. "I want you to have eaten everything by the time we start," he says. There has been some concern that I am too skinny, in addition to the strange illness.

Feeling feeble, but, to all outward appearances, seeming to be on the mend, I continue setting up in the southwest corner of the gym. There is a small stage, a stationary bike, a couch where witnesses can hang out (two of them must remain here for four hours at a time), a large HD TV for entertainment, web cameras to record and broadcast the record attempt online and a small curtained-off area behind which I will urinate and sleep. Going "number two" and showering requires a short run to the men's change room.

Scott comes over to me again in between training clients. I'm holding on to a railing for balance, still feeling nauseous. On seeing this, he shoots me a look that says, *That doesn't look like "ready" to me.*

"I'm at a seven out of ten right now in coming back around," I reassure him. "It's good enough to start." The room continues to spin, possibly from dehydration and not being able to keep enough food down. I feel drunk.

It's not ideal. But I'm concerned about inconveniencing all the volunteers who have taken time off work. There is a 24-hour schedule, filled out for the next week, that includes the names of witnesses and additional support, over and above a core group of people who will be around continuously, like Scott. *It would be impossible to reschedule everyone.*

OCTOBER 6, 2010

It is 7:58 a.m. A few early morning gym members go about their regular routines, casually eyeing the small corner gathering of family and volunteers.

I'm seated on the bike with both feet clipped in, steadfast. The official race clock is in my periphery.

Come on, Ryan, you can do this.

Scott gives me an affirming nod. "Begin pedalling in three, two, one, GO!"

CHAPTER 24

ATTEMPT TO KILL MYSELF

STATIONARY CYCLING ATTEMPT – DAY 2

After 48 hours of almost non-stop riding, I peel myself off the stationary bike and hobble a couple of feet to the curtained-off area behind the stage. One of my crew hands me a set of earplugs as I wearily pass by.

I collapse on a sleeping bag, face down on the floor. My mouth hangs open, my breathing is heavy and a string of drool slowly soaks down. I can feel my heartbeat and the light thump of Top 40 music from the gym's sound system vibrating on the floor. My clothing and cycling shoes are still on. It is 9:00 a.m. *Sleep now.*

There is peace of mind in knowing I have built up a rest buffer. Out of 240 accumulated minutes, 180 minutes remain after 12 washroom breaks. To save time, there is a portable urinal that I can take back with me behind the curtain. The humble task of draining and disinfecting it falls on my support crew.

My former RAAM crewmember Megan is joined by her mom and stepdad, from Calgary. The trio has been able to trade off for short breaks at the Comfort Inn & Suites next door. The hotel manager has generously donated a room for their use.

Just as I begin to feel settled, there is a tug at my arm. Megan calmly tells me it is time to get up. I stare up at her with a quizzical look. *Wait, did I even have a chance to rest?*

"You have been asleep for almost 20 minutes," she confirms.

I take off my eye mask and my vision adjusts to the light. I stand, taking a second to catch my balance, then hobble back to the bike. "You have two minutes before you need to begin. Might as well stretch for a second," says Megan in a comforting, yet tough-love sort of way. I came to know this demeanour well on RAAM. She's not going to give an inch.

"Okay, wow, already?" I look stupefied.

Twenty minutes off the bike is the magic number that was set by two previous record holders. The pair also agrees on building up a time buffer in the opening days of the record attempt, both for these short sleep breaks and for the unexpected. The chief concern seems to be hallucinations.

During RAAM, I remember hearing reports of riders confusing mailboxes for monsters in the dark. And just last month, the DEA agent had to cut his latest attempt at the record short when he hit a similar hallucination wall. He was attempting to reclaim the record from German endurance freak Frank Trtschka.

Unlike a cramp or a painful saddle sore, unknowingly losing my mind is new endurance territory for me. *Maybe it only happens to certain people?* The crew also remains hopeful, on rotation and happily in the here and now.

STATIONARY CYCLING ATTEMPT – DAY 3

The main question on day three is not *if* I will break the record, but rather, by how much? Those watching from the sidelines have said I look strong. And I feel it. But there is still another five days of "going nowhere," as someone put it eloquently. *Or is there more?* If I pass the record mark of eight days and eight hours and continue to feel in relatively good condition, *when do you know to stop?*

Based on how I'm feeling, I half expect to go beyond nine days. *But shit, do I really want to?* And if I do stop earlier when I feel like I can keep going, is it an injustice to the world record, like retiring after six Tour de France victories when you know that a seventh is possible?

This question opens up an interesting debate on Facebook. I throw in my two cents while I answer e-mails on a newly purchased iPad. The device fits snugly in a perch created by my cushioned aero bars.

Also featured in the "cockpit" is an odometer with my current speed and distance listed. Each hour, to the minute, two witnesses and a crewmember check that I have reached the 19 kilometres required. It hasn't been a problem so far.

With no tension, the challenge is actually not to overshoot the mark by too much. Riding an extra kilometre or two is ideal, the crew and I decide. "Cross the 19-kilometre point at 45 minutes and then just coast to the end of the hour," Scott suggests. Trying to achieve the mileage right at the hour puts everyone unnecessarily on edge.

Awareness of my record attempt is increasing each day. Having people continually stare at me as they work out, or people who just pop in to speak with the crew (from behind a barrier), is also becoming more the norm. If I need to pick my nose or fart in plain view, *so be it*. This is not a public exposition on being proper.

In the early days of discussing this record attempt, most people assumed I would go home when the gym closed each night. *No sir*, this ride goes 24 hours a day. When you're sleeping at 2:00 a.m., I'm riding. When you get up early for work, feeling cranky, yep, I'm still on the bike.

The small crowd of spectators, which began as gym

members and gym coworkers, has grown. These same people now bring their kids by to watch for 15 to 20 minutes at a time. I try to be alert and friendly for everyone, especially for the younger children. "Come on over," I encourage the shy ones.

It was not so long ago that I was in their shoes, sitting cross-legged on a hard gymnasium floor in elementary school, patiently waiting for a guest speaker to clear his or her throat. I remember hearing stories of climbing Mount Everest, of canoe trips along uncharted rivers and of humanitarian work in places with unpronounceable names.

I always felt inspired by these talks. I hope this ride will have a similar impact on the young people who come to watch me.

Sensing that I am in it for the long haul, many of our volunteers begin to sign up for extra witness or support shifts, as not all spots were filled when we began. "Whatever you need," is the sentiment often echoed. "Can I work both positions?" is the follow-up question.

Unfortunately, you must choose one or the other. It is a conflict of interest to both aid my progress and objectively account for it. Witnesses are also not allowed to help with back-to-back shifts. Yet, for the strong-willed, it is becoming increasingly common to see them around in the early morning, then again after work. "I was up anyway," they smile, brushing aside any concern on my end about their time commitment.

With the support schedule full, I turn my attention forward again and wave.

Stats on the live video stream are increasing exponentially. After only a dozen people watching on the opening day, we have jumped to over a thousand active viewers. "I leave you up on my desktop at work," one guy says. "It's hard to look away," he laughs, acknowledging the absurdity outright. The camera angle is a pixelated shot of me pedalling, and it never changes. It's a peep show for endurance junkies.

If I ever need to talk strategy or "adjust" myself, one of the crew strategically stands in front of the web camera. For those that may wonder if I ever stop pedalling during these moments, there is a second camera with an unobstructed view of me. It records to a hard drive (not broadcast online). This second camera was installed so we could provide additional evidence of the authenticity of the record attempt, if necessary.

The sound on both cameras is somewhat muffled.

It is entertaining to read comments from friends on Facebook as they try to guess what movie or show I am watching at any given moment. We push the programming with harsher language to the later hours. Still, even with an active audience, no one questions the content, even my mom, who has just arrived from British Columbia with my father.

The two of them cringe at the blood-splattered bondage scene in *Pulp Fiction*. "Necessary viewing," I tell them. It's all intended to keep my mind engaged. The soft stuff just doesn't cut it after three days on the bike.

STATIONARY CYCLING ATTEMPT – DAY 4

I wake up from a 20-minute sleep break feeling nauseous and overheated. A crewmember opens the emergency exit door, a welcome nearby source of uncirculated fresh air, and turns a fan in my direction. Still, I don't feel well.

The severity of my symptoms becomes even more apparent if I stand to pedal. Almost immediately, the black rubber floor mats appear to shift beneath me, instilling a panicked sense of vertigo. It is an entirely new and horrible sensation for me.

My attention turns away from the watchful gym members and other supporters. "If you could, please hold people back from talking to me today," I ask one crewmember. It is a shame, as more parents have brought their kids in to meet me. There are also some reporters on site. "But not today, please," I reiterate.

Escaping to the iPad, I notice that my vision is also blurred. I quickly pass the device back, so I don't vomit. Messages of support are instead read out loud to me by my mom and sister. Scott and my father step in to be the public voice for everything else.

Staring away from it all, my head anchored on one arm, I begin to feel emotional.

That same afternoon, my friend Sharon and her mother come in for their witness shift and to console me. Sharon has been an active participant in my spin classes. She also teaches yoga at the gym. And although she is ten-plus years my senior, she is in excellent shape and a close mountain biking companion.

For the next hour and a half, a new Ryan swears at her, while speaking in gibberish.

I notice her concerned look as I begin to come back around. "Did that just happen?" I whisper quietly. She politely deflects my question.

I'm confused. "We were on a rooftop talking. I was swearing a lot – sorry for that, by the way." Speaking of the scene out loud, I begin to realize how foolish it all sounds. I'm still on the bike, not a rooftop.

What the hell just happened? I apologize again to Sharon. It's not like me to swear out loud, not since RAAM anyway.

My father walks over with an awkward grin. "Have I been speaking funny?" I ask him. He smiles and pats me on the back. There is no answer.

I'm starting to get angry now. I want to know if something is up.

All the crew hears the shift in my tone. "No, seriously, have I been speaking funny?" They play it off again, as if I'm a friend who has just woken up from a drunken stupor. All the while, Sharon stands off to the side, still looking concerned.

"Someone say something!" I say sternly. *Was it a hallucination?!*

There is a disconnect in my brain. It feels like a waking dream. I could have a face-to-face conversation with a person, then five minutes later be unsure of what we talked about or where our conversation took place – only remembering that I was somehow involved. *This is no laughing matter.*

I think of my grandma. She is now in a retirement home, living with dementia. *Is this what Alzheimer's feels like?*

The crew tightens up on a few variables that had been relatively slack, such as me having control over what I was in the mood to eat. On that particular point, Scott calls up Steve Born, the "Fueling Guru" for Hammer Nutrition, who is now sponsoring me. Like me, Steve has a storied history with RAAM and other ultra events. Questions pertaining to the nutritional needs of Steve, me and other elite athletes are not the type of thing you take to just any nutritionist.

Scott and Steve run through my diet thus far. It once again includes the Hammer products, but also a greater concentration of whole foods, as my stomach allows them. Steve says we are on the right track. My nutrition is not his main concern, though.

Moving away from my eating regime, he advises that if we can, we should try to schedule a couple of longer sleep breaks, and soon. Based on his experience, this will be our best chance at breaking the hallucination cycle.

STATIONARY CYCLING ATTEMPT – DAY 5

I'm woken from a 30-minute rest, groggy and hallucinating once again. It takes another ten minutes and a handful of smelling salts to get me consciously pedalling.

"Oh yeaahh," I remember what we are doing now.

As difficult as it is to admit, the crew and I agree that the extra ten minutes of sleep was too much. This conclusion is supported by the results of a conversation with an oil rig worker who is knowledgeable about the effects of sleep deprivation. My body started falling into a REM (rapid eye movement) sleep cycle. As a result, I can't expect to begin riding again so quickly.

In addition to my puffy-eyed, grimacing state, I lean over and tell my father that my feet have been going increasingly numb and that they also hurt.

I have tried changing into my running shoes on occasion. They allow my arch to flex and relax, whereas custom-fitted mountain-bike shoes are fully rigid. But the increased comfort comes with a trade-off: the running shoes do not pedal as efficiently as the cycling shoes. They lose power in the flex. Cycling shoes channel all the downward force into the ball of the foot and the pedal beneath.

This is an important consideration, even with next to no tension applied – just enough to keep my muscles engaged, and to prevent atrophy.

After months of dissecting the previous record holders' attempts, it dawned on me that with so little resistance on the bike, it would actually make more sense for me to pedal with one leg at a time. The other could rest on the frame. I would switch legs periodically, which would mean both legs would remain fresher, longer.

None of the previous contenders had tried this before. Whether or not it would be allowed was up for debate. But after some back and forth with the Guinness record department, they agreed to our plan.

At the time, I considered it a stroke of brilliance.

STATIONARY CYCLING ATTEMPT – DAY 6

Every minute counts.

It is becoming increasingly difficult to stay on the bike for hours on end. I start using up more of my five-minute breaks as they are awarded.

We have it timed that I can run, assisted, across the gym to the men's change room, where it is ten minutes for "number two," or 15 minutes for a shower and a change of clothes. Two people always run alongside me with stopwatches. One of them is a witness; the other is a member of my crew. They stand outside the change room and yell, "You are at two minutes, three to go!"

Adding to the time crunch, I missed reaching my hourly mileage requirement for the first time last night. I was half asleep, caught up in a story that an elderly witness was telling. And, ironically, I was also the first to catch the slip-up. "We missed it," I admitted out loud, half-frightened that the record attempt was over.

But no, we are just penalized an hour. I have roughly 45 minutes left in the bank.

Knowing that another slip-up cannot occur, the crew takes on the agonizing task of enforcing mileage targets every 15 minutes, as my own ability to do the math slips further. Someone is almost always at my side now, saying things like,

"You need to pick up your speed … yep, that's good. Keep up that rhythm."

Everyone that comes into the gym is invested now. They see me struggling and understand that I cannot do this alone.

My vision grows increasingly blurry and my attention span wanes. "Pick it up," my father says, concerned. I snap a look back, short on temper after being constantly watched for so long. *Fuck!* He throws his hands up and walks away.

Leland steps in in his place, trying a different approach. "A little bit quicker, come on," he says softly.

I am on the verge of crying.

The crew takes turns gently rubbing my back and massaging my shoulders. "You're doing good," they tell me. "Keep going, come on."

My condition begins to dramatically waver by the hour. Heading to the back for a hurried break, I mistakenly piss all over my sleeping area, missing the portable urine bottle. "Don't worry, we got it," Leland calms.

Shortly afterward, two police officers stop by to have a casual chat with the crew. Looking directly at the uniformed pair, my mind's eye sees a vibrant city park instead of rows of treadmills and weight machines. I'm losing my grip.

STATIONARY CYCLING ATTEMPT – DAY 7

The first staff and early gym members arrive at 5:30 a.m. Each of them is relieved to see that I am still pedalling away. There is an increasingly stressed look on my face, though, at least on the half of my face that can be seen. The other half is buried in my arms, hidden below a hunched torso.

Music is still a ray of light, thankfully. "Clocks" (my

self-professed theme song, by Coldplay) comes on and I can no longer hold back any emotion. *Please let me see this through.*

The gronks notice my breakdown and are the first to pass along their praise to Scott and my parents. Stepping beyond the barrier, one of them walks over to me. "I have witnessed true greatness," he says, with tears in his eyes. "Hold on, brother!"

STATIONARY CYCLING ATTEMPT – 4:00 A.M., OCTOBER 13

I have been stuck in a hallucination for the last several hours. "You have to keep pedalling," my crew takes turns repeating.

"Why??" I moan back. *It doesn't make any sense.* As far as I can remember, I completed the record attempt many years ago.

Looking around the room, I see that we are in a spaceship. The people I knew as friends and family are actually holograms with an uncertain agenda. *They appear to be tricking me into powering the ship by pedalling. Any time I slow down, they begin yelling. Are they the enemy?*

In response to incessant pleas, I swear and yell back, "It doesn't make any fucking sense. Why are you forcing me to do this?!"

I get off the bike and try to run away.

Someone grabs me, sits me down and puts my running shoes on. Next, I feel my spaghetti arms placed around two sets of strong shoulders.

One of my arms is around my father, the other hangs heavy around the largest black man I have ever seen, an oil worker by trade, but with a teddy-bear demeanour. "Just had to come see how Ryan was doing," he speaks softly to my father.

I feel a breeze.

It is dark out. The two men help me across the gym parking lot and over to the hotel next door. The gravity of the situation hasn't hit me. I'm just relieved to no longer be powering the ship. But that hallucination is waning.

Inside the hotel, I begin to sense that something has gone wrong. Unfortunately, fatigue inhibits a connection back to reality. I'm quickly falling asleep.

Moments later, I am lying down in a bed. I hear people around me speaking in whispers, praising my effort. But none of what they are saying sticks in my mind long enough for me to process a response. My body is in full shutdown mode.

Fading out of consciousness, I recognize the voice of a key volunteer asking my parents if she can say a prayer. She makes a plea for my health, speaking quietly by my side, "Please, we ask that you watch over him…"

My father writes on my Facebook wall:

> You fought the good fight for many days and nights on end, when many lesser people would have quit. You didn't quit. Your mind and body just lost the ability to come together one last time. So be it. No one died. You will reflect on this experience as another great adventure. Mom, Trish, Lee and I were honored to be part of the whole experience. You accomplished your goal of helping to bring the community of Sylvan Lake together. The fine staff and customers of Best Body Fitness are to be commended. It has been a long

time since I have witnessed so many people doing so much for another.

Love,
Dad

I rode for 6 days and 20 hours, and covered 3292.5 kilometres.

CHAPTER 25

FINDING BALANCE

OCTOBER 13, 2010

My eyes begin to open after a couple hours of rest. I still feel dazed.

From a chair beside the bed, my mother asks, "Do you know where you are?" It takes me a moment to realize that I am in a hotel room and no longer on the stationary bike.

"Yes," I reply, with tears welling up. *I didn't make it.*

"We tried everything we could to keep you on the bike," my mother continues. "You kept trying to run away – one time you even got off the bike and ran out the emergency exit. We thought the cool air would be good for you, but no. You continued to believe that your support crew was the enemy."

I feel incredibly embarrassed that my mind went to the places that it did. "It was like a waking dream," I reiterate. It is the only time in my entire life that I can recall losing control in such a dramatic fashion. The few times I have been drunk, they don't even compare.

My mother asks if it would be all right if Scott stops by to check on me. "A lot of people are really worried about you."

"Of course," I respond.

Scott comes by the room an hour later. I hobble timidly toward his brotherly hug. "I'm sorry," I tell him, referring to all the wasted energy on his part.

"For what?!" he shoots back. "You have inspired a ton of

people, bro. There is an incredible energy in the gym and in the community. It took me an hour just to get up to my office this morning. Everyone is asking about you!"

We hug again.

Later that morning, my father helps me back out into the sunlight and fresh fall air. My sister and Leland recently purchased a home in the small town of Lacombe, about twenty minutes east of Bentley. The plan is to spend the next couple of days recovering at their place. "There are a couple of supplies to pick up at the gym first, if you're all right with that?" he asks, opening the Jeep door for me to get in. Scott has done most of the cleaning up already.

"I'll stay in the car," I say, feeling awkward.

At that moment, a mother and daughter who helped as witnesses walk out from the gym. I slump down in the seat so as not to be seen. No matter what Scott says, I still feel like I let a lot of people down.

OCTOBER 15, 2010

I don't have any feeling in my body from my hips down. Still, my muscle memory has a mind of its own.

The last couple of nights, I have woken on my side, my legs pedalling around in phantom circles. The bedsheet is often tangled around my feet, just like after RAAM, like dough caught in a mixer. But this is the least of my worries.

My mind is accustomed to being awake for over 23 hours a day. This unfortunate rhythm is not a lever that can be turned on and off at will. And yet, my body still cries out for the downtime to recover.

Sleep is a luxury now.

Lying in bed on another restless night, I scroll through hundreds of e-mails and Facebook messages. It is heart-warming to see the outpouring of support, both from the community and from new friends as far away as Europe who followed the live video feed. No one looks down on me for having stopped early. *But, damn it*, I wish I could have pulled it off.

Many "what if" scenarios fill my thoughts.

What if I hadn't been sick before the attempt began? What if I had slept a little during the first two days of the ride? Were my cycling shoes too small? Was pedalling with one leg the right strategy? What if I hadn't missed my mileage that one time, had not been penalized an hour and had the opportunity to have a longer rest in the 11th hour? *What if...*

My parents stay with me in Lacombe for the week to make sure I'm okay. I'm set up in a spare bedroom, temporarily.

Other than the lack of sleep and no feeling in my legs, everything else appears normal. Granted, continuing to stub my toes on table and chair legs is a running joke. Since I'm not able to properly coordinate my movements, I have to whip my legs forward like a wooden toy soldier. It's amusing, at first.

My mother makes a grocery run to stock the empty fridge in Bentley. I am now the condo's sole occupant. Returning to Lacombe, she offers to stay with me once I move back on my own. "To help nurse you back to health," she pleads.

In the background, my father defaults to a more subdued, "Get off the tit." He's playing nice.

I assure her that I will be fine. "But could you maybe drive me home?" I ask. I'm not yet in a position to transport myself.

They give me a lift back that afternoon, each of them giving me a longer hug than usual as they say goodbye.

In the condo alone, I soak in the silence.

I attempt to kneel and untie my shoes, but I wobble at first, then buckle to the ground. *This lack of feeling is only temporary*, I tell myself.

Getting back into my bachelor routine, I download a bunch of old movies to watch with a bowl of easy-to-make, microwave popcorn. Past the opening credits, however, I just blankly stare at the images flickering across my computer screen.

Later that night, unable to sleep, I start hobbling around the condo.

I end up in the spare room, not remembering why I originally came in there. The feeling is reminiscent of waking up at my parents' lake home after RAAM – in a cold sweat, staring at a blinking LED light in the dark and feeling like I was supposed to be somewhere.

OCTOBER 18, 2010
I receive a visit from Scott and a reporter from the *Sylvan Lake News*. They come as friends first, but also to conduct a follow-up interview with me while my memories are fresh.

They are both very respectful of the recovery process, not wanting to barge in if I am unwilling, and neither of them assumes I will be back to work anytime soon. Hugging again, Scott tells me, "Take all the time you need. We have a collection jar going at the front desk to help pay your bills."

In the midst of feeling bashful, the three of us sit down on a pair of old leather couches in my living room. It is a while before the recording device comes out.

There are quotes that will never make it into the newspaper – those lines that help lighten the mood when dealing with such an emotional and heavy subject. The process of allowing ourselves to open up is much different from reporting on the local sports beat.

And then we begin.

Scott provides an account of how the record attempt has affected the community. "Members who haven't worked out in ages are back. The heavy lifting guys are being more talkative. And it's hard to walk in and out of the building without at least a couple of people asking how Ryan is doing."

My public display of suffering came as a shock to a lot of people. It also brought together in a volunteer capacity many people who had often kept to themselves. "There is a much more caring attitude in both the gym and the community," Scott continues. The reporter couldn't agree more.

As for the inevitable question of where the path leads next, I respond, "My focus is on a full recovery, then continuing toward my goal of making the 2012 Olympic team for London." *Onward.*

NOVEMBER 1, 2010

MY LEGS ARE ON FIRE! I tear the bedsheets away in a frantic search for the mystery heat source but am confused to find that my limbs are lying there all the same: pale, white and without any sign of a flame. There is instead a war waging inside my legs. My unresponsive nerves are now waking up in the least friendly way possible.

I hobble in pain toward a cool shower.

Cautious not to slip, I sit down in the tub with my knees held up in a defensive position. No amount of water can wash away the panic on my face, however. This unrelenting hurt is new to me. It is not an obvious scrape or bruise that can be attended to.

I stay in that position until an uncontrolled shiver forces me out of the tub. *What the hell is going on?*

I experienced a partial loss of feeling in my hands and feet after RAAM, *but nothing like this*. This feels like a severe burn that is nowhere near calming. The feeling in my hands and feet gradually returned after RAAM, but what about this time?

Rubbing my arms and chest, I am on the lookout for any further symptoms. *Should I be worried?*

Probably not. I'm young and have had no previous health concerns. But, for good measure, Scott suggests I take a little longer to recover at home. "It should only be another week before I can return to work," I tell him.

THE NEXT FEW WEEKS
The painful neuropathy continues, unrelenting. Socks are too painful to wear, and even the thinnest of bedsheets feels too heavy on my fiery toes. So, I lie in my boxers, frustrated, wearing several warm layers up top.

Once or twice an hour, half asleep, I'll hobble over to the cool tile floor outside the bedroom and just stand there for relief. Remaining upright for any length of time is a challenge, however.

Cooking, driving and going for walks are now out of the question. So I stay in the condo like a hermit, surviving off of Hammer Bars left over from the record attempt and other easy-to-eat meals like pizza and canned soup.

A month slips away in this lonely bubble. Snow now falls outside my window.

Looking in the mirror one afternoon, I notice my sunken eyes and yellow complexion. My ribs have also begun to protrude. I can't recall ever being so skinny. I'm down to 153 pounds.

Scott stops by on what has become a regular weekly visit and says that I look like a zombie. "You should go see a doctor," he tells me. But I am ignorant when it comes to hospitals. So my friend Sharon points me toward the local walk-in clinic and makes me promise I will go. She follows up every couple of days to see that I have called for an appointment. "Yes, yes, it's done," I finally reassure her.

The clinic is located in a retirement residence a few blocks down from the condo. Normally, such a walk would take me less than five minutes. Now, bundled from the cold, and taking painstaking steps through hard-packed snow, it takes an additional 15 minutes.

Inside the clinic, a handful of sad-looking seniors in stationary wheelchairs mumble to themselves. I find a bench in a dimly lit corner, away from it all, and hold on to the hope that a cure for my own depression will soon be at hand.

A nurse calls my name.

Inside a sterile blue room, an older doctor looks me over, asks about my medical history and quickly dismisses any long-term damage. "You're a young guy," he encourages. "There's nothing to worry about. But let me prescribe some medication for the nerve pain and another to help you sleep."

I shuffle down the street to the corner store, which also houses a pharmacy.

"How does this work?" I ask at the counter, having never purchased anything other than Aspirin. The pharmacist asks for my prescription slip and healthcare card, then portions pills into two small containers.

As per the doctor's directions, I swallow both pills with a glass of water after returning home. *Of course*, the doctor said that it might take a little while for the medication to build up in my system.

I give it a couple nights. There is still no change in my sleep or my nerve pain.

I double the dosage. Still nothing. "Fuck this shit!" I yell out in defiance of modern medicine. I've been playing this waiting game for a month, and I'm becoming more and more concerned about my severely atrophied muscles.

Just get out there, make it happen!

I begin a walking regime to the end of the block and back every day. Returning home, I take a foam roller to my legs and try to massage the nerve pain away. Like a hot shower that eventually feels cool, I surmise that continually stimulating the nerves will eventually dull the pain. However, my teeth grind in agony at even the slightest bit of pressure.

Following that routine, I sit in a cool bath with a pillow propped behind my head. Classical music plays in the background. The goal is to calm my thoughts, if even just for a half hour.

After a month and a half of waking nights, I finally sleep for three hours straight. It is a huge breakthrough in regaining my health. Our hormones, cells and immune systems depend largely on sleep in order to recover. My mood immediately lifts at the prospect of progress being made, however small.

Eager to break out of the condo routine, the next morning I call Scott and tell him it's time for me to come back to work.

In anticipation of being around people again, I attempt to stand and tie my shoes, after weeks of sitting on the ground to do so. Crouching down, my legs still shake and I again begin to lose balance. No matter, I focus on trying to find a stable centre. *Come on, you can do this.*

Driving to the gym, I find it is too painful to press on the gas pedal for any length of time, especially along snowy country roads with no stoplights. I flip on the cruise control to help. *Don't worry, you'll get there.*

Pulling up to my second home in Sylvan Lake, I turn off the engine and pause for a moment. I'm hesitant to face potential embarrassment inside. It is still unclear what exactly happened during my hallucinations and how other moments of weakness were perceived. *But remember, everyone has been supportive so far.*

Limping to the front door, I realize that my fitted uniform now hangs off of me. *Hopefully no one pays attention to the weight loss.* My incessant need to rub my legs and feet, to help curb the nerve pain, is also a concern.

My hobble slows. And finally the glass doors open to a host of friendly smiles at the front desk. "Welcome back!" a younger female staff member squeals. Her smile sets off an alarm, quickly alerting others to my presence.

Gym members soon surround me.

They shower me with hugs, handshakes and a most humble sense of appreciation. "I have never seen anything like what you did ... I've got a ton of questions," one member starts in.

"Can I buy you lunch?" asks another.

Working his way through the crowd, Scott laughs, "It's going to be a while before you can get any work done. Welcome back, buddy!"

I smile.

The main question on everyone's mind is whether I should make a second attempt at the record. "Perhaps in a couple of months, or next year," I generally respond.

Volunteers and witnesses who were closest to the unfolding drama are among those with the most varied opinions. I would have thought that my wildly fluctuating mood and hallucinations would have been enough to scare them all away. Not so.

As I lean on the front counter, trying to keep most of my weight off those sore feet, one of the more invested witnesses starts in, leaning on the other side of the counter: "Here's how I think we should do it next time..." He describes a militarily precise operation with no room for laziness or mistakes by my support crew, which he now wants to be a part of. "I hated standing on the sidelines, only allowed to watch," he says.

I look into his eyes as he stares off to "my corner" of the gym, already deeply invested, and think, *You know what? Maybe I will.*

Others approach me with a quieter demeanour, feeling both sadness and relief. "You're done, right? There is no possible way you would put yourself through that again, would you?" they ask me. And still, I let my ego feign a cheeky grin. "Please don't," they plead. But my mind is not made up.

Despite the agonizing pain I feel daily, the stinging prospect of coming so close has infused my thoughts with a half-cocked optimism.

The conversations come to a head one morning as I hobble down into the gym from the upstairs office. As per the new routine, I brace much of my weight on the metal railing, while my weak legs struggle to find balance, one narrow step at a time. Watching from the bottom of the stairs, a large black man surveys my struggle. It is the same man that helped me to the hotel with my father in the early morning hours after the record attempt.

Seeing him, I straighten up.

We shake hands before speaking for the first time directly. "That was pretty intense, man. I didn't know a person could push themselves to that kind of darkness." He looks me over, seeming genuinely concerned. "How are you holding up?"

"Not so great at the moment. But I hope to bounce back in a few weeks," I tell him.

Yet, having been one of just a few people to observe my final few hours on the bike, as well as having witnessed many on-site oil field injuries, his face cringes in sorrowful disagreement: "I don't know about that..."

Is he suggesting permanent damage?

My role at the gym has evolved into a management position. Better pay and the opportunity to help Scott build the business has made painful days pass much more quickly. Mind you, my strained nerves only allow me to work for three hours at a time. I also have to remove my shoes for much of it.

Embarrassed to continually wince and look weak around members, I often close the door to the office I share with the other manager and buckle down on a couple of new projects, including data entry and the implementation of new gym-management software. I also don't want members to witness my evolving depressive state.

And my health is only getting worse. Enter, the "reaction."

DECEMBER 8, 2010

Returning home from work one afternoon, I reach for a glass of water, take one sip and immediately begin to feel faint. I have to lie down on the tile floor and close my eyes, or otherwise, vomit.

Soon, I begin to shiver. My heart rate has also skyrocketed. I can feel my heart pounding in my ears.

I crawl to the shower, turn on the warm water and slip into the stall, curling into the fetal position. Crippled and unable to call anyone, a very real series of thoughts crosses my mind. *Is this it? Am I about to die?*

I crawl back along the floor to my bed, stripping wet clothes off every few feet. Under the covers, I mull over other ultra recovery stories. But no relevant examples come to mind.

Eight excruciating hours pass before the severity of the reaction lessens and the familiar wave of nerve pain floods back in – now the lesser of two evils.

DECEMBER 11, 2010

The first time my reaction happens in public, it's during our Saturday morning spin class at the gym.

My sister Trisha and I riding our first bikes, 1989

Dad and I riding down Haleakala volcano in Maui, 1991

Dad and I finishing our second big tour – Prince Edward Island to Grimsby, Ontario, in 1997

Being held by Dad as a baby

Assistant captain with the Calgary Royals, 1998

Completing Ride for Life beside the Olympic columns
in Calgary, 2002

Dana and I skating at the Olympic Oval in Calgary, 2005

Driving along the dusty Dalton Highway in Alaska, en route to Prudhoe Bay, 2005

Inquisitive kid wearing my sunglasses in Ollantaytambo, Peru, 2005

Reaching Ushuaia, Argentina –
"The End of the World" – 2005

Dad offering encouragement on a Race Across Oregon climb,
2007

Race Across Oregon finish, 2007 – RAAM Qualified

Race Across America, 2008, start in Oceanside, California

Scorching Arizona climb, Race Across America, 2008

Debbie meeting up with us in Arizona, Race Across America, 2008

Killer heat and sleep deprivation, Race Across America, 2008

Riding into Monument Valley,
Utah, Race Across America, 2008

The simple pleasures

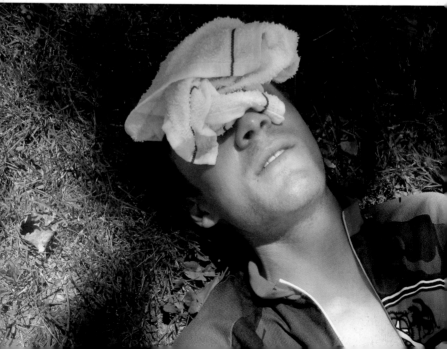

Youngest Finisher

With Mom and Dad at the finish in Annapolis

Suiting up for the Marathon World Championships in Montello, Italy, 2010

Moving up the Alberta mountain-bike ranks, 2009

With Brian at TransRockies, 2009

Scott and my father holding steady, stationary spin attempt, 2010

Leland and I goofing around, 2011

Hike-a-bike atop a frigid Cabin Pass, Tour Divide, 2012

McDonald's binge after the Great Basin, Tour Divide, 2012

Reaching the Brush Mountain Lodge, Colorado
(halfway point), Tour Divide, 2012

New Mexico "road," Tour Divide, 2012

Reaching the finish, Antelope Wells, New Mexico, Tour Divide, 2012

Coldplay with Sarah after the race, 2012

Slowly pedalling next to Scott, I take one sip of my water bottle and immediately feel dizzy again.

For the next six hours, I lie on his office floor with my eyes closed. Scott asks that I go and get my blood tested.

The test reveals nothing.

I inquire with poison control as to whether there is anything wrong with the Bentley city water. Unfortunately, that's another dead end.

The reaction starts occurring daily, and not always after I drink water. Sometimes it happens with food, too. The only consistent variable is consumption.

JANUARY, 2011

I become scared to eat anything that does not come out of a wrapper. I'm paranoid that someone is poisoning me. There is a small group of unnamed cowards who have spoken out against my efforts.

One person went so far as to post signs around Sylvan Lake, including on the front door of the gym, saying I am being investigated by the RCMP on potential charges of child molestation. That lovely news was forwarded to me while on Christmas vacation with my parents in Arizona. Of course, none of it is true. The police are on my side now. Scott is too.

This is serious.

When I come home from work, I now check to see if anyone is hiding in the condo. A creepy ex-roommate (who happens to be a pharmaceuticals rep) once pulled that stunt, brushing the incident off as, "I was going to tell you, but…"

"Get the fuck out!" I yelled, pushing him toward the door. "And give me the goddamn key back."

Suspicion continues when my new road bike is stolen out of my locked truck.

Letting new people into my inner circle is a long process for me. It's something I rarely seek out. I often keep my blinds closed, just in case someone is looking.

My eyes have become dark rings of paranoia.

I begin eating out at Tim Hortons every day. My snacks consist of whatever we have on hand at the gym: protein bars, shakes and energy drinks. Having one of each becomes a daily routine, not a reward as they would be for many people. The amount of caffeine coming into my body is ridiculous.

I hobble to the grocery store and buy the easiest, ready-to-eat calories I can find. The fatty carbohydrate source doesn't really matter: an unfriendly side effect of the reaction is being forced to empty my bowels right away. It's more to satisfy a temporary hunger.

My body turns to devouring its own limited muscle in place of fatty stores, which are now fully depleted. I'm a skeleton.

Every couple of days, the front desk receives a call, "Please tell Scott I can't make it in today." Everyone knows what that means: I've had another reaction and/or sleepless night. Unfortunately, no doctor is able to diagnose the problem.

Stuck in the dark doldrums, I'm faced with questions about my own mortality and my future purpose. And in those moments, one last bright thought makes an effort to shine through. It screams out, *I don't want to be alone any longer.*

APRIL 12, 2011

I giddily check my e-mail inbox for *her* reply.

A few days ago, I happened across the online dating profile of a beautiful young woman in Ontario. She is a triathlete, she likes to travel *and she has been to Peru?*

I break the ice by asking if one of her pictures was taken in Ollantaytambo. I tell her that my support driver, Mark, and I stayed in the beautiful town on a break from the Pan-American Highway ride before making the trek to the ruins at Machu Picchu.

I had not expected to hear back from her. *She's too beautiful*, I thought. Yet she surprises me by responding with enthusiasm, saying, yes, the picture was in fact taken at that spot.

Her name is Sarah.

CHAPTER 26

POSTHOLE

MARCH, 2011

I'm still injured. Nevertheless, I apply to represent the national team at the UCI Mountain Bike Marathon World Championships in Montello, Italy, in June.

I worked hard to earn those UCI world-ranking points at TransRockies last year. And deep down I know this opportunity is the closest I will ever get to the Olympic dream. I'm a good racer but nowhere near the top five in Canada. And I have since screwed over my potential to be better.

Reviewing the completed application, my listed racing credentials are noticeably different from the norm (most racers would have been part of a number of mass-participation events), though no less telling of my focus and dedication.

FIRST WEEK OF MAY, 2011

Word comes back from the national team that I have been selected for Italy. Sarah is the first person I share the news with. I'm excited to make her proud.

Our online shorthand has evolved into a new Facebook friendship, including lengthy messages written daily. After a month of typing back and forth, she finally agrees to a "first date" on Skype. She lives over 3600 kilometres away, in Toronto.

"How times have changed," my mother says with a questioning smirk, still trying to process the idea of two people courting each other over a computer. I dare not say the word "relationship" out loud.

MAY 7, 2011

The morning of the big date, I head out with Scott on an ambitious 200-kilometre ride in the countryside. It's part of his training for Ultraman Canada, a multi-day triathlon event held in Penticton, British Columbia, covering triple the distance of Ironman. The dream of competing in Kona, Hawaii, at the Ultraman World Championships, lives on.

Riding in pairs provides a sense of security when exposed to the early-season elements. And, as should be expected on a rural Alberta ride in early May, the weather can, and most likely will, be unpredictable.

Just before our halfway turnaround in the small farming community of Alix, the sky to the east grows dark and we begin to get pelted by cool rain. The situation is exacerbated by frigid westerly winds. "It might as well be snowing," I half joke.

Scott and I ride elbow to elbow, encouraging one another to get to Alix, and shelter, as quickly as we can. We're both shivering. Our extremities are also numb with near frostbitten pain. And of course, there is the matter of my feet.

Walking barefoot is out of the question due to exposed nerve sensitivity. Trouncing around in ordinary shoes also remains a challenge. But somewhere in between, and for reasons that are not totally clear to me, I can manage stiff-soled cycling shoes with only minor discomfort.

I have been told by a couple of doctors that it is not advisable to continue the same activity that put me in this position. Yet, ironically, cycling remains the only form of active recovery I can handle, since running and weight-bearing exercises feel so much worse. Swimming doesn't even cross my mind, likely because of some deep-seated fear of turning to the dark side of triathlon. "It's where bike handling and apparel fashion sense go to die," I often joke with Scott.

We find sanctuary in a Chinese-food restaurant attached to the village gas station.

Inside, we immediately begin stripping off our damp layers and go about finding a portable heater to have at our table. An elderly couple and group of drunken cowboys stare at us over their shoulders for a moment, then turn back to hunching over their lunches. Dim sum and cheeseburgers appear to be the mismatched meal of choice.

Scott and I each consume a bowl of chicken fried rice and won ton soup. All the while, we stare out in silence at the dim weather prospects. Upon further contemplation, we have another round of the steaming combo. Then I suggest, "Maybe one more?"

When it becomes apparent that the weather is not going to improve, and that there are only so many menu items to be sampled, I ask our friendly server if she has any garbage bags we can have, which we will fashion into makeshift rain jackets. "Of course," she smiles, appearing sympathetic to our cause.

Scott and I hurry home in the rain.

We make it back just in time for my call with Sarah. "Are you ready?" I text her, scrambling to my computer desk, still in my damp cycling shorts and socks.

"I think so," she hesitantly replies, knowing that this new connection will likely cause our relationship to evolve, for better or for worse. *I hope he/she still likes me after.*

The Skype dial tone rings. And finally, Sarah and I con-nect face to face for the first time.

Immediately following the two-hour marathon of grin-ning, we text each other again. "My cheeks hurt," I type.

"Ha ha, so do mine!" Sarah replies.

My face is still sore the following day.

EARLY JUNE, 2011

Scott and my friend Sharon are overjoyed to hear that things are going so well. *But where do we go from here?* Sooner or later, a physical connection must come into play for things to continue moving forward.

As it happens, Sarah's mom is in Edmonton for a work conference in mid-June. I offer to drive north to the "City of Champions" to meet with her.

The online gap closes further over friendly dinner conver-sation with Mary-Anne, Sarah's mom, and her friend Jane, along as a co-pilot; then a thwarted attempt on my part to pay for the meal, followed by a short walk and parting hugs.

Sarah texts me on my rainy hour-and-a-half drive home to Bentley: "My mother has never spoken so highly of a guy. She really likes you!"

Wow, this is really happening.

JUNE 22, 2011

Sharon drives me to the Calgary International Airport for my lengthy flight to Italy.

Before pulling out of the short-term parking lot, she gives me a warm hug and a bag of travel goodies. Included in it is a large pack of licorice, a risqué magazine and some money to help cover some of my expenses. *What a great friend.*

As the plane is boarding, I suddenly feel the weight, and potential risk, that comes with flying half a world away.

Infused with strong emotions, I decide to go for broke and text Sarah my deepest, most guarded feelings. Should something happen mid-flight, I would be heartbroken to have never said, "I love you." *Send.*

There is not an immediate response. "Now, please turn off your electronic devices," the female flight attendant directs. I'll be in a communication blackout for the next day.

Upon arriving at the Venice Airport Marco Polo, in northern Italy, I pick up my suitcase and my oversized bike box and make my way directly to the tiny car rental desk. The middle-aged attendant speaks only Italian, passionately flailing her hands while doing so. She hands me a set of keys to an economical little car and points to a lot outside. Small sedans are apparently the norm here.

I pull out a stack of printed Google travel directions from my carry-on bag. Walking out to the highway entrance to get my bearings, it quickly occurs to me that some of the directional cues for the drive ahead may be lost in translation. I also declined to get an international data plan for my phone, which would have been helpful for GPS navigation to the hotel.

My scheduled two-hour drive to Montello turns into four hours of continuous backtracking along narrow, old-world streets. Ancient cathedrals, quaint stone buildings and dimly lit outdoor cafés line the way.

Frustrated, I pull over to ask for help.

A young woman behind the counter of a curbside gelato shop tries to interpret where I am headed. She points farther to the west, and again, to emphasize *even farther.*

I begin back down the main highway, in darkness.

At 1:00 a.m., I pull over at a concealed grouping of quint-essentially Italian cypress trees and get out of the car to take a piss. I begin to accept the fact that I might be sleeping in that car tonight. *Just a little farther*, I tell myself.

Deep in the countryside, much farther than I expected to drive, I instinctively, and finally, roll up to the tiny two-storey accommodation. *It's the right place, thank god.*

An older woman in her pajamas walks toward me and un-locks a pair of heavy glass doors. In broken English she ex-presses having waited up just for me. "Thank you so much," I acknowledge with sincerity, breathing a huge sigh of relief.

She helps me up a couple flights of stairs to a small room with a traditional lock and key. Inside is a bed that takes up most of the room, a small antenna TV and a tiled toilet offshoot.

Lying curiously on the bed is a printed note.

I pick it up, smiling as I read the first few words. It is an e-mail message that my new friend in the pajamas was asked to print in advance. It reads: "All I need is you ... Love, Sarah."

My head is spinning.

UCI MOUNTAIN BIKE MARATHON WORLD CHAMPIONSHIPS – JUNE 26, 2011

I flat three times in the opening stage of the race and end up touring much of the 116-kilometre World Championships course. The pack of seasoned professionals leaves me in a wake of amateurism.

Putting the opportunity in perspective, I accept the mis-fortune and realize I can either make the best of a once-in-a-lifetime trip to Italy, or mope around and drop out.

Just have some fun with it.

The water stations have packed up by the time I arrive. My only option is to knock on the doors of neighbouring vineyard homes. "Please, water," I point to my two empty bottles.

In another instance, a couple out enjoying a picnic lunch offers me an apple and some animal crackers. "*Buona fortuna!* (good luck!)," they yell out as I pedal away, headed upward along a hot and dusty path.

A motorcycle sweep vehicle soon doubles back to ask if I am finished. "No!" I yell, enjoying my new solo adventure. He speeds away in frustration.

Arriving back at the Montello town square with no other racers in sight, I cross under a nearly dismantled finish arch. The race crew has also begun taking down the spectator stands and sponsor banners. No one turns to acknowledge my effort.

Instead of wallowing in some misplaced shame, I lift my arms up to the sky and proclaim with great pride, "Love, I have arrived!"

JULY 8, 2011

Sarah and I anxiously meet for the first time in person. She has agreed to accompany me to my cousin's wedding near Barrie, Ontario, two hours north of Toronto.

Our first few moments together are spent in a loving embrace outside her hotel. A kiss helps to break the nervous anticipation. "Hey, you," I say with a smile.

We agree to move in together.

AUGUST 21, 2011

I begin my last day at Best Body Fitness in Sylvan Lake. That afternoon, my friend Sharon takes me out for lunch. With encouraging tears, she hands me a blank journal. "Write your story," she tells me.

Scott and I have a chance to catch up later that evening as I'm filling out my last time sheet. It has been exactly three years since I was hired over the phone. We hug, each of us thankful for the friendship that has developed over the course of many highs and lows. *It's been a journey.*

After one last handshake, I hop into my truck, close the door and eagerly text Sarah, "I'm coming!"

Scott waves as I pull out of the gym parking lot. He soon disappears in my rear-view mirror, replaced by the sight of a trunk full of moving boxes and three bikes in tow. *Be well, my friend.*

I drive through the night, stopping only for gas and brief interludes of rest along the Trans-Canada Highway. On the evening of the third day, I'm warmly welcomed with a hug at Sarah's new Lakeshore apartment. The charbroiled aroma of "Burlington Ribfest" wafts through our now shared bedroom window. Fireworks round out the humid summer evening.

It is a dream.

In the week that follows, we go for long walks along Lake Ontario and speak romantically about our exciting life ahead. Back in the reality of the apartment, I continue to unpack my clothes, my cycling gear, my IKEA home office, my computer and my newly acquired Hammer Nutrition career path.

Two months before leaving for Ontario, Darren Thompson, the owner of the Canadian arm of Hammer Nutrition, asked if I would be interested in helping with sales in the eastern part of the country. He also offers me the position of "Fueling Guru" for the entire Canadian business. This position would make me the go-to individual for providing answers to questions about using the Hammer Nutrition products in particular, but also about sport nutrition in general. I don't say yes immediately, though, as I do not have a professional sales background, nor a formal education in nutrition. *Am I qualified?*

Darren does not hesitate. "Think about it," he responds. "You *are* a salesman. You have been marketing yourself for many years, including to me. And as for being a nutrition expert, I appreciate that your knowledge is more of the practical variety. Especially with ultra racing, however, I cannot think of another cyclist with more hard-earned knowledge."

He's right. I've puked, shit out and performed on every energy mix on the market. "Okay," I tell him "I'm in!" It seems I have finally found a career path that complements my passion for cycling.

OCTOBER, 2011
Spurred on by this new-found stability in my personal and professional life, I begin writing a long-promised book about my adventures, titled *A Purpose Ridden*, a process that had stopped and restarted several times over after I cycled the Pan-American Highway in 2005. Close family and friends are supportive of the new project. That is, until they have the chance to read the first draft chapters.

JANUARY 26, 2012
I meet up with my parents in Tucson while attending a Hammer Nutrition-sponsored cycling camp. They are visibly frustrated by the fact that I plan to write about my baby brother, Nathan, and of some of our family's growing pains.

Holding back their tears, they implore me to find a way

around some of the more sensitive parts of the story. "For one, you do not have the maturity to write about these things," my father says bluntly.

I try to explain. "My goal is not to hurt our family, Dad. It's to tell a great story, one that is honest about both the highs and the lows, and to bring it all around in the end. You need to trust me."

But they cannot.

My father is terribly hurt by the way I speak of our relationship. He also doesn't agree with my recollection of our tense hockey exchanges.

After a few tension-filled e-mails and one dropped call, I'm told that if I want to have a relationship with my parents, I am not to write about Nathan, at the very least. The confrontation leaves me feeling angry and disheartened. I tell Sarah that I'm going to stop writing. "It's not worth the heartache," I confess to her.

She encourages me to push on, as does a small group of friends and relatives who have signed on as "book sponsors," providing a $100 contribution in return for weekly updates and an acknowledgement in the published version. They hold me accountable and reassure me that not all stories worth telling are spoken about with ease.

My parents stop speaking to me.

Still, I continue writing every day. Four hours in the morning, and sometimes more at night. *But how does this story of cycling and grand ambition come together in the end?*

CHAPTER 27

THE GREAT DIVIDE

JUNE 8, 2012

I ride up Banff Avenue (in touristy Banff, Alberta) on my fully loaded Giant XTC 29er mountain bike.

The early morning sun shines through crisp Rocky Mountain air, encompassing my being with a new-found joy. I have been away from the rugged western topography for almost nine months now, and I find I have a greater appreciation for its natural beauty.

At the south end of town, I come across another "kitted out" rider. He's carrying at least an extra 20 pounds of weight (using the backpack approach, which I have purposely avoided). He's a non-contender, most likely. I say "Good morning!" just the same. "Looks like we are headed to the same place."

Noticing my minimalist approach, the older, perhaps wiser, rider inquires as to where the rest of my gear is. "This is all I need," I tell him. *I'm here to race the Tour Divide.*

We cross over the emerald-green Bow River, turn left at a T-intersection on a quiet Spray Avenue and immediately pull up to a scene of approximately 100 anxious riders outside the decidedly low-key start line at the Banff Y Mountain Lodge, a YMCA hostel, which also has subsidized housing available.

It is impressive to witness first-hand how this underground race has evolved from a lonely few riders, beginning in 2008. The spike in popularity has much to do with the release of a feature film about the annual event, called *Ride the Divide*. Admittedly, my own conviction was sealed after watching the film. It follows a group of amateur riders as they race 4418 kilometres along the remote Continental Divide, from Banff, Alberta, to Antelope Wells, New Mexico.

"How was the warm-up ride?" Sarah greets me with an enthusiastic hug. She and her parents flew in from Ontario to see me off.

"Good, good," I nervously pace side to side, now also starting to shiver from a chill in the air. It feels surreal to finally be at this place in time. The seed for me to take on the Tour Divide was first planted in 2009 while I was racing TransRockies. I remember the Rocky Mountain Bicycles rep, Keith Brodsky, and his Tour Divide veteran teammate Jill Homer telling me: "Your tendencies toward the ambitious and obscure are perfectly suited."

Having since damaged my feet and lost much of my fast-twitch muscle, among other related ailments still left undiagnosed after the stationary cycling record attempt, I'm now forced to pull away from the shorter, faster events and refocus my Olympic priorities around those skills left undamaged, including backcountry survival and an unwavering ability to punish myself.

Every fibre of my being says I can win this race – as much as one can be a victor in an event with no official race roster, entry fee or prize purse.

Preparations kicked into high gear after coming to terms with my physical limitations, and my unmistakable flat tire luck, in Italy. I devoted at least three hours each day to reviewing waterproof maps from the Adventure Cycling Association, to creating custom cues, to training, to researching gear, to reviewing past race forums, to ordering custom packs for my bike and to figuring out how to best organize it all. Unfortunately, I only allowed myself one overnight test run.

With two minutes to go until 8:00 a.m., the official start time, Sarah and I say our final goodbye. "I love you," I gush again, *a thousand times over.*

Unlocking from our tearful embrace, I walk over and hug Sarah's mom in the background, then surprise her father with one too. I'm extremely thankful that they came all this way to see me off. My own parents are still not speaking to me. Tucson was more than four months ago now.

Time further slows. I feel an equally nervous and excited heart beating inside my chest. Adrenaline causes my hands to tremble, *like getting shot out of a cannon.*

Crazy Larry, the resident long-haired eccentric, local cycling advocate and unofficial start official, stands on top of a box and yells, at the top of his lungs: "Are you guys ready?!?"

I look back at Sarah one more time and smile.

Larry shouts out: "Three, two, one ... SEE YOU IN MEXICO!!" *And we're off.*

TOUR DIVIDE, DAY 2

At 1:00 o'clock the following morning, my legs are still pumping. Not far ahead, in the pitch black, I can see another rider's flashing red taillight.

I have only stopped a handful of times since Banff, to urinate and quickly try to consume as many packaged calories as possible. I've stopped at a camp store in Peter Lougheed Provincial Park and at a convenience store in Elkford, British Columbia. I've downed some burgers at an A&W in the town of Sparwood, British Columbia, where I also repaired a precarious sidewall puncture to my front tire. That fix required some MacGyver know-how, placing an empty Hammer Bar wrapper on the inside of the tire in order to stop the new inner tube from poking through and pinch-flatting.

The mountain weather has been cold and rainy since the start of the race. My once-pristine bike is covered in an extra five pounds of mud from the rugged forest service roads and backpacker trails. At least my bike and components are up to the challenge, though, since I've only ridden it a couple of times. The bike I first had in mind for this race was stolen out of a storage locker in my apartment complex in March. That brings the tally to two robberies in one year. *I would love five minutes alone with these assholes.*

The rider and I catch up to one another. The burly Serge and I had separated for a short while after filling our faces at the burger joint in Sparwood (a rare intersection with civilization). Our paths converged once again at the abandoned mining town of Corbin, just two hours later and at a decisive race decision.

Together we stood silent, our headlamps gently shining into the dark abyss. Finding solace in the hollow sounds of the industrial graveyard, Serge wisely chose to seek refuge. "Enough for one day," he said wearily. I paused for a moment, and then told him that I would continue on, foolishly perhaps, alone into the dark and increasingly dangerous terrain.

The Flathead River Valley has the largest population of grizzly bears in all of North America. Many consider sleeping exposed in the woods to be an unnecessary risk – a sleeping bag alone does very little to protect you from an animal attracted to the scent of sweat and junk food. Adding further insult to the more risk-averse, I have chosen not to carry bear spray (also known as pepper spray) because of a minimalist, weight-saving approach and a general lack of fear of the large animal.

Hours tick by in the darkness.

The forest service road devolves into an exhausting bushwhack through brawny coniferous trees on a steep hillside. With adrenaline fading, I stop, and question the logic of continuing to grasp for slippery roots on my hands and knees. *This doesn't feel safe*, I remind my ego.

Earlier in the day, at the beginning of the race, I had relied on a line of sight to the race leaders, their muddy tracks as a backup breadcrumb trail. But in the dark and alone, my navigation skills appear fruitless. *Yes, I am on the highlighted GPS route.* The reality of an imposing rock face says otherwise, though. Worse yet, there is no obvious workaround.

Delirium encroaches as I continue pacing back and forth in search of an alternative through the thick foliage. At 3:00 a.m., I catch a hopeful glimpse of a second set of tracks in the moonlit snow. I immediately drop my bike and leap over to the exposed plateau. *Finally*, a solution to this lost wander. But, *Fuck*, no, the tread pattern reveals the side by side of my own clumsy footprints. I have hiked in a complete circle.

Back on track the following afternoon, a dusting of snow crystals falls from a frozen shoe turned upside down. I place the rugged size 12 on a nearby boulder and hold up my pruned foot for closer examination. Running a thumb over the emaciated white toes, I feel the joints all pop and crack like a cheap home appliance running thin on oil.

The sound is a staunch reminder. Two years ago, I found myself in a state of desperation, crawling helplessly alone across a cold tile floor, gaunt, with my vision spiralling and my heart racing. I was sure that the side effects of adventure had finally caught up with me. But I never fully crossed *that* line. Instead, I lay bedridden for three months and in pain for two years, and on this day, my comeback, it is everything to me.

As if on cue, a light rain begins to fall from the greying sky.

I pull out a ball of cheap grocery bags from my pack, wring out my wool socks, slide them back on, wrap the plastic over top of the socks, then slip my feet back into those cold lugs. A strand of duct tape around each ankle helps create a moisture seal. This solution should keep the wind and aggravated arthritis at bay.

I stand and grit my teeth, feeling fiery nerve pain nonetheless.

Scanning back down through the drizzle, I see no riders coming up the mountain. Though there was no official start list, I'm aware of at least 100 bikepacking renegades scattered in the brutal wilderness, slowly worming their way south. Groups of similar abilities are likely working together now, pooling resources, building fires and keeping safe. Should I indulge?

No. Keep moving.

At 2:00 p.m. an unexpected blizzard descends on the brutal mountain. My teeth chatter uncontrollably as warm blood retreats from my extremities, which are beginning to go into hypothermic shock. I am feeling desperate. Still, forward momentum seems the logical choice.

I continue postholing through the knee-deep snowpack, shaking my head with each laboured step. *Not even fucking close.*

The *Ride the Divide* camera crew failed to capture scenes like this. Any shots of snow looked playful, showing riders stumbling around like Chaplin in the sunshine. The brutal reality at higher elevations will therefore come as a horrendous surprise to any rider – especially one from a southern climate – who is unable to descend to the relative safety of a warm motel before nightfall.

Concern befalls.

Around a switchback, I notice multiple sets of snowed-over tracks leading downward through the flurries. With an elated, yet cautious, breath, my laboured push through the pack quickly transitions into a hurried step-and-slide. My bike, aptly nicknamed "The Tumbler," after Batman's black war machine, serves as a makeshift snowplow and brace.

Crunch, slide. Crunch, slide.

The onslaught of flurries begins to calm below the treeline. Out of the storm, I pause to unzip my expensive GORE-TEX jacket. A cloud of pent-up heat and perspiration comes billowing out.

Taking the minimalist approach has forced me to pay particular attention to layering, for which my clothing options are limited. There is always the concern that my inner warming layer will become saturated in sweat. When at rest, this moisture steals away precious body heat. And surprisingly, a drop in body temperature of more than a few degrees is deadly.

Get back on the bike. Keep moving.

The snowpack gives way to a muddy forest road with veins of runoff water that criss-cross each other to form wheel-sucking rivulets. Normally, there would be no hesitation to attack. The relative safety of a one-day race (and medical crew on standby) negates such concern. But out here in the wild, there is just stupidity and death.

I proceed in a controlled slide.

Saturated earth sprays off the knobby front tire, hitting me square in the face. Instinctively, my clunky frozen hand mashes on the right brake to try and regain control. But like a car caught hydroplaning, the back wheel locks, causing the Tumbler to fishtail nervously. "Come on," I murmur, squinting through the sludge splashing up.

The sub-zero spray is a harsh reminder of the frigid mountain stream that also sloshes inside my bowels, cooling from the inside out. *Pee now, dammit!*

I dig my right heel into the ground and mash again with whatever stopping force remains. The Tumbler nervously slides to a halt at the valley floor, allowing me to unsaddle and dash into the adjacent woods.

Running through the deadfall, instinct states the next most obvious solution. *Fuck, I need fire.*

I fumble through one of my packs for a cheap Bic lighter. With a flick, I turn up the intensity to full, pointing the orange flame underneath a small pile of springy saps. The wood begins to smoke, igniting a small spark of hope, and then nothing. *It's too wet. Fuck.*

My chest and arms begin shivering violently.

I scream out loud, resorting to Plan B – exposing my withered appendage to the unforgiving wind. The simple act of relieving myself warms my core a little, but not nearly enough.

I straddle the bike again and yell out, "PLEASE!"

Tears of dwindling optimism stream down my cheeks as I reach for the emergency beacon strapped to the top of my saddle pack. I don't want to quit the race but I'm afraid that not doing so would be "stupid," as my father would state. "And selfish," he would add, referring to the potentially fatal consequences and ensuing family fallout.

My thumb shivers indecisively over the plastic rescue button, ready to signal for a helicopter savior, just one press away. An inch to the left, the tracking LED display flashes in my narrowed peripheral vision. It waits for forward progress,

taunting my conviction to tackle the world's toughest mountain-bike race.

I have never faced a greater challenge.

"Please…"

As I gaze up the next mountain pass, the snow appears
deeper, the distance extra long. I do not envy the poor bastard that trenched through here first. I look to see how much
new snow has collected in the sunken tracks. *The next rider
can only be 20 minutes ahead of me.*

Fatigue holds me back from taking any more than a few
steps in one push. Exaggerated knee lifts and a steady balance are required. My quad muscles tremble as one leg kicks
through the air and the other is forced to hold my body
weight. The action is made more challenging by the fully
loaded Tumbler, which continually falls through the top
snow layers and digs in like an anchor.

As with the two previous mountain passes, the tracks me-
ander around a series of teasing switchbacks. The summit remains shrouded in fog and falling snow.

Formulating a plan of attack for when I get through this
shit is all that keeps me sane. There is no way I am turning down the chance of a hot shower and warm bed. It's not
safe to push on tonight, especially with my sleeping bag still
damp from the night before. I'll become hypothermic again
in no time.

Three determined hours later, I reach the summit.

Regrouping like a brutish caveman, I smack my helmet
with frozen fingers, knock the ice off my shoes, clip my feet
back into the pedals and scream, "Fucking warm shower!!"

I again shiver uncontrollably as my wheels spin more quickly under steep momentum.

The cue sheet says the 16-kilometre gradient down Galton Pass is extreme, and to watch for cattle. Those riders behind me will likely have to walk this section in the dark. Fortunately, the highway leading to the United States border is now within my grasp.

The tattered road hits a paved junction with Highway 93 South. In incredible pain, I immediately tuck down in my aero bars and push on to the border with haste.

At the Roosville, Montana, border crossing, a stern customs agent watches me with interest as I pull up in the rain. "Hell-o, lemme juss grabububub muh my pssport," I initiate.

Following the customary once-over, he points to a door. "Go ahead and take a break inside. The first few riders did." This border crossing is well accustomed to seeing riders racing the Tour Divide.

I promptly prop my bike up against the brick building.

Inside, a janitor sees me in shambles and motions toward a metal bench along the far wall. My shoes leave behind a trail of mud and slush, as my battered cleats click along. "I'm soorrrry," I tell him. He smiles, letting me know that it's not a problem.

A few customs officers congregate around a window in the back behind a long service counter with no one in line. One of them makes an offhand remark about the dreary weather and lack of traffic today. *You should see what it's like up on the mountain.*

Having difficulty controlling my shivers, I turn my attention to a wall-mounted TV. It happens to be playing *127*

Hours, the film version of Aron Ralston's incredible tale of survival. I remember reading his book, *Between a Rock and a Hard Place,* during my ride from Alaska to Argentina, in 2005. I have grown to appreciate that experience more over time, especially the palm trees.

I am still shivering 15 minutes later when a female customs agent asks if she can get me anything. "Coffee, do you have any ... or anything warm?" I respond, twitching as I speak. The spasms are starting to cause muscle strain in my neck and shoulders.

She comes back with a steaming cup, which I shoot back right away, despite the "scalding hot" disclaimer. "Another?" she asks.

"Please, yes," I nod, despite the burning sensation now coursing its way up from my stomach.

My core begins to warm slowly, from the inside out.

I sit back down to consider my next move. Looking at the map cues, I see there is a small motel only a couple of blocks away. A few more options exist 13 kilometres down the road, in the town of Eureka. That option also has a couple of stores to restock my food supplies.

Eureka! I ask the lady if I can use her phone book.

I feel like an asshole but decide it is in my best interests to call ahead. It dawns on me that there may be limited rooms available in the more commercial area. As soon as the others get within cell range, they will likely do the same. *I need to look out for myself.*

It just so happens that there is *one* room left in Eureka. The proprietor tells me the place is already teeming with frozen racers. He also mentions there is a Subway restaurant and convenience store in the same building. *Perfect,* all I have had to eat during the last 24 hours is Hammer Bars. My body craves meaty protein, succulent vegetables and a variety of sugary treats that have no other purpose than to serve as a reward for conquering the Flathead River Valley.

I grit my teeth and head back out in the rain.

WARMING UP IN EUREKA

The motel shower turns lukewarm, then slowly cools. I scramble out in frustration and desperation, still shivering, and jump under the bed covers.

Lying in the cotton cocoon, I stare at a pile of food, just out of reach. In a plastic bag are two foot-long sandwiches, a container of chocolate milk, a couple of Snickers bars, a bag of licorice and more. Still, I shiver at the thought of extending a bare arm for sustenance. *I should have bought hot soup.*

Fighting against my warming instincts, I crawl out from under the covers and begin unpacking my appetite and damp gear. "Water-resistant" gear bags do not equate to "Waterproof" gear bags, so I have learned.

It is important to take extra care in how things are dried, instead of just tossing them on the floor. I put newspaper in my shoes, wring out my clothes, wipe off my electronics and tools, clean out my pack innards, then hang everything up to dry. Last but not least, I set about cleaning off my bike with a set of ill-fated white hotel towels.

By the time I have lubed my chain with a fresh coat of oil and coughed my lungs clear of mucus, which accumulated from the cold and elevation, my wristwatch reads 1:00 a.m. I settle back into bed and close my eyes.

"YES, YES, YES!!" I wake to incessantly loud humping coming from the room above me. A woman screams with great enthusiasm as she slams the headboard repeatedly against the wall. It is a groggy 3:30 a.m. below.

At 4:00, the couple shows no signs of stopping.

Son of a bitch. I look at my watch, do the math and decide it's time to get up and repack my gear explosion. The bigger items are still damp, no doubt.

I turn on the TV for white noise. My options are *infomercial, infomercial* and everyone's favourite late-night comfort movie, *JAWS: The Revenge. Awesome.*

Still the humping continues.

Pulling back the window curtains to take a look outside as I mentally prepare for the next leg of the race, I notice that the moonlit shadows are saturated in cold fog but are no longer blurred by rain. Next door, I see two bikes lying against the building. And if I listen closely, I can hear the rustling of competitors packing.

I'm thankful I did not have to cram in with them (*them*, who, perhaps because of budgetary considerations, were forced to pack in like sardines), wet gear all over the place, everyone cold and cranky, fighting over that joke of a shower. But that does not mean I am without compassion for my fellow riders.

Setting out at 5:30 a.m., I look back into the room from the doorway and scan it one last time. A forgotten sock, battery or light has lasting consequences.

Just as I straddle my bike to clip in, a weary rider pulls off the highway and makes a beeline for me. Shivering, he tells a horrific tale of being stranded overnight, just now coming off the mountain. "Would itit be alrighttt if I used youryouryour room? ... I can give you $20," he pleads.

I motion him inside. "It's yours! Don't worry about the money."

CHAPTER 28

THE GREAT BASIN

TOUR DIVIDE, DAY 3

It's 5:30 a.m. in Eureka, Montana.

Despite getting very little sleep last night, starting the day on asphalt puts me in a better mood. I roll up to where I last left the route, across the motel parking lot, turn on my GPS and wait for my position arrow to line up with the highlighted Tour Divide race route.

Okay, I think I'm getting the hang of this.

I roll straight through the highway intersection, down a hill and quickly see that my arrow is headed in the wrong direction. *Shoot.*

I backtrack to the highway, stop again and double check with my printed cues, propped in a clear waterproof insert on my handlebars. I'm supposed to turn right (left, now) on Highway 93. *Check.*

Headed south, two Divide racers soon ride rapidly past me, headed in the opposite direction. *Come on, am I wrong again?* I look over my shoulder and see one of them veer into the motel parking lot. I'm guessing he forgot something. I conduct my own mental checklist, just to be sure. *Wallet, check. iPhone, check. SPOT tracker on and set to tracking. Cue sheet flipped to the current section, yep. Bags zipped up, good. And Snickers at the ready in my bento box.*

I'd been doing well with my Hammer Bars and Perpetuem (a "meal in a bottle" produced by Hammer Nutrition), but I notice that my stockpile is depleted. I quickly transition into a new realm of convenience store fuelling.

For breakfast, I rip into a foil pack of stale Pop-Tarts with the corner of my mouth. In doing so, half of the "Wildlicious Wild! Berry" concoction falls to the ground. Without hesitation, I brake mid-pedal-stroke and walk back to pick up the Pop-Tart. Calories of any variety are scarce, I'm quickly understanding.

Turning uphill on a side road, a nagging pain awakens along both Achilles tendons. The backs of my ankles feel overstretched and torn, most likely from all the hike-a-bike yesterday. And now, I fear I may have done some damage. The pain worsens with each elongated pedal stroke.

I decide to sacrifice my form to accommodate the injury. The inconsistency makes me dwell on the need to cover at least 245 kilometres each day to finish within my goal of 18 days. Winning times are generally within 16 to 18 days, depending largely on how much snow the northern regions receive, and conversely on how many forest fire reroutes farther south may be required (if any).

The Achilles pain digs in deeper during the next major ascent, up the Whitefish Divide. Four hours of hiking through deep snow ensue.

Feeling sluggish, I look back to see if I can spot any other riders coming up behind me. I assume I'm falling behind. But only deep grizzly bear tracks are scattered nearby for company. A sign sticking out of fresh avalanche debris warns hikers not to stop, for this reason.

Summiting the Whitefish Divide a second time after dipping down to the far side, overlooking Glacier National Park, I sit down in snow that is so deep that I barely have to bend my knees to make contact. I allow my ankles to ice while appreciating a frozen view of Red Meadow Lake, surrounded by fresh white. There is not another person in sight.

The descent into the town of Whitefish is filled with irony. The main headquarters of Hammer Nutrition are located here. Still, I cannot take advantage of restocking my endurance fuels. Individual riders must not be given any special privilege. Everyone must have the same access to commercial restock points. Hammer would normally be closed on the weekend anyway. Option B is the next-closest grocer.

My dinner in the neighbouring town of Columbia Falls consists of chicken nuggets and fries. "I'll give them to you at a discount," the Smith's Food & Drug manager concedes. The deep-fried rejects have apparently been sitting under a heat lamp all day. It's the only warm meal left, however.

I slouch down on the curb outside and begin gnawing on the stale entrée at dusk.

A group of dishevelled teens drives up beside me in a beat-up station wagon, rowdy, barely taking notice of the fully loaded Tumbler and unique story unfolding in plain view. "Who's gettin' the beers?!" one of the girls yells out.

"I got the fucking chips," another replies.

TOUR DIVIDE, DAY 4

After riding for six straight hours, I'm thankful for a much heartier meal late the next morning at the picturesque Holland Lake Lodge. I'm also thankful for the proprietor's extra care: "I've got plenty of chocolate bars and chips that you can purchase after you're done your lunch. You'll need the energy for the next push." He points to Richmond Peak on the opposite side of the pristine Holland Lake.

Talking with the only other person seated at the rustic wooden bar (an employee of the Adventure Cycling

Association, as it happens), he tells me to expect more snow up top. "We tried our best to clear a path with shovels for you guys, but it's still a little sketchy."

I thank them both as I head back out into relative sunshine, my belly full like a king's.

As was the case with each previous climb at elevation, hours of winding forest service roads eventually intersect with knee-high snow. This time, however, the trail is much narrower and perched on a ledge with a steep drop-off. I pay particular attention not to misstep, still weary from riding along rolling high terrain in the Swan Range in the rain all morning, and from more coughing fits in my cold bivy sack the night before.

I reach the snowy summit on my hands and knees, dragging my bike up behind me. How the one tandem team, piloted by last year's winner, Kurt Refsnider, will navigate this section is beyond me.

Tracks lead in a multitude of confused directions. Gazing at the options, each appears to be searching for the best way up and over the last lip. The most worn path requires that I drop my bike five feet off one ledge to another, and pray I do not stumble off the side.

I follow the lemmings before me.

The dirt descent is fast and painful. My brakes squeal, due to worn calipers pressing furiously against worn-out pads. With the extra weight of my gear, it is next to impossible to slow myself fully once momentum has taken hold. Steering wide-eyed through tight conifers smacking my arms and face, I feel several jolting whips, grinding my teeth as I realize that this overgrown bumpy brush trail is the only way down. "FUUUUUUCK!" I cry out in pain.

Slowing toward the bottom, I immediately crumple off the Tumbler, rocking back and forth on the muddy forest floor in demoralized agony. My knees and tender feet are rattled raw. *This only feels like it is going to get worse...*

I reach into my handlebar pack, yank out a travel-sized Advil container, pop three pills and store the rest in my back jersey pocket (for easy access). Then, making a conscious effort to regain control of my shit, I thrust back upright and tell myself to get a move on.

Two riders pass me in my moment of weakness. They make the customary "Everything okay?" check-in sign in my direction, though the rules dictate that they don't necessarily need to help. *Yeah, yeah*, I wave, hunched over my bike, realizing that I just dropped off the leaderboard to 11th place.

My thoughts are deep in contemplation as I trudge along on foot for the next hour. Doing the mental math, I begin to accept that this might have just become a concerted effort to simply finish this race, not necessarily place. Sarah communicated by text that the front of the pack is already a day ahead of me.

Darkness descends on the forest road.

Sitting cross-legged in the gravel, looking at my map cues by headlight, I decide to push on 42 kilometres to the town of Ovando. It is located along a highway intersection and is bound to have services.

My spirits lift at the thought of chowing down on a greasy diner meal.

Forcing myself back onto the bike, I stuff a handful of gummy bear incentives into my jersey. Then, pushing off with a delirious smile, I say out loud, "At the top of this hill, you get to eat some damn candy." The hilltop reach-back becomes routine.

Within the hour, the rolling forest road opens to farmland and wheat fields accentuated by starlight. In the distance, I take note of only one small patch of man-made lights. *Ovando is close.*

I reach a four-way stop, and stop as I always do. Turning left after crossing the highway, I scan down a quiet main street. A few dim porch lights line the way into town. *This is not looking so good.*

Reaching what appears to be the town square, I see that the inn has already closed down for the night. Adding insult to injury, the neighbouring restaurant, called the Stray Bullet Café, does not open again until 8:00 a.m. *Dammit, I'll be long gone by then. Or at least, I need to be.*

My cold belly growls with disenchantment.

I scan the dark shadows for a suitable place to bed down. A rocky crawlspace at the back of the town post office is where I am headed next.

TOUR DIVIDE, DAY 5

Coming down off a bone-rattling mountain pass en route to the Montana capital of Helena on Day 5, I rejoice at the sight of pavement, several convenience stores and four bars of cell reception. I promptly text Sarah, "Have reached Helena. Am okay. Anyone here right now?"

I happen to catch her at the end of her workday. After sharing an electronic embrace, she checks the Spot tracker page and sees there is only one other rider in town: a guy named Josh from Gunnison, Colorado. Josh initially passed me on a long climb out of Elkford, British Columbia, on Day 1.

Knowing that a front-runner is back within my reach, my competitive side kicks in. "How long has he been here?" I prod with great intrigue.

"There are reports through bikepacking.net and mtbcast. com that he crashed yesterday. Something about riding off a cliff. He is stopped at a local bike shop for repairs but has considered dropping out because of injury." Sarah further explains.

I can picture the rough gravel descent that may have been Josh's undoing. "Thermarest Hill" claimed some crucial components of my cold-weather riding gear, as well as a large Powerade. Without my knowing it at the time, my tightly bound seat pack had burst open from constant jostling. I am now without leg warmers and proper riding gloves.

As the cooler twilight hour descends on Montana, I have an important decision to make. Option A: stay overnight in Helena and wait to replace the clothing as soon as a bike shop opens in the morning; or Option B: improvise.

The thought of making up time on Josh spurs me on.

Stopped at the first convenience store in town, I quickly stock up on Snickers, Gatorade, salty nuts, AA batteries, sugary energy drinks and one of those sad, plastic-wrapped salami sandwiches on bleached white bread.

Chugging back an energy drink, I let out an uninhibited carbonated belch, and quickly review my clothing options. *Okay, this is doable.*

Going against fashion sense, I proceed to slide on my thermal underwear, which I normally use for sleeping, and a pair of thin glove liners for my hands. Then, after one final loving text to Sarah, I push off with vigour.

City asphalt transitions into rural wilderness within the hour.

Rolling back over familiar gravel hills, a young couple in a Jeep pulls up and makes me an offer: "If you want, you can stay at our place tonight." I guess they figured out that I am a Divide rider. "We've got pizza, beer and a warm shower waiting."

I must politely decline, however. Accepting this kind of help, also known as "trail magic," is a grey area in the race rules, and one that I would rather not challenge.

As the sun finally slips below the mountain horizon, a second driver pulls up beside me. He is decidedly more ominous in his craggy approach: "You better be careful out here at night," the old man warns.

I nod in acknowledgement, quickening my pace with a renewed feeling of nighttime anxiety. My sense of hearing and touch intensify in order to compensate for my vision, which has only a solitary headlight to dimly show the way.

At first, there is the sound of crickets, my two wheels churning on gravel and my own deep breathing. Looking behind me with dilated pupils, I scan the road for more vehicle headlights. I keep a special eye out for drunken assholes. *Settle down, there is no one else out here.*

I crest a high peak and stop to gaze back at the faint Helena city lights, now over 40 kilometres behind me. *It's peaceful*, I think, feeling a light misting of rain accentuate a rare moment of Zen.

An unexpected downpour follows.

I begin riding again, in a hurried search for shelter. The flash storm obscures my vision, however. And soon my mountain calmness hearkens back to the panicked chill I experienced on Day 2, hiking up and over the snowy mountain passes, scrambling to the United States border. There is no motel waiting for me this time, though.

The muddy track becomes too dangerous to navigate.

Fuck, I scramble off the road into a patch of young coniferous trees.

Trembling under sparse sapling limbs, I immediately unravel my bivy sack. Any chance of warming up is dashed, though: my sleeping bag is nearly saturated by the time I'm tucked inside.

The situation becomes more severe, as I make the foolish mistake of keeping my wet clothes on, not yet committed to the idea of staying put. Meanwhile, pools of rainfall begin to toy with the integrity of my "water-resistant" sack.

Rainwater from higher up the mountain rushes alongside me.

Feeling genuinely scared, I clench the palm-sized Spot tracker, one finger on the sos button, another pointed in defiance. I think back to the couple and their offer: "We've got pizza, beer and a warm shower waiting."

TOUR DIVIDE, DAY 6

Five agonizing hours later, I drift in and out of consciousness as a hint of sunlight pierces through the green bivy mesh.

I'm still wet and shivering.

My best option is to begin riding as quickly as possible. The brisk morning air will initially pull more heat from my wet core, causing blood and oxygen to retreat from my extremities. The warming process will kick in slowly afterward.

Just do it!

I unzip the bivy sack, stand up in fresh dew and strap on my mud-clogged shoes. "Fuuckk!" I yell out, immediately feeling the anticipated cold. It takes another 15 minutes to pack up my waterlogged gear.

Back on the road, it appears I ended yesterday at one of the few singletrack climbs, headed up a slushy Lava Mountain.

The increasingly rough terrain ultimately becomes too difficult to ride in my challenged state.

I defer to an arduous hike-a-bike.

Riding everything, or "clearing it," is a badge of honour in the mountain-bike world. Doing so showcases your technical prowess. But out here, and alone, I have nothing to prove to anyone. So I keep jogging toward the winding forest summit.

My sore Achilles tendons and increasingly tight legs scream with each step. It feels like someone has been punching my muscles for days on end. *Jesus Christ.*

I stop and pop a couple of Advil.

For the sake of making up time, I try to clear the slippery root descent as quickly as possible, thrusting my back end, and centre of gravity, far behind the seat as I squeeze both brakes, sliding downward in an uncomfortable, breakneck plunge. "How the hell is the tandem team going to get through here?" I let out a mystified chuckle.

Said tandem team, made up of Kurt and his wife/stoker Caroline, are somewhere close behind me. We first crossed paths early yesterday morning outside a small grocer in Lincoln. All three of us had deep bags under our eyes from a rough Ovando pit stop, climbing over Huckleberry Pass in desperate search of breakfast.

When he first laid eyes on me in Lincoln, Kurt had called out, laughing, "Was that you behind the post office in Ovando?" Apparently, they were camped nearby that night.

"Nice to meet you," I smile, extending a hand.

In between filling my face with turkey cold cuts and chocolate milk, I'm intrigued to ask Caroline more about their setup. She details her nauseating lack of steering ability, and how she often closes her eyes as Kurt navigates down the fast descents. "It's scary! We also have to pedal in unison. I can't just stand or coast whenever I want," she explains.

Finding momentum farther down Lava Mountain, I think about the relationship challenges they must also contend with daily, including disagreements on direction and strategy, plus any routine marital squabbling. *No thanks.*

I reach the nearly abandoned mining town of Basin, Montana, and the Silver Saddle Club in time for its 8:00 a.m. opening. Fresh-cooked eggs, warm toast, non-stop coffee, crispy bacon and a side of doughy pancakes are promptly served up.

The opportunity to kick off my shoes and indulge is a godsend. It is also a rare opportunity to charge my iPod and cellphone, though reception is generally limited to a small radius around more commercial centres, which equates to less than 15 per cent of the total race route.

A table of friendly local seniors breaks from their morning catch-up to ask where I am headed. "To Butte this afternoon. I'm hoping to get my bike serviced, and then on to Mexico." I smile.

"You're doing this alone?" one of the women asks in a raspy, though unquestionably curious, smoker's cough.

I nod, *Yes, ma'am.*

"You got to be tough," her husband states, pointing a finger of mental integrity to his temple.

"I'm trying," I reply.

They wish me safe travels as I pay my bill. Their faces betray a concerned look for the young rider with puffy eyes, who appears gaunt, alone and is limping slightly. *I asked for this*, I assure them with one last parting nod.

The Divide route parallels Interstate 15 the rest of the way into Butte. Looking up at the hills running alongside the highway, I fondly recall a precarious night out on my first solo tour to Arizona, to surprise Kelly. I was 18 years old, and the wilderness broke me that evening, forcing me to beg my parents to pay for a hotel room after spending a fearful night wrapped in my pup tent. My wilderness instincts have since evolved.

After a much-needed tune-up at the aptly named Outdoorsman bike shop, I continue on with my ego intact.

The tandem team catches up to me on the outskirts of town, headed up Mount Fleecer.

Grinding in the granny gear, we exchange rainy stories of the past few days and laugh about *that* infamous film. Less experienced riders, who were initially drawn in by the film's inspired imagery, are probably hating life right now, we lament.

The tandem team pulls ahead of me in view of a scenic mountain vista and the sun beginning to set on what my map cues list as an "extremely steep downhill" off an exposed Fleecer ridge. Kurt emphasizes the need to get through this technical section before nightfall. "Thank you," I respond. The insights of a race veteran, let alone a previous winner, are invaluable.

My new friends disappear into the woods below.

Taking a moment to massage my sore feet, I slip into my thermal underwear, remove my sunglasses and remind myself to keep a keen eye out for obstructions hidden in the low light.

Not far along the saturated valley floor, the path once again connects with a paved artery.

In the nearby village of Wise River, I come across a lone bar/motel. The tandem bike is parked out front.

Kurt and Caroline are enjoying a warm meal. Away from

their view, I contemplate my next move. It is an important decision. Do I stop early for drinks, more helpful conversation and potentially a bed for the night? Or do I push past temptation and continue riding for another hour or two?

This is still a race.

Under the guidance of my one headlight, I turn south down a vacant State Route 73 and continue through the darkness until my usual stopping time of 10:00 p.m. With limited visibility, there is a strong likelihood that I might crash. Riding this late requires more energy and it will take longer to cover the same distance as I could during daylight hours. Those with better lights continue to pull ahead.

Having made up 16 kilometres on the tandem team, I unclip from the Tumbler and hike into a patch of forest. I then proceed with what has become a familiar routine: I unravel my bivy, strip out of my sweaty clothing, clean myself with a baby wipe (while I stand naked in the wind), worm my way down into my sleeping bag, set my iPhone alarm and try to fall asleep on a makeshift arm pillow.

My mind feels more at ease knowing I have gained some ground tonight.

TOUR DIVIDE, DAY 10

There is a pack of three riders that have been trailing me closely since the town of Lima, Montana, right before the Idaho border. They catch me with my guard down a day later, when I'd decided to stay wrapped in my warm sleeping bag for an extra 30 minutes past my 5:30 a.m. wake-up time.

They ride by me, unaware that I am watching them from my Grand Teton hideaway.

Last night I crossed into Wyoming and set up camp below the infamous mountain spine. Among the group of three riders is the second-place female and two veteran riders from Colorado, including Josh Shifferly (whom I passed in Helena). They likely know this section of the route better than anyone.

Once they are out of sight, I pack up my gear and begin the tough grind over the range.

Surprisingly, there are still patches of snow to carefully negotiate. My legs and arms are now littered with scrapes and bruises from sliding out and crashing on this type of debris.

I catch up to the group an hour later on the east side of the mountain range, at the Flagg Ranch resort.

Aware that I was near, the dishevelled band of "Three Amigos" is quick to welcome me at their breakfast table. "Hey, how's it going, man?!" we all shake hands.

Seeing their smiles, it is apparent that they have found a source of strength in working together, especially in Josh's case. The group has convinced him to keep riding past the doldrums of injury in Montana.

I listen intently to the plan ahead.

Next to plates full of pancakes and rich maple syrup, they begin plotting the next four days, paying particular attention to a barren stretch known as the "Great Basin." Knowledge of the terrain, as well as knowing where to restock is a tremendous advantage. I'm thankful they are being so open around me.

The four of us ride on together for the rest of the afternoon. I too appreciate the company.

In the early evening hours, we begin a long slog up Union Pass, at an elevation of 9,210 feet. One of the "Amigos," Dylan Taylor, is keen to ride a little faster. He encourages "Amiga" Katherine Wallace to ride ahead with him to safer ground. He is worried about bears in the area. Josh and I opt to spend some time at a tranquil mountaintop lake, albeit in prime bear territory, yelling ahead that we will catch up in the morning.

We agree on a 5:30 a.m. start.

TOUR DIVIDE, DAY 11

At 5:00 the next morning, Josh is already up, packed and ready to go. "Go ahead, I don't want to keep you," I tell him. He hesitates for a moment, caught between holding to our agreement of leaving together at 5:30 a.m. and not letting the other "Amigos" get too far ahead.

Go ahead, I motion again.

The 96-kilometre morning ride to the Basin perimeter town of Pinedale gradually drops in elevation. I cross through grassy valley farmlands, segregated by steam rising along tiny irrigation canals. The air feels fresh against my exposed cheeks.

I can't help but smile while navigating through a pack of a couple hundred cattle, slowly walking toward me on the road. They moo and I "moooooo" back. Two herding ranchmen on horseback tip their cowboy hats.

Turning left onto main street, Pinedale, achy and relieved to be around fast food prospects, I'm thinking about current race leader Craig Stappler and his failed attempt at a record for fastest overall time in last year's race. He chose to pull out before the next two-day stretch of isolation.

Pinedale is a benchmark for many riders.

In addition to being on the edge of the Great Basin, it is also one of the few restock points that is situated on a bus line. It's an easy out for those who wish to abandon the race. Already, a few riders ahead of me have dropped out for some pretty common reasons, such as Achilles tendon inflammation, scheduling conflicts (taking longer than they expected to complete the race) and overly expensive bike fixes.

I have no intention of quitting.

I do, however, need to figure out a solution to my foot pain. The fleshy pads under my two big toes are beginning to bruise – a concerning new symptom with no clear solution. I'm convinced they may have been damaged from the frozen hiking conditions up north *(remnants of frostbite, perhaps?)*. My strained Achilles tendons also remain a concern.

First, food. My attention is drawn toward a nearby Subway restaurant and convenience store.

Inside the aisles of recirculated air, tacky trinkets and minimum-wage angst, I'm surprised to run across Katherine Wallace in a damper mood than me. She stands at the cash register with two subs and a handcart full of candy indulgence, looking somewhat dejected. "The guys went on ahead about an hour ago," she says, upon seeing me. The "Amigos" are splintering.

"See you in a bit," she says, referring to the fact that I'll likely catch up to her after finishing my messy meatball sub.

I immediately plug my iPhone in and text Sarah. "There is another rider in Pinedale," she notes right away. "And two not far ahead…" *Don't worry, I know.*

I fill her in on my encounter with the "Three Amigos," the interesting dynamic of having company for a short while and what I learned about the stretch ahead. "Heading into the Great Basin this afternoon. Probably out of cell range for at least a day … love you," I respond, as always.

At a pharmacy down the street, I peruse a little farther down the Advil aisle in search of a non-medicated solution for my lower half.

There is a shelf with black Kinesio tape, made of supportive, flexible strands that can reduce my Achilles stretch and pain. I also buy some cheap gel orthotics to replace my gloves, which I have mashed into makeshift arch supports up until this point. I'm banking on the Dr. Scholl's to redistribute some of that painful toe pressure.

Applying my new supports on a bench outside, I happen to notice a pile of 5-Hour Energy drinks and plastic orthotics packaging similar to mine, thrown on the ground. *Josh has been here.* Coincidentally, he shares the same symptoms as me.

There is a fantastic tailwind leaving Pinedale.

I stop again to double-check my packs before proceeding into good fortune. The seams are bursting with eight Gatorades, ten chocolate bars, four large burritos, gum and two packages of gummy candies. *Good to go!*

With a new confidence stoked by the immediate relief I feel as a result of the Kinesio tape on my Achilles tendons, I dive headfirst into the Great Basin.

Pedalling to a methodical electronic beat, I catch Katherine within the hour. The Phoenix native is slouched over her handlebars as I approach. "I'm not feeling well," she explains, appearing frustrated. *Of all the places.* I show concern.

She encourages me to push on.

She wants to be alone.

Only after I'm assured of her safety do I power ahead over the sterile landscape at full capacity. My odometer lists a staggering 288 kilometres by day's end.

TOUR DIVIDE, DAY 12
The sun rises over the open Great Basin landscape.

Sitting up in my bivy sack on the side of the deserted sage-brush road, completely exposed, I unwrap my last remaining burrito, take in a deep breath of appreciation and bite into the desert tranquility. *I feel well rested.* Unfortunately, the tremendous tailwind that carried me here yesterday has changed direction.

Okay, here we go.

With dry eyes watering, my thoughts immediately shift to conservation mode.

I'm down to two water bottles and I have 62 kilometres to cover before I reach the next town of Rawlins, Wyoming. At a slower average speed of 10 km/h, riding into a headwind, it will take me at least six hours to reach my next Big Gulp.

The wind feels like a warm hairdryer.

Scanning the horizon for any sign of a water source, and finding none, I kick myself for not placing more emphasis on scouting the remote wells that my map cues listed yesterday. Granted, my odometer would need to have been perfectly synced – which it rarely is. And so the cue "Water source: off route one mile straight ahead, source supplied from rain and snow melt" means very little if it's not in plain sight.

Within the hour, my mouth and throat feel like dry cotton. Swallowing requires an exaggerated effort.

By hour two, my lips have dried and are starting to crack. I can also feel a headache coming on.

All I can think about is lining up a row of Gatorades like shot glasses, then diving into a frenzy of greasy fast food. I'm famished.

By hour three, all my bottles are empty.

Skittering back and forth along the road, looking franti-cally behind for oncoming riders (*they surely can't be going this slow*) and ahead for any sign that the route will soon shift out of the wind, I find my attention span waning.

Drifts of sand sweep across the road in no discernible pattern, challenging my bike's traction with each gust. I grow concerned about the amount of time it is taking me to complete the remaining miles.

By hour six, I have begun walking alongside my bike.

And then, after far too many dashed hopes and prayers, a paved intersection finally appears on the eastern horizon: "the end of the Great Basin," so says my cue sheet.

Wary of my bike-handling skills in this depleted state, I proceed south on Highway 287, riding on the far edge of the shoulder. The wind has shifted again, to a crosswind. It now shoves me sporadically back and forth over the white line.

Feeling my hands beginning to tremble with a cold, clammy shake, I realize I'm about to pass out. *You need to do something about this now.*

Scanning my surroundings, I happen across a small clump of trees and what looks like an industrial water tank nestled on the hill.

I desperately scramble off my bike with as many bottles as I can carry.

Faded stickers on the outside of the green plastic tank indicate that the solution is (*was?*) unsuitable for drinking, and most likely used for irrigation. Unscrewing the large lid, I peer inside and get a whiff of diluted chemicals. Dead bugs and dirty leaves float on the surface.

You can force vomit, if need be.

CHAPTER 29

THAT AIN'T CHOCOLATE MILK

TOUR DIVIDE, DAY 12, CONTINUED

I'm particularly fond of the new McDonald's McCafé Frappé Mocha. The best part is not caring how many calories are in the creamy, caffeinated drink (over 680 in a large). So, "I'll have another," my inner kid beams after finally reaching Rawlins, Wyoming, on the far side of the Great Basin. "Please also add some extra chocolate curls," I interrupt the cashier, rubbing my protruding ribs in delight.

The comfortable plastic booth quickly becomes littered with empty drink containers and yellow wrapper entrails. Each piece of trash accounts for at least 600 calories, 3,000 calories all in – a staggering figure, considering that most nutrition programs advocate a 2,000-calorie-a-day balanced diet.

I rub the greasy leftovers from the ginger beard that has overtaken my normally clean-shaven appearance. *Where to next?*

There is a moment during each sit-down meal, in contrast to the grab-and-go convenience variety, when my thought process switches from embracing a deserved break to understanding the strategic need to maintain forward momentum. Elite endurance athletes are usually very disciplined in this regard.

There's no better time than the present.

Leaving the restaurant, Sarah confirms by text that both

Dylan and Josh have continued on. Katherine is over half a day back now, having lost a worrisome amount of time in the Basin, but she is still moving and is close enough to catch up.

I take one more look at the prospective hotel across the street and bid it a fond farewell. "Over halfway through the race now," I text back.

"You can do it!!" She encourages.

Rolling to the western edge of town, I stop again at one of the awkwardly named Kum & Go convenience stores to restock my packs. Enjoying just one more ice cream sandwich on the curb outside before heading back into the remote yonder, my vanilla hit is rudely interrupted by white-trash America.

Ahead on the street corner, I witness a rusted Oldsmobile plow into a pickup truck. An obese woman storms out of the sedan, surveys the damage, then proceeds to swear at the overweight male in the driver's seat of the Olds, both lighting up a cigarette mid-feud.

It occurs to me that I might get off my butt and offer some assistance. *But no*, I'm happy to sit this one out.

I come across a muddy little mountain stream along one of the rolling, grassy valleys 53 kilometres south of Rawlins. It is nearly dried up but apparently worth mentioning on my cue sheet.

Such water sources have become a numbing relief for my sore feet. I'll often pull over and dangle my naked toes in the cool water for 15 minutes at a time. Now, the priority is to try and clean myself. My last shower was in Lima, Montana, nearly three days ago. And there have been few streams since.

The smell aside, I'm concerned with keeping my nether region rash-free. Baby wipes and water bottle rinse-downs do little to clean the buildup of sweat and road grime that has fused onto my cycling short chamois. The spotty brown aesthetic of my cycling jersey isn't anything to write home about, either. Hardened stains from meals past dot the front. Each is a casualty of desperate ingestion.

After finding a hiding spot for my bike, I remove my dusty shoes and tight cycling socks, and walk barefoot to the trickling edge. With another step, my feet and ankles are sucked into a thick, taffy-like mud. I try to awkwardly manoeuvre to where the silt water is deepest – no more than six inches.

Inside a four-foot storm drain below the trail, I squat and give myself a thorough rinse with my right hand. My left hand grips onto the metal shell all the while, steadying the humbling, bare-assed effort. I dip my chamois into the stream, making sure to wash away any shit stains, dried sweat and bloody friction points.

I smile at the thought of Sarah's arachnophobia. *It's a good thing there aren't any spiders crawling around down here.* A few days before flying out west, she jumped at the sight of a six-legged fiend crawling along her car door just as she was heading to work. "Get it! Get it! Get it!" she pleaded. *But race a difficult triathlon, no problem.*

I continue back along Sage Creek Road.

Come nightfall, the Gatorades from the Kum & Go are nearly empty. And judging by the ominous signs of drought, I decide it is best to refill my reserves at every natural source instead of waiting until they are empty.

Part way up a challenging gravel climb, I spot another small creek at the foot of a steep grassy embankment.

I load an armful of empty Hammer Nutrition and Gatorade bottles, along with water purification tablets, and butt-scoot down to the water's edge. Next, I dip each bottle into the stream, staying away from stagnant pools, which could contain parasites.

The sound of water trickling in over the rocks is calming. It makes me appreciate the remote simplicity of the Divide.

The challenge has awoken in me many of the primal instincts which every rider seems to relish, even those that have been unlucky in their quest to complete the distance. One such rider, Dave Nice (also known as "Fixie Dave"), is on his sixth attempt. Stolen gear and lost motivation have hampered Dave's past efforts.

It's getting dark now.

Out of the barren Basin and the surrounding flatlands of Rawlins, I enter a forest of aspen trees atop the foothills bordering Colorado. Perched on the side of a valley cliff, I find a small bivy spot tucked out of view, hidden behind the hulking trunk of a fallen tree. Sleep comes easily in the cooler, forested surroundings.

TOUR DIVIDE, DAY 13

Early the next morning, my arrival into the mountainous state of Colorado is met with a near head-on collision with a herd of cattle crossing Interstate 70, headed west. My warning "Mooooo" spooks the slow movers, unfortunately, sending them back in my direction, rather than off into the ditch as I had hoped. I can't help but laugh at their uncoordinated companionship.

I make a left on Slater Creek Road, headed for a hearty breakfast at the infamous Brush Mountain Lodge. Staff at the "Divide-friendly" hunting establishment actively watch for riders passing through via the Spot tracker page, often going out of their way to ready a warm bed and home-cooked meal, at all hours. Tour Divide race director Matthew Lee and his family have travelled from North Carolina to help run the much-anticipated "Halfway" layover.

Searching online to learn more about Matt's connection to the race, you would be hard-pressed to come across much detail. He has purposely kept the race website devoid of new content, including any information about him as director. There is a badge of honour in restricting access to the mainstream, so I have learned.

Matt is like Oz behind the curtain. He knows every bump and turn along the route.

It should come as no surprise that Lee has also won the event five times since its inception, in 2003, when it was called the "Great Divide Race" and started farther south, at the Canada-United States border. It is only in the last two years that Lee has taken a step back from pushing the pace, choosing instead to focus on nurturing a young family.

A row of interconnected log cabins appears over a bluff.

Much to my surprise, a weary Josh is shuffling around inside when I ride up to the main entrance of the lodge. He shakes his head, even after a full night in comfort. "I don't know if I can go on," he says, pointing at his feet. Sounding even further defeated, he tells me that Dylan left alone this morning. I picture Dylan pumping his fists in the early light, his Eminem playlist blaring.

My back-and-forth companion steps gingerly outside and readies his bike for possibly one last push into the town of Steamboat.

I choke down a stack of home-cooked pancakes in anticipation of riding together again. Matt pulls me aside, however. "You just got here. He's been here since last night – so rest a minute." His delivery is rather straightforward. Still, I feel conflicted.

I'm reminded of a conversation Josh and I had grinding up Union Pass three days ago. Since he had to drop out of the Divide twice before, Josh is more determined than ever to finish this time. Waiting at home for him is stressful part-time work, a rocky relationship and unexpected fatherhood. The Divide is a means to regain control of his life.

I let Josh go ahead.

As I chew more slowly, Matt and I chat about some of the armchair debates raging online, especially on bikepacking. net, which attracts a lot of Divide enthusiasts. Among the hot topics of conversation include whether riders should be allowed to carry smartphones in order to receive race updates; whether the fact that the two race leaders are joined at the hip constitutes an unfair advantage; and frustration at the lack of web updates. Matt reconfirms that being aloof is beneficial for keeping participation numbers low and likely under the radar of forest permits, expensive liabilities and the like.

Sipping on a second cup of coffee, I catch a glimpse of someone outside. Stretching to look over Matt's shoulder, I see Josh still sitting on the front lawn, his upper body in a depressed slump. "I think he's waiting up for me." I cut the conversation short.

I place a $20 bill on the table and thank Matt's wife for her hospitality.

Back outside with Josh, Matt tells us of a small rafting business along the Colorado River in Radium, an ambitious 176 kilometres farther down the route. "Just mention my name. They can hook you up with a place to stay tonight. They also have chips and Red Bull for purchase."

Finding energy in Matt's optimism, Josh proclaims, "We should try and catch Eszter Horanyi."

The two of us are being "chicked" by the female race leader, now in ninth place. Superhuman Eszter also happens to be the 2009 24-Hour Solo National Champion as well as the women's record holder for the 789-kilometre Colorado Trail Race. Her abilities are not to be taken lightly.

"I don't know about that," I reply with practical concern.

Heading back out on the dusty road, I emphasize to Josh that if we're going to ride together, it must be at "broken foot speed." Meaning, he needs to come down to my (more) consistent pace. And I believe it is in his best interest to do so. He agrees.

We ride side by side for an hour, all the way to the base of Hahn's Peak. Ahead is a steep 2.4-kilometre "pusher," as described by the cue sheet. Surprisingly, Josh continues to pound ahead in an attempt to clear the climb, riding all the way up in one go. *Why overexert yourself? And with your foot pain?*

He has been resting for 20 minutes by the time I reach the mountain summit. He has also been taking advantage of the clearer cell reception.

While changing out the batteries in my GPS unit and Spot tracker, I overhear him talking to his new girlfriend. "I'm going to ride into Steamboat and see how I feel. My feet are killing me." *Huh.*

We descend down an extremely rough ATV track.

My bones and packs rattle as I bounce from one boulder to the next, barely under control. The force causes my front shocks to bottom out, rubbing my handlebar bag against the front tire. The scent of hot metal and burning mesh ultimately signals me to stop. I allow enough time for my brake pads and frustration to cool. *Motherfuck, my feet hurt.*

Josh shoots ahead to a corner store at the bottom of our long descent. Once again, I arrive to a scene of him hunched over his knees, like dead weight, this time with an ice cream sandwich in hand. I drop down beside him with my own bag of groceries.

Staring off down the next stretch of paved country road, we each massage our sore feet. Josh tells me he tried to pop the masses underneath his toes (which, in both our cases, have evolved from bruises to puss-filled daggers), but that didn't really help. His eyes are glossed over now.

We ride on, aided by a tailwind and sunshine.

Nearing the edge of Steamboat, Josh tells me exactly what to expect for the next couple of days. "There is a dam, roughly 30 miles up. That would be a good spot to set up camp tonight," he instructs. I ask him about the roads going farther south. "They only get worse from here. New Mexico is all washboard ... it's brutal," he says, thinking of the increased foot pain that ride would entail.

Parked at a Subway with a much-anticipated messy meatball sandwich in hand, I look on as my downtrodden comrade makes a couple of calls from outside the restaurant. The scene is eerily similar to the time I came across the other "Amigo," Katherine, at the Subway in Pinedale. I'm pretty sure I know what conversation comes next.

Dejected, Josh tells me his Divide quest is over. "I'm sorry to hear that, man," I say, genuinely disappointed for him.

He's going to try and hitchhike to his home in Gunnison, Colorado. Steamboat is in the same county, so his chances are good. "As for tonight," he says glumly, "I'm going to go sit at that bar next door until it gets dark, then probably find a public park to set up my bivy."

In place of a conciliatory hug, we shake hands, no longer as gentlemen competitors, now as just friends.

TOUR DIVIDE, DAY 14
A couple of Breckenridge ski town tourists walk by with questionable looks on their faces, no doubt curious as to why

I am prodding my bare feet on the ritzy main street. "Can you do a little research on this?" I text Sarah a picture of my blackened toes. I'm hoping that something might come from floating the oddity out on the race forum.

My last climb before nightfall lies beyond the far edge of town: up and over Boreas Pass, at an elevation of 3499 metres. Josh referred to it as "railroad grade," meaning that a railway once used the same path and that the pitch will be easily managed.

As for timing, I'm more concerned about the required race detour from the main Adventure Cycling route that lies on the back side of the range. It leads riders down three miles of "Gold Dust Trail" (single-track trail), which becomes more dangerous in the dark. Granted, I could stop before that section, but the Como bed and breakfast is within reach. My last slice of comfort was one week ago at that motel in Lima, Montana.

To help ensure that a bed and shower will be waiting for me, I text Sarah to see if she can call ahead and let the owner know I am on my way. She hesitates. "I think that would be against the rules. I'm sorry, Babe ... you can call them, though."

"You're absolutely right! Thank you for the reminder," I tell her. But unfortunately, my thrifty side ultimately wins out against the prospect of the long-distance charge. *I should be okay.*

The sunny Colorado afternoon fades to dusk.

Wiping my brow at the top of Boreas Pass, the sweaty exhilaration I feel after a strong climb quickly transitions to feeling chilled from the exposure. I waste no time unpacking my GORE-TEX jacket, thermal layers and an energy bar to scarf down.

Zipping up, I take time for one last mental photograph.

The expansive valley view back down into Breckenridge is incredible. The setting sun perfectly highlights the coniferous greens, the log architecture of the mountainside homes and the contrasting rocky ski slopes. *I could live here.*

My attention turns to the opposite side of the pass, and for signs of the Gold Dust Trail. *Shit,* of course it is not as obvious as I would like it to be. Single-track trails are often confused with commonly used animal paths, of which there are a few to choose from.

I make an educated guess. As I roll down and along, all remaining daylight quickly fades behind the mountain.

For the next hour, I bounce off trees and sweeping muddy embankments like a pinball in the dark, guided by an ever-weakening headlight. Nearing the trail terminus, having momentarily dropped my guard, I crash into one of the 90-degree sloped rails and bail over my handlebars, hard.

Lying face down in the dirt, I rotate my joints and feel only mild stiffness. *Thank god.* Watching the Gold Dust settle in the otherwise pitch black forest surroundings, I grow wide-eyed at the sight of my handlebars, also lying contorted from the crash.

Apprehensively, I approach the wounded Tumbler, which reminds me of a wounded dog lying on the side of the road. *Please, let this be an easy Allen key fix,* I pray.

Fortunately, luck is on my side, at least for mechanical issues. Any chance of reaching the B&B before closing is quickly slipping away, however.

My watch reads 10:00 p.m.

Speeding downhill toward sanctuary, I peer into the widening dry-eye gravel void, blinking continuously, and try to anticipate the shadows beyond my headlight. *Where is this place?* I am just one pothole away from catastrophe. *Maybe I should look for a good bivy spot instead?*

Out of the forest, I spot a two-storey home outlined by a solitary exterior light. Just another rural subdivision, I assume. Yet, in the blink of an eye, I catch a glimpse of a small white sign at the end of the driveway. It reads, "Como Depot." "Holy shit!" I proclaim happily, out loud. *I made it!*

Stepping up to the wooden door of the historic-looking building, I knock, half expecting no one to answer at this late hour. Yet, surprisingly, owner Dave Tomkins greets me with an English accent: "Are you Ryan?" He has been following the race online and anticipated my late arrival. My mind immediately feels more at ease.

David leads me to a vacant bar adjacent to the lobby area. "An anonymous donor has sponsored beers for every rider – here you go," he says, handing me a cool pint. "I'll go and cook up some dinner. You can drop your dirty clothes in the hamper. I'll have them cleaned for you by the morning. And how does a 5:30 a.m. wake-up and pancake breakfast sound?"

"Good," I nod, somewhat stunned by this good fortune.

TOUR DIVIDE, DAY 15

I can feel the environment I'm riding in growing more desperate.

Heading into southern Colorado, there are fewer farms, fewer drainage basins and even fewer streams with flowing water. *Come to think of it*, the only water source I have seen in the last two days was a small reservoir along an arid plain this morning. I'm kicking myself now for not stopping. *There has to be something flowing ahead*, I remember telling myself. Stagnant water is my last go-to.

A rider headed in the opposite direction passed me earlier, one of the few taking on the Divide in reverse order. He was lugging a pair of heavy, four-litre water jugs behind him in a trailer. It occurred to me that I should ask for help, but I didn't want to seem unnecessarily wimpy, nor impinge upon his limited supply. Instead, my dehydrated grimace morphed into a challenged smile, followed by a wave.

Now, caught in a network of dusty hills in the Rio Grande National Forest, which is noticeably devoid of shaded woods, I scout ahead from a plateau and see no solution to my current predicament. Every potential water source that my map cues list has dried.

My pace slows as survival mode takes over from racing mode. I hold on to the hope that a nearby campsite will have water. Unfortunately, there is a sign at the gate that reads, "CLOSED." Drought seems partly to blame.

Looking across the street, a small family of bony cattle mills about in a muddy field, looking like beef jerky with a heartbeat. I stare at the animals pushing through the soft mud and debate the merits of enduring a Giardia infection to temporarily ward off dehydration. I remember hearing about how a former race leader was forced to drop out of the Divide just 480 kilometres from the finish and make an emergency trip to the hospital. It is thought that he ingested the debilitating parasite through specks of cow manure that had flung up on his water bottles while he was riding. I often rub the rubber spouts clean for this reason.

Option B is to wait until the evening hours and try to make up some ground when temperatures cool. As far as I know, the next restock point is at least 80 kilometres away, in Del Norte. The city is close enough that I will likely not perish before I reach it. It is far enough away, however, that this will no doubt be a character-building experience.

Fuck, I stare some more at the cow pasture and let out a heavy sigh. The novelty of the Divide is starting to wear thin.

I walk over to where the mud looks freshest and shoo the

cattle away. Kneeling down in frustration, I begin digging through the mess with both hands. The top layer is a mixture of grass and mud, with manure scattered nearby. Each successive layer appears cleaner.

A small pool of water begins to form at my fingertips. I keep digging another two feet until the hole is deep enough to fully submerge one of my bottles on its side. I screw off the plastic top.

Next, I remove my cycling jersey and stretch it over an empty bottle. Holding the full bottle overtop, I begin spraying water down through the makeshift filter.

Holding the considerably cleaner water up to the sun, I inspect the field blend once more, and then drop in two water purification tablets (one extra to be sure). I patiently wait the prescribed 30 minutes before I begin drinking.

I find a sparse piece of shade and lie down to rest in a full spread-eagle, still thirsty after consuming two full bottles of the water. *I'll set my alarm to go off in 15 minutes.*

"Ryan?" I hear someone yell out.

In a sleepy daze, I look back down the path to see another rider slowly pulling up. It's Eric Schraufnagel, from Denver. He was one of two riders who passed me as we were leaving Roosville, Montana. I overtook him in Steamboat, after saying goodbye to Josh. Eric apparently had stopped at a local hospital to receive treatment for fluid in his lungs. But as Sarah mentioned by text, at some point he got ahead of me again. So it comes as a surprise to see him trailing me now.

He sounds concerned. "Are you okay?" I realize now that it might appear as though I had been hit by a car.

"Yeah, yeah. Just taking a quick break … I thought you

were ahead of me." I quickly change gears and stand up to shake his hand.

He lets out a phlegmy cough. "I was. The Tomichi Creek Trading Post owner told me you passed me this morning at Sargents. I was camped behind the store and slept in this morning. Of course, I assumed they wouldn't open their doors until 8 a.m."

I smile, now understanding what happened. I unknowingly got the jump on Eric when I rolled up early and caught the owner of the trading post in a good mood. In addition to opening the general store early, he also let me have first crack at a pan of freshly baked cinnamon buns. Those dense doughy calories have since burned into the ether.

Eric and I continue on together, both desperate for food and water. At the first paved junction, we scramble off route a couple of miles to the La Garita Trading Post, listed on our cue sheet.

As we roll in one hour before close, the owner and her elderly parents look on happily from a table next to us. Her two young kids take charge of entering our candy and coke order into the cash register. Their formality adds an extra sweet touch. "Thank you both for your help," I smile, dropping a small tip into a jar. The kids both jump at the loot.

"What are your thoughts on tonight?" Eric asks me, sitting down with his stash.

The town of Del Norte is another 32 kilometres south on what appears to be rough track. It will take us about two hours to get there. My cue sheet says we will "pass through an open badlands gap. As you descend, watch for sharp rocks, sand and washouts."

"Del Norte makes sense. I'm not going to bother riding past dark, and up the next mountain pass, just to get a hotel room and call it a night," I concede. It's already 7:00 p.m.

"Okay, yeah, I'm cool with that," Eric agrees. The race is now neutralized. We can ride on as just friends and without concern for race tactics.

Regardless of intent, it is apparent that Eric is riding just a little bit stronger than me. In a battle of his lungs against my feet, he's winning out. So again, I admit, "You're going a little too fast for me. Go on ahead, Eric."

"Are you sure?" he questions, ready to slow down.

"Yeah, go for it!" I wave him off.

In good faith, Eric suggests we will see each other again soon enough, probably in Del Norte or on the impending climb up Indiana Pass to an elevation of 3630 metres, which is also the longest climb of the entire race, at 37 kilometres.

I'm left alone to slide out in the sand and jagged rock, just as my cue sheet warned.

Feeling a cursed stab on my right side, I see that a wound on my hip, which I received en route to Como in the dark, has torn open again and has grown larger than a fist in size. Blood now seeps through a torn white panel on my cycling shorts, drying and stinging like clockwork on each pedal stroke.

I try to remember that this type of wound is more of an annoyance, not something to get angry about. *Take a look around*, I tell myself. The sun sets on a beautiful red rock desert scene. *Even better, take a picture.*

Connecting again with smooth asphalt and unfortunate small-town poverty, a bright yellow Subway sign neverthe-less shines through the darkness at an intersection along the main street of Del Norte. Scanning up and down the dark U.S. Route 160, no other dinner choices are apparent.

First, having learned that small-town accommodations

are often limited, I make my way to a dive down the street. "It's the last room," the attendant confirms.

Stepping into comfort, I'm greeted by many stereotypical reasons to stay away from such establishments, including a TV that doesn't work, a bed that is covered in slippery plastic and the ever-present, musty smell of shag carpet and leaky showers. But it's heaven for the weary and wounded.

I get back on my bike and head toward the Subway.

Inside, I meet up with Eric again. He passes me with two subs in hand. I'm not so lucky, though. The bumbling pair behind the counter have just closed up shop. A partly frozen convenience store burrito and chocolate milk are available in the adjoining grocery aisle.

I sit down at a window booth to eat.

Loading up his packs outside, not stopping to eat, Eric appears to have gotten a second wind. He tells me he might continue on tonight and try to make up some distance over Indiana Pass. "If I could just get a shower first, that would be awesome. I'm going to head over to the motel a couple blocks down," he tells me.

Sensing his race instincts kicking in, I decide to play a card of my own. "Yeah, I think I might head there too." I hold back from divulging that no rooms are available, or offering to share my own.

The relationship among the race leaders is a unique one. Sometimes we work with each other, sometimes against. All of us want to see the other reach the finish, however – there is no question about that. But it is often something more than pure cycling ability that determines the winner.

Tenth place is back up for grabs.

CHAPTER 30

HUMBLE PIE

While on the phone with Sarah in my Del Norte motel room last night, I remember overhearing the caretaker open a nearby door for Eric. As I listened to his wheels tick in, I realized that my room apparently wasn't the last available.

He's up there now, somewhere.

With my nose tilted toward the high roads of Indiana Pass, I can taste a slow drip of silky red iron draining down my throat. I use the back of my cycling glove to wipe away the blood.

The air is especially dry today.

Stopped at the foot of the first steep pitch, 18 kilometres out of town, I see a male and female rider speeding down toward me on a pair of fully loaded mountain bikes: yet another couple that has chosen to test the integrity of their relationship on the Divide, heading north. "Everything okay?" the bearded boyfriend asks.

"Yeah, just a bloody nose," I huff.

"Aww, muffin," says his wiry female companion, taunting my nothing sideline. *Yeah, yeah.* I'm not looking for sympathy.

"Have you seen any other riders this morning?" I ask.

They tell me that Eric is about an hour ahead of me.

As for the front of the pack, Sarah informed me that New Zealander Ollie Whalley will cross the finish line in

Antelope Wells sometime this morning. He's on track for a record-setting 16-day pace, riding an average of 276 kilometres each day.

Calgarian Craig Stappler is not far behind him, having unfortunately dropped from winning contention after breaking a pedal and having to hitchhike to the nearest New Mexico bike shop. *That's too bad.* I was rooting for my former adversary to win. Craig and I traded podium finishes during the 2009–2010 Alberta racing season.

Unfortunately, my sore feet and poor lighting have prevented me from keeping up this time. I resolve to simply finish well.

It is a humble recognition, though still something very much worth fighting for. "We're rooting for you," Sarah tells me.

"And we want you to know that we love you," Sarah's mom adds.

Their love, it means the world to me. And to think, just over a year ago we were strangers living at opposite ends of the country.

The blood begins to congeal. *It's time to get moving again.*

Climbing has always been a strength of mine. But climbing is a push against gravity that requires me to mash on the pedals instead of pulling up. *Fuck,* I grit my teeth, feeling my undiagnosed toe pain sink deeper.

One hour down.

Two, and *look at that view.*

Three is a drag.

And four, the windy summit. Its jagged peak has been sliced open to expose greedy iron innards. The site of the Summitville mine is located directly below.

My cue sheet warns that absolutely none of the runoff water in the area is drinkable. In the 1980s, the then active gold mine accidentally leaked toxic by-products into the watershed pathways, killing fish and livestock downstream. Toxic red minerals continue to flow through the creeks today.

Carrying on, feeling dehydrated and uneasy, I miss a turn, double back and then hit my crotch on the handlebar after nailing a misjudged pothole. "Son of a bitch!" I yell into the barren destruction.

The bumpy trail descends to the village of Plataro and continues through the Conejos River valley on what I deem to be the Worst Fucking Road of the Divide.

It is like a rocky creekbed. I can only travel a short distance before having to stop for 15 minutes to massage my feet and allow time for a mental break. Meanwhile, trout fishermen cast away in otherwise beautiful waters running parallel to where I am riding.

By the time I reach the intersection for Colorado State Highway 17, three hours later, I don't even care that the next ten kilometres are straight up and over La Manga Pass, at an elevation of 3118 metres. *At least it's paved.*

At the adjacent corner store, I resupply on gummy candy and energy drinks. *There isn't really anything else to choose from*, I justify. And even if there was, I'm back on *the kick*: "When I get to the top of this hill, I'm going to eat some damn candy." The cheer is accompanied by bouts of swearing, of which Mom would not approve.

Cresting La Manga with Red Bull wings, I calmly exhale at the sight of a beautiful sunset. Turning up the volume on my iPod, I infuse the ensuing downhill ride with the upbeat "Charlie Brown," from Coldplay's new album, *Mylo Xyloto*, and love-filled dreams.

Elaborate proposals have filled my thoughts for the last

several days. I'm confident now that Sarah is the one that I want to spend my life with. In fact, it is impossible not to smile just a little brighter at the thought of her beauty and compassion.

I'm coming for you, Babe.

Twenty minutes later, I veer off the smooth asphalt and onto a rambling ATV trail. The narrow path winds through a grassy landscape with no particular rhyme or reason. *Where to next*, I wonder with anticipation and delight. An important landmark approaches.

Around a steep corner, at the cattle guard park boundary for Carson National Forest, I officially enter the final state of New Mexico. Approximately 1120 kilometres are all that stand between me and the finish at Antelope Wells.

TOUR DIVIDE, DAY 17

I sit on the step of a quiet mini-market in the sparsely populated Navajo Nation at dusk. Tumbleweed blows across the sunbaked two-lane highway running alongside where I sit.

Standing in silhouette at the far corner of the blue stucco building, a weathered Native American waits patiently for his next opportunity to hitch a ride. His leathery brown skin and sunken eyes tell of a challenging life.

I give him a small wave. He does not acknowledge me.

The Elder seems content to remain in his own thoughts, never uttering a word, despite our unique familiarity. He and I have been leapfrogging each other for the last 43 kilometres, all the way from the small restock town of Cuba, New Mexico. My quiet companion has hitched at least four different rides since then.

Up until now, I have yet to observe his method.

Two husky Navajo teens drive up in a dusty sedan, blasting obscene hip-hop music from tattered backseat speakers. He does not budge.

Not long after this happens, an elderly woman and another woman, who is overweight, likely her daughter, pull up for gas. The daughter motions toward the man for him to join them. He walks over and climbs into the open cab, still without speaking a single word.

Unsure of how my presence on this land is regarded, I remain quietly respectful. Catching the daughter's eye, I offer a small smile and a nod. She surprises me by asking me if I need a ride somewhere. *Huh*, "No, thank you. I'm on my way to Mexico."

"How far you going tonight?" she asks.

"Oh … until I get tired, usually," I smile again.

"Well, good luck to you. This here is Navajo land. We are good people. You will be safe," she reassures me. The next 130 kilometres of the road are also paved. And, combined with the warm evening air, I'm optimistic about riding later than usual.

She waves goodbye as I adjust my makeshift glove orthotics, in addition to the cheap Pinedale slips, and give my feet one last good rub. As usual, I cringe as my ankles and all my toes crack painfully. *Cartilage is overrated, anyway.*

I switch on my headlights an hour earlier than normal.

I ride on, slightly paranoid about the path ahead. My thoughts turn to that *other* family tragedy. I haven't thought about it for a while.

My cousin Jonathan and his fiancée Laura were killed on a Native reservation in Arizona, just over 17 years ago now. A drunk Native American man crossed the highway median at sunset, slamming into their van and trapping them inside. The Native American and Jonathan died on impact.

As the van caught fire, a passerby tried to get Laura out, who was still alive, but it was too late.

My parents, my sister and I were spending Christmas down south that year. We were on our way home to Calgary, driving. My parents were asked to divert to a police station in Flagstaff, Arizona, in order to represent the family in the identification process. I was 12 years old and I remember sitting in the police station for several hours, quietly waiting, in shock. My parents would come out of a nondescript room every so often to give my sister and me coins for the lobby vending machine.

Corn chips, that's what I remember eating.

As I chow down on convenience fare again, this time, back on the Tour Divide, I reflect on how my opinions about Native Americans have been shaped by this event. But, *We are good people*, I must remember.

Only a truck or two passes me as I continue on.

Since my view is unobstructed by mountains or city smog, I can see a great distance in every direction, even in the low light. The faint glow of TV sitcoms is visible through the windows of reservation homes, scattered far apart. Dogs bark as I approach, which appears to signal nearby crickets to call out to the sun, now falling below the western horizon.

It is a foreign land, yet vaguely familiar.

Stopped for another short break on the side of the road, I scratch my scruffy ginger beard. The annoyingly coarse hairs are almost an inch long now – ganglier than I have ever let them grow. But I dare not shave this token of wilderness survival, not yet anyway.

Prancing through the dark ditch on my right, a pack of antelope teases me toward the finish, still a few days away. Their eyes glow white like the reflective material on my clothing. When our eyes meet, they freeze. They soon recognize me as a fellow traveller of the night, however, as they dance effortlessly over a farmer's barbed wire fence and on to certain solitude.

The wind whistles as I coast away from them.

Enter, my old nightmare from solo touring: high beams come blaring up behind me. For an unknown reason, they choose to stick on my wheel, just a short distance behind. *They could easily pass me. What are they doing?*

The stalking truck remains in position for ten minutes before falling back, now obscured by a ridge.

A second car speeds past.

A few minutes later, the truck in question comes revving back. I look over my left shoulder, holding up a right hand to try and block some of the blinding light. I cannot make out the assailant, or their intent. *Maintaining a defensive speed seems smarter than pulling over.*

The truck finally pulls up beside me. I get ready to bail into the ditch and run.

Someone rolls down the passenger window. I squint, trying to see. "No way," I laugh out loud, breathing a huge sigh of relief at the sight of the young woman from the gas station. She waves. Remember, *We are good people.*

Without saying anything for the next hour, she remains protectively on my wheel – just like my support crew on the Race Across America. The spotlight affords me the opportunity to speed ahead in aero, unconcerned about any cars coming up behind me. *This is awesome!*

And then, without notice, the truck pulls off into darkness and does not return. My elusive Navajo goodwill appears to have run its course.

Feeling my eyes growing heavy, I begin scanning the shoulder for an increasingly rare patch of desert trees or an obscured ridge to hide away. *Bedtime.*

After a full day of relatively friendly asphalt, in addition to last night's Navajo stretch, my cue sheet finally guides me to make a left turn on what appears to be an elongated sand trap and 48 kilometres of salivation. Pie Town, New Mexico, taunts on the horizon.

Every kilometre marked is an achievement made possible at this point by a mix of walking my bike and finding compact sections to coast a short distance. The lack of momentum tests my patience. And with fluid reserves running low, the immediate goal becomes very simple: *that signpost in the distance, that's all you think about.*

It takes me two hours to cover the first 16 kilometres.

Collapsing down on an aborted tire tread, I sip on my last bottle of Gatorade with a resentful appreciation for the infertile farming landscape before me. A few familiar cattle stand scattered about in the late afternoon heat, searching for grass among the lunar apocalypse. *There has got to be a water trough somewhere.*

The last drop of orange sport drink slides down my throat. "Fuck you!" I finally unglue, tossing the clear plastic bottle into the New Mexico abyss. It is unlike me to litter. My voice of reason has reached a breaking point, however. I'm frustrated with my sore feet, for falling out of contention, with the horrible road conditions, for all the dried-up creekbeds and because the Divide is now keeping me from Sarah.

Pushing on, the map cues list a windmill (with a broken water pump), an abandoned farmhouse, a private acreage for supposed religious fanatics, and a cemetery, on the left. I finally find salvation at a sign on a gate that reads, "CDT (Continental Divide Trail) Riders, Stop Here." Steps away, there's a farm building with running water and a curious mule for company.

One step at a time.

At 8:30 p.m., I roll into Pie Town. Unfortunately, all three of its prized pie shops have closed for the evening, only 30 minutes prior to my arrival. Doubling back on the dusty main street, there do not appear to be any other services, just a few scraggly dogs pacing through the evening alleyways on their own agendas.

My cue sheet lists no other restock points for the next 160 kilometres. *Ah, shit,* I'm going to have to hole up here until the pie shops open in the morning. In doing so, I'll lose two hours of riding tonight, and another impatient three early tomorrow morning.

I ride over to the town's RV campground.

No one answers when I knock on the office door. There are no campers parked in the lot, either. *It's like a ghost town around here.*

I walk over to the small one-stall washroom building on site. Scrunching my bike inside, I proceed to lock the door and slide down to the floor. *Okay, now what?*

I take stock of the humid amenities. There is a tiny shower and a sink in which to clean up. *Guess I'm staying,* I sigh, out of both boredom and frustration. It is unfortunate that I cannot spend this downtime being more productive, by doing proper laundry, buying groceries, phoning Sarah and getting a good night's rest in a fully horizontal position. *Pie Town, I expected more.*

Twenty minutes into purgatory, I hear footsteps crunching on the gravel outside. I unlock the door to a friendly smile and handshake from the RV park manager. Thankfully, no stranger to the vagabond cyclist, he tells me that most riders stay at a place called the Toaster House, just down the road. There are beds, a shower and free food. I'm dumbfounded. "It's hard to miss," he points me in the direction.

I head optimistically back out into the evening.

A few homes down, I come across an eccentric yard with old toasters hanging from the walkway gate – *Ah, yes, the Toaster House.* No one answers when I knock on the front door of the brown wooden shack. Taped above the knob is a handwritten note. It informs me that the side door is unlocked, and to come in. *Okay, this is different.*

I walk around to the right of the building and proceed to let myself in. "Hello?" I call out. No one answers.

I flick on a couple of lights.

A second note on the kitchen table says to help myself to any food in the fridge. It further explains that Nita, the kind owner, no longer lives here, and that this home is a safe haven for weary travellers of the Continental Divide (thru-hike) Trail.

Smiling in disbelief, I walk into a room with a bed. In another room, musty furniture surrounds stacks of *National Geographic* magazines and old board games. Shelves are lined with candles, items left behind by others and knickknacks belonging to, I guess, the elusive Hawaiian owner.

Inside a fridge situated out back on a porch overlooking the New Mexico wild, my eyes grow wide at the sight of homemade pies, frozen pizzas, pop and ice cream sandwiches ... *the trail magic motherlode!*

After a warm shower and a cheesy skillet amalgamation, I set about filling my water bottles and restocking my food reserves. Naturally, I pack the densest calorie option available: two mixed berry pies folded over in their tin plates and mashed inside a grocery bag. Tomorrow, I'll ration a small slice for each hour of riding. I'm banking on 16 hours without any services.

Before drifting off to sleep, I drop a $20 bill in the donation jar sitting on the kitchen table and write a small thank-you message in Nita's guest book.

I'll be ready to go at daybreak.

TOUR DIVIDE, DAY 20

All worries generally subside when a restock point is nearby. It therefore comes as a surprise to look down on a thirsty morning to see that my highlighted GPS route is about to take an abrupt turn left, instead of continuing 11 kilometres straight toward services as my cues suggest. *That can't be right!*

Scanning my surroundings, I notice a sign for the Sapillo Group Area Campground. *Shit, this is the turn.* I must have made an error inserting the final detour into my cues. Matthew Lee has specified four detours from the main Adventure Cycling route, often to avoid paved riding. "AMPLE water is needed for this section," my cues further warn. The next 19 kilometres follows a difficult single-track section with plenty of hike-a-bike.

The question now becomes, am I prepared to go without water for the next two to three hours? I drank my reserves in anticipation of the nearby restock point, now at least a two-hour detour. *What would Eric have done?* I strategize, knowing he is still within reach.

The afternoon sun blazes down, testing my resolve.

I decide to take the gamble, first checking for water in the campsite. Unfortunately, each of the water pumps is out of order.

I push past the ominous signs.

The first climb is incredibly steep. I take one step forward, thrust my bike a couple of inches forward, apply the brakes (to prevent the Tumbler from sliding back), step ahead with my other foot and then take a deep breath.

It takes over an hour to hike even a small distance. And already my throat feels like dry cotton.

Looking ahead to the jagged mountain terrain of the Gila National Forest, I grow frustrated by the amount of hard work I've invested in what now seems like a bad decision. Flashes of wilderness survival stories begin to flood through my thoughts. This is one of those victim stories you hear about in the news: "The 20-something was disoriented, with a broken leg and no water, and was forced to crawl in search of help."

I screwed up.

Turning around, not once do I let up on my disk brakes. Still, my locked wheels slide along the steep sandy cliff, nervously careening around narrow embankments lined with cacti. I grind my teeth in anger.

I ride through the campsite and back out onto the paved Highway 35, then speed 40 minutes ahead to a small grouping of guest cabins at Lake Roberts. Inside the general store, I relax when I see a cooler filled with ice cream and Gatorade, and shelves lined with chips and chocolate. My body has become a candy-metabolizing machine.

"Are you doing that crazy bike ride to Mexico?" the owner asks.

"Yeah, I am. Have you seen anyone else come through?"

She tells me they haven't, not since the detour was added. "And it's a shame. We've cooked up a huge tin of lasagna for you guys – it's on us." *No way!* Glorious trail magic is at work once again.

I proceed to fill my face in their back room.

Looking out a small window from inside the smoky lounge, I take note of the hot sun and consider how the heat will only make things worse if I choose to hike back up the mountain in midday. *I already made one poor decision. Don't make another.*

If no one else has come through (the only restock point since Pie Town, as far as I know), that means Eric must have made it through the Gila and on to the final restock at Silver City this morning. He's probably gearing up now to make a nighttime push to Antelope Wells. *It is unlikely that I will catch him.*

LATER THAT EVENING

My bike navigates on instinct toward the first greasy McDonald's in Silver City. On arrival, I order my usual Quarter Pounder meal, large soda and frappé on the side.

I'm relieved to eat and to have made it through the remote Gila National Forest in one piece.

In between bites, the restaurant manager walks over and makes light chit-chat. He confirms that one rider came through this morning, another two on a tandem bike last night, the last of my competition ahead (and now likely finished). *Good for them*, I smile.

I lean back in the booth and kick up my feet. *You gave it your all. There's nothing to be ashamed of ... It's just you against the clock now.*

My iPhone boots up after a quick charge. A text from Sarah immediately buzzes on screen. "Everything okay? Saw you went off course. Eric is in Silver City! He has been there all day – there is no word as to why," she writes. My adrenaline immediately surges.

I'm guessing he paid for not going off route to restock. If so, he may have spent the last several hours trying to recover in a local hotel room. Thinking ahead, it is unlikely he will wait until tomorrow to take off again. Riding under the cover of darkness is optimal for this exposed final section. *Yes, bring it!*

After 20 days and 4220 kilometres, the Tour Divide has come down to a sprint finish for tenth place and a spot on the leaderboard. It is an exhilarating feeling.

I quickly text Sarah back, "I'm going to go for it. Going to try and ride through the night, just like RAAM." Antelope Wells is another 198 kilometres to the south. And fortunately, my map cues list no mountains ahead, just "smooth surface heading through high desert." Granted, I need to be mindful that there are no services from here on out.

The convenience store across the street is my next stop. Under white neon exterior lights, I stock my packs with eight sugary Gatorades, ten small cinnamon buns, two beefy burritos, some gum and a couple packs of addictive gummy candy. If I could carry more, I would – there is not time enough for a return trip, though.

The sweltering desert heat has cooled to just the right temperature. Gazing up at the cloudless night sky, I see an especially bright waxing moon. It illuminates the speedy path before me – the next 29 kilometres out of town are all paved.

Seizing the moment, I text Sarah one final goodbye before cell service drops. "Gotta go, Babe! I LOVE YOU!!!" *More than you know.*

With the slow-moving, stop-and-go intersections behind me, I settle down into my aero bars and begin pedalling with renewed vigour. Taking deep, consistent breaths, I hover just below the red line, carefully taunting the lactic acid that readies to shut down my muscles, should I go anaerobic.

Far removed from the lights of Silver City, my cues direct me to turn left onto a remote sandy path.

Pulling away from all signs of traffic, I power down my

red blinking light attached to my seat pack. If Eric is behind me, I don't want to provide a visual cue for him to go faster. Our blinkers can be seen for miles in these clear conditions. I'll also moderate the use of my headlight.

TOUR DIVIDE, DAY 21

As I continue on, the moonlight stretches across a sea of sand dunes and scraggly farmland. I pay extra attention to the dried riverbed washes that pull at my wheels. Rolling faster now, with a tailwind, further hampers my ability to anticipate such danger in time. It is nonetheless exciting to feel speed on my side once again.

Three hours into the desert darkness, my front end begins to bob up and down. Because of the soft trail, I'm not immediately certain that it is a flat. *Please don't be.*

I turn on my headlight and inspect the front tire, still rolling along. *Shoot,* it bloats underneath my added forward weight. Pulling over, I find that a lone cactus needle has pierced through the extremely worn, once knobby tread.

I turn off my iPod and scan the relatively flat 360-degree horizon for Eric's lights. Standing still, my elevated pulse and increased sweat rate are racing with anticipation. *Where are you? I know you're out here somewhere.*

I immediately start fixing the tire.

Concerned for lost time, I keep one eye pointed down the road. *Still no Eric?*

I either sped way ahead of him or am actually behind him. There is also a chance that Eric's Spot tracker isn't working properly. The GPS technology can send out a delayed signal, or sometimes none at all, depending on battery strength and the line of sight to the sky. Sarah may have been working with outdated information.

At 1:00 a.m. I stop to massage my feet and chow down on one of the gas station cinnamon buns. *Eat only half now, the other half in an hour.* I have learned to use food as a reward system, including an incentive to stay awake.

I stop again at 2:30, my attention span now waning.

In the far distance, I see a line of car and semi-trailer truck headlights, the first sign of civilization in over four hours. Reading ahead on my map cues, I surmise it is traffic on Interstate 10.

Continuing on, the perpendicular stretch of illumination becomes my next visible target. And maybe, despite my cues warning me otherwise, I might be able to stock up at the Continental Divide Trading Post, near where I cross under the highway. *I need an influx of gummy bears and energy drinks to break the sleep monster.*

The line of lights toys with my weary eyes. I slap my face hard – *If I am tired, so is he. You have a chance to finish in the top ten. Keep going.*

I emerge out of the darkness and cross underneath the Interstate. On the other side is the Divide tourist trap, now closed, and a line of dim parking lot lights hanging high in the sky. Two large semi-trailer trucks stand still, idling their engines nearby.

I let out an unsatisfied exhale. *No gummies.*

Sitting on the asphalt next to my bike for a moment, I turn on my cell and check for reception. Surprisingly, a text from Sarah appears. "I'm sorry, Babe. Eric reached the finish line an hour ago. His tracker wasn't working properly."

With my race momentum quickly deflating, I sigh again. Antelope Wells is still another 117 kilometres to the south. *You tried your best.*

I ride another 13 kilometres east on a dark frontage road. Turning right at the intersecting Highway 146, headed south, a large sign on the corner reads, "Antelope Wells Port of Entry, 65 Miles; Open 8:00 a.m. to 4:00 p.m." I smile with an exhausted sense of pride.

Turning my attention away from Interstate traffic whizzing by, my eyes grow heavy in view of two lonely lanes ahead.

Unconsciously looking for a reason to sleep, I hold up my watch for confirmation of the early hour – it's 4:00 a.m. *Yep, I think I'm done for now.*

I slide off my bike and walk a short distance into exposed desert. Hunched behind a patch of sagebrush, barely hidden, I pull out my sleeping pad and lie down in the warm sand, without the need of my sleeping bag or bivy. Lastly, as a matter of hygiene and routine, I roll down my sweaty cycling shorts, allowing "the boys," and numerous festering wounds, to breath freely under the exposed sky.

The stars are a wonder to behold.

THE LAST STRETCH

At 5:30 a brilliant sunrise awakens across the desert to the east. I turn onto my side and stare for a moment. With no mountains to climb over, its warm rays soon reach the highway. *Here we go, my last day.*

By 8:00, sweat is already beading on my arms and legs as they pump away.

Nightmares of riding through Death Valley on the Race Across America, and of sweating buckets through Mexico on the Pan-American Highway, come painfully flooding back. Both times, I cramped to the point of falling off my bike, and on both of those occasions, I had a support crew.

There is absolutely no shelter out here. Also, not a single car has passed all morning. Huh.

I had incorrectly assumed there was going to be more traffic around the border crossing, mainly for hitchhiking potential back to the town of Lordsburg, 45 minutes southwest of Silver City. From there, I had planned on taking a four-hour bus ride to Tucson and flying home to Ontario. Now I'm just focused on asking a passerby for water.

A black helicopter circles in the distance, no doubt searching for illegal immigrants trying to cross the border. Next, two fighter jets thunder overhead. *Holy shit*, I grip my bars, startled by their stealth approach.

A white truck passes me just minutes later. Two men wearing dark sunglasses scan me up and down with serious expressions, seemingly annoyed by my presence. *The border patrol trifecta.*

I scan the shoulder for cacti large enough to seek shelter under. *If only I could just cover my head*, the slightest amount of shade would allow me to take a sip of water, swirl it around and swallow just before it evaporates away.

I now ration one sip every 30 minutes.

As I close in on the marker signalling 30 miles before the race finish, another cactus needle stops me in my tracks. The hot asphalt has made my tires more vulnerable. In fact, I couldn't imagine either wheel lasting another day. This brings new meaning to the expression "leave it all out on the course."

Desperation rises higher in the sky, bleaching out what texture and colour remain in the desolate landscape. I squint ahead in the sun, even with sunglasses on.

There is a sign for 15 miles to go, and then one for every mile thereafter.

My tire goes flat again! *Fuck.*

I lick my cracked lips incessantly.

And then, for the first time in three weeks, I see a checkered finish flag on the GPS horizon. It is no longer a question of *if* I will finish, but *when*.

A group of metallic grey buildings appears around a hill. *You did it.*

Smiling like an idiot, I pass into a gated area, and stop at the door of the United States customs office. The outside of the building has familiar lettering sprawled across one of the brick walls, stating "United States Border Inspection Station, Antelope Wells, N.M." Nearly every Divide finish picture uses it as a backdrop. As I look down at the GPS again, however, the finish still shows as being ahead.

I ride ten feet farther and scoot underneath a security gate into Mexico. Their stucco border station looks surprisingly archaic in contrast. I would be surprised if they have electricity.

Three armed men in army fatigues stand under a lone tree for shade. "*Hola,*" I wave at them.

One of them walks over to me and begins speaking in authoritative Spanish. I point back toward the United States, and smile, *Thank you, but no thank you.* The man looks puzzled as I return to the land of the free.

Fist pump, *booya.*

It looks like my finish call to Sarah will have to wait, however, as I hold my iPhone up to the sky and am met with only one fluttering bar. No matter, she has probably been tracking me all morning from work. A bouncing blue dot indicates an official finish, and soon after, a return to civilization.

I walk my bike up to the United States customs office.

Holding out my iPhone again, I pose for a well-deserved selfie in front of the Antelope sign. While I'm doing so, one of the officers steps outside and offers to take my picture. He then invites me inside the small air-conditioned building for a complimentary cold soda and ice cream sandwich. "Oh, wow," I shake his hand.

The friendly welcome seems abnormal for the stale border patrol brethren, yet fitting, considering the remote conditions: only a few cars pass through here each day. My inevitable next question comes: "How do most riders get home from here?" I wonder out loud. The process remains somewhat of an anomaly on race forums.

"Many seem to have rides coordinated in advance," the officer explains. Unfortunately, my closest friends live in Phoenix, over 600 kilometres away to the northwest.

"There is also a shuttle service that is scheduled to come up from Mexico this afternoon. You might be able to get on with them. I know that they stop off in Phoenix," the officer says encouragingly.

"Wow, okay, perfect," I respond with relief.

"It's not a guarantee you will get on," he cautions. "It depends on whether they have room and how they feel about transporting your bike. I can ask for you. The shuttle drivers do not speak English."

Biding my time, I walk around to the back of the building to clean the Tumbler off with a small garden hose. Rubbing my hand across its black metal frame, washing away three weeks of accumulated dirt, sticky tar, baked cow manure and spilled sport drink splotches, I acknowledge my bike with respect. *We did it.*

A white passenger van pulls up three hours later. It is loaded with Mexicans headed to visit family in Arizona.

I approach respectfully, unsure of protocol.

Tension in the office rises as the officers ready their game faces, and guns. It is apparent that this can sometimes be a tense exchange. "You can't be here when we search the vehicle and check everyone's documentation," the officer warns me, and tells me to go back around.

Twenty minutes later, the officer comes around back and says the shuttle driver will take me for US$50 paid in cash. Thankfully, I have kept US$200 hidden away in my pack for instances where a credit card could not be used – which were surprisingly few.

"*Hola*," I extend my hand to the overweight gentleman in charge of transport. Nodding, taking my cash, he helps cram my bike into the back of a cargo trailer, already tightly packed with suitcases and water jugs.

"*Vámonos*," he points ahead.

I hop into the hot van and shimmy awkwardly to the sweaty back seat. The plainly dressed Mexican passengers all sit quietly, barely acknowledging the odd man out. *The gringo in Spandex.*

With my legs propped up, I quickly drift off to sleep.

After five stuffy hours on the fast-flowing Interstate 10, we reach what appears to be the shuttle terminal. The one-room, dimly lit building is located in a Hispanic neighbourhood somewhere in south Phoenix. Where we are in relation to the airport, I'm not exactly sure.

The driver walks to the back of the shuttle and helps pull out the Tumbler. I thank him, "*Gracias.*"

"*De nada* (you're welcome)," he nods politely. Our last verbal exchange was in Antelope Wells.

Meanwhile, anxious family members reunite in the background. I walk away from the animated Spanish conversations, wheeling my bike out to a quiet, unfamiliar city street. *Which way now?*

I pause for a minute and take a deep breath.

As if summoned in that moment, a large airplane passes overhead in the calm evening sky. It glides downward to what I can only assume is the Phoenix International Airport.

I begin rolling in hot pursuit.

With great pride.

———

CHAPTER 31

COMING HOME

OCTOBER 29, 2012

It has been four months since I completed the Tour Divide. Still, my sore toes continue to make walking difficult. A doctor recently took a scalpel to what she diagnosed as blood blisters overtop of painful corns. Unfortunately, like so many of my previous visits to experts in the medical field, the problem remains mostly unsolved.

But I'm home.

The leaves are turning yellow along Lake Ontario in Burlington, and it's warm. I'm convinced we'll never get snow, not like in Alberta, anyway. "Just you wait and see," Sarah taunts, as we walk hand-in-hand to our regular Saturday morning espresso diversion.

I order a plain Americano with no milk or sugar. I'm still recovering from three weeks of non-stop sweets. She gets her regular skinny vanilla latte.

Sitting outside with our hot drinks, I'm distracted by the morning sun catching Sarah's dark hair and gentle cheekbones in just the right light. She doesn't see me peeking over a document on my iPad, smiling obnoxiously. I continue to stare until she catches on.

She finally puts down her magazine and whispers softly, "How's it going, silly?"

I have almost finished writing a book about my adventures – this book. "Good," I reply. "I think I finally know how it should end."

It has been difficult to find a crescendo. My cycling adventures and other life events were never conceived with a story arc in mind. They just happened.

I wonder what my 13-year-old self would think now?

There is no sports car in the driveway, I'm not a pro cyclist and the world is far from changed. In fact, I highly doubt that any of the over-caffeinated faces in line know anything of the distances I have pedalled – over 100,000 kilometres now, including training mileage.

It invites the question W*hat is the greater purpose of it all?*

Thinking back to the Tour Divide, I recall my second-last evening, following that fortuitous encounter with the Toaster House in Pie Town, New Mexico.

TOUR DIVIDE, DAY 19

I turn on my headlight and squint into the mounting darkness. With the same naïveté that I have expressed each evening before, I tell myself *This is the night that I ride through till morning. This is the night that I show what I'm made of.*

Lost in an inspired thought, I drop my focus for a mere second.

Ahead, a frightened antelope jumps across my path.

"Fuck!" I yell out, jamming on the brakes.

Consequently, the Tumbler begins to slide sideways in the sand and gravel, its wheels soon giving out in dreaded succession.

My left hip, ribs and exposed elbow break the fall. The tender contact points rip open, creating rich, bloody wounds, now packed with dirt.

Lying on the ground, still clipped in, with the heavy Tumbler pinning me down, I curse with frustration.

I remain still for a moment.

Wiggling my fingers and toes, I feel no pain.

As I rotate my free knee, hips, shoulders and elbows, however, that familiar stiffness and stinging pain come flooding in. But nothing is broken.

Lying in the middle of the remote service road, I stare off into a nearby meadow opening, and see the antelope standing peacefully in the moonlight, stoically alone and appearing to look back at me.

Maybe I should stop.

Walking over to the forest edge, I prop the dusty Tumbler against a fallen tree. Throwing down my bivy sack and sleeping bag behind, I proceed to strip naked.

Sitting cross-legged in the buff, I reach inside my frame pack for a crumpled tin plate, what's left of the berry pie that I commandeered from the Toaster House back porch fridge. Feeling my belly rumble, it's easy to justify eating the remaining quarter of flaky delight.

My mood lightens, high on indulgence.

Munching in deep, slow chews, I stare around at the Gila forest surroundings. No longer moving, my eyes have begun to adjust to the low light.

The still air is peaceful.

This feels right.

And I realize, although I have often been hungry and in pain during this endeavour, it is invigorating to be out in the wild and to have to fend for myself. Not having any reward or media coverage dangling at the finish has also made this a uniquely personal endeavour, and pure in nature, just like when my father and I first toured across Canada.

I have missed this.

My father is the keystone in all this. He and I haven't spoken much since I started writing. It was a tremendous oversight on my part to not think his feelings would be hurt by speaking of him as a hard-ass, of our family's struggle surrounding the death of my baby brother and of our disagreements over my unconventional path. *But you can't have the good without the bad*, I justified.

Perhaps I should include more *good*.

For starters, he taught me how to skate.

As a small child, I remember stumbling across a pond in Edmonton, looking up into his large glasses as he got ready to catch me. His wavy dark hair was already starting to grey. *Funny, he would have been about the age I am now.*

From stumbling to striding, I remember my father coaching almost every sports team I was on.

He gave all the players an equal chance to play, and often rotated our positions. He was conscious of the opposing team in that regard, too. If my baseball team was outscoring the other squad, he had us switch batting positions to help teach us an important lesson in sportsmanship. He wanted us to have fun, not beat each other into the ground.

My hormonal years were no doubt a difficult next chapter.

Like most teens, my limited attention span was drawn to video games instead of schoolwork. I remember my father throwing out my Game Boy while on a road trip, telling me to look out the window instead. I threw a hissy fit that lasted at least a week. But ever since, the game of life has been of far greater interest to me.

The ideal of continuing to play that game as a team, and to support others through charity, I now realize, began before learning about Terry Fox and Lance Armstrong.

I remember my father hiring a schizophrenic who could

not get employment elsewhere. They worked together doing yard work at our acreage in Calgary, which seemed like a dicey move on my father's part, at the time, considering his young family playing nearby. But sometimes you need to have faith.

No newspaper articles ever awarded him for such charitable work. But that was never the point.

My father has always had integrity.

As a challenged teen, it was not always easy for me to understand this unwavering hard edge.

I remember him being a fierce protector of my mom, especially from my angst. He stood by her side when I became selfish over the handling of my baby brother. We fought on several occasions because of this.

Still, through all that shit, he made an effort to reconcile with his own father to some degree, and provide a comfortable life for both my grandparents in British Columbia. He maintained their yard, drove them to doctor's appointments and even loaned them our family dog for company.

My grandfather would retreat to the woods for long hikes alone.

That man who survived the Second World War, he was a bit of a rambling anomaly. We all cringed whenever he whistled for my grandmother, rudely pointing out that he needed something, or telling her to "hush" mid-sentence.

When my grandmother suddenly passed away, my grandfather hastily assumed ownership of our dog, in the process of moving to an unknown address. We immediately lost all contact with him.

My father's estranged sister told us later that he had lived somewhere on the west coast and passed away a few years later. Our dog too.

In the end, my father and my grandfather became a stark

contrast between caring, and caring only for oneself. My father would exemplify this by saying, "How many fathers do you know who would ride across Canada with their son?"

He changed my world.

And I am forever indebted.

There is no story without two wheels, or without my father's eternal wisdom trailing somewhere close behind. He taught me how to play fair, to go to where the puck is going to be (not where it is), to live a life of purpose and, most importantly, to not just be a man but, through his example, be a good man

A better man.

Holding onto Sarah's hand as we stand up to leave the coffee shop, I smile, my thoughts still caught deep in introspection.

"Next, we should talk about our plan," she playfully reminds me.

"Which plan are you referring to, Babe?" I snap to.

"Our triathlon training plan for next year, silly."

Ah, yes.

And, I'll add, a man who would try anything at least once.

A SPECIAL ACKNOWLEDGEMENT

I would like to especially thank these special people and organizations for encouraging me to complete *A Purpose Ridden:*

Peter and Brenda Correy, Leland Pall and Trisha Correy-Pall, Jim and Mary-Anne Hornby, Sarah Hornby, the Thompson Family, Hammer Nutrition Canada, Scott McDermott, Debbie Dowd, Kelly Dowd, Sharon, Terry Stone, Gail Whiteford, David White, Mike Bermingham, Lisa Cichelly, John Proc, Andrea Graham, Sue and Maurice Richard, Bruce Kirkby, Melanie Rutledge, Don Gorman and everyone at RMB | Rocky Mountain Books.